PLUTARCH

LIFE OF DION

PLUTARCH

LIFE OF DION

WITH INTRODUCTION AND NOTES

BY

W. H. PORTER

ARNO PRESS
A New York Times Company
New York • 1979

Reprint Edition 1979 by Arno Press Inc.

Reprinted from a copy in the University of
        Wisconsin-Madison Library

GREEK TEXTS AND COMMENTARIES
ISBN for complete set: 0-405-11412-5
See last pages of this volume for titles.

Manufactured in the United States of America

———◆———

Library of Congress Cataloging in Publication Data

Plutarchus.
    Plutarch's life of Dion.

    (Greek texts and commentaries)
    Reprint of the 1952 ed. published by Hodges, Figgis,
Dublin, under title: Life of Dion.
    Bibliography: p.
    1. Dion, tyrant of Syracuse, 408-353 B.C. 2. Sicily--
History--To 800. 3. Greece--History--To 146 B.C.
4. Sicily--Kings and rulers--Biography. I. Porter,
William Holt. II. Title. III. Title: Life of Dion.
IV. Series.
DG55.S9D56613   1979   937'.8 [B]   78-18594
ISBN 0-405-11435-4

PLUTARCH:

LIFE OF DION

PLUTARCH:
LIFE OF DION

WITH INTRODUCTION AND NOTES

BY

W. H. PORTER

M.A., Dublin ; D.Litt., National University of Ireland
Formerly Professor in University College, Cork
Editor of Plutarch's Life of Aratus

DUBLIN

HODGES, FIGGIS & CO., LTD.

6 DAWSON STREET

1952

PREFACE.

Two of Plutarch's biographies are concerned with Sicily. The second of these, the Life of Timoleon, was edited many years ago by Dr. H. A. Holden, but the Life of Dion, though not inferior in interest or value, has hitherto lacked an annotated edition in English.

The text of the *Dion* edited by K. Ziegler (Teubner, Leipzig) shows a great improvement on its predecessors and only in a small number of passages have I found reason to diverge from it.

My Introduction is mainly concerned with the question of ' Sources '. Matters of historical interest are discussed in the ' Supplementary Notes ' inserted in the commentary at appropriate places.

My thanks are due to the Senate of the National University of Ireland for a grant towards the expenses of publication ; also to Professor H. D. Westlake, for a copy of his short but valuable paper, *Dion of Syracuse : A study in Liberation.*

This book has benefited much from suggestions and criticisms received from Dr. Maurice Duggan, whose edition of Plutarch's *Philopoemen and Flamininus* is now ready for the press ; Professors H. W. Parke, T. A. Sinclair and W. B. Stanford, of whom the last has read the whole of the annotations in manuscript ; the President of University College, Dublin (Dr. Michael Tierney), and Professor D. E. W. Wormell.

W. H. P.

DALKEY, CO. DUBLIN.

CONTENTS.

CORRIGENDA

P. xx, 9th line, *insert comma after the word* representative.

P. 60, 10th line from bottom under Supplementary Note iii, insert *Dion at Court.*

P. 73, line 32, for *persons qualified.* To act, read *persons qualified* to act . . .

P. 74, 16th line from bottom, for *deliberate* read *deliberative.*

P. 76, note on 24, 5, for *see on 5, 7* read *see on 3, 4.*

INTRODUCTION.

SECTION I.—*Summary of Plutarch's Narrative.*

The first two chapters form an Introduction to the Lives of Dion and Brutus, which together made up the Twelfth Book of the Parallel Lives. This Introduction is balanced by the comparison at the end of the *Brutus.*

Chapters 3–16 treat of Dion's life at the court of the Dionysii.

Dion was the son of Hipparinus, a Syracusan noble, who had helped the elder Dionysius to make himself Tyrant.

Dionysius was a bigamist. His wives were Aristomache, Dion's sister, and Doris of Locri in Italy. Aristomache was without children for many years. Doris was the mother of Dionysius' eldest son. When Dion was a young man Plato visited Syracuse, and under his influence Dion became an adherent of Philosophy. His strictness of conduct combined with his natural reserve made him unpopular at court, but he gained and kept the tyrant's confidence in spite of his habit of speaking his mind without respect of persons. He came to be employed on important affairs of state, in particular as envoy to the Carthaginians, by whom he was highly esteemed. At the time of the tyrant's death he was in command of the fleet.

The new tyrant, Dionysius the younger, knowing himself to be inexperienced and ill educated, was induced by Dion to invite Plato from Athens to direct his studies. Plato came, but his aims were soon frustrated. Dionysius on his accession reinstated Philistus, whom his father had sent into exile ; and Philistus on his return persuaded Dionysius that Dion was scheming to oust him from power, and was trusting to Plato's visit to divert attention from his own intrigues. Some four months after Plato's arrival, commissioners came from Carthage to arrange terms of peace between their government and Dionysius. To them Dion wrote a letter urging them not to engage in ' conversations ' about a settlement unless he should be present. The letter was intercepted by Dionysius' spies and furnished him with a pretext for deporting Dion to Italy. At this stage, however, he allowed Dion to retain the revenues of his estates.

[Sources : Platonic Epistles : Timaeus' History—see below, Section 3.]

CHRONOLOGICAL TABLE.

SOME MODERN WORKS CONSULTED.

(Generally cited by name of author.)

Historical. E. Meyer, *Geschichte des Alterthums* v (1903) ; K. J. Beloch *Griechische Geschichte*[2] iii (in two parts), 1923 ; W. Hüttl, *Verfassungsgeschichte von Syrakus* (1929) ; *Cambridge Ancient History* vi (esp. ch. 16 by R. Hackforth) (1928) ; H. W. Parke, *Greek Mercenary Soldiers* (1933) ; M. W. Laistner, *History of the Greek World from 479 to 323 B.C.* (1936) ; also G. Grote, *History of Greece*, vol. ix ; A. Holm, *Geschichte von Siciliens*, vol. ii (1874) ; E. A. Freeman, *History of Sicily*, vol. iv (1894) ; T. A. Sinclair, *A History of Greek Political Thought* (1952),

Topographical. Fabricius, *Das Antike Syrakus* (*Klio* 1932. Beih. 28).

On the Platonic Epistles. Annotated Edition of the Epistles by F. Novotny (1930) ; of *Epists.* 7 and 8, by R. S. Bluck (1948) ; Loeb *Plato*, vii (1929) with *Introduction*, R. G. Bury ; Translation and Commentary, by J. Harward (1932); by G. R. Morrow (1935).

Miscellaneous. Wilamowitz, *Platon* (esp., vol. ii), 1929 ; G. C. Field, *Plato and his Contemporaries* (1930) ; E. Barker, *Greek Political Theory* ; *Plato and his Predecessors*,[3] (1947) ; A. E. Taylor, *Plato the Man* (1926) ; E. Frank, *Platon und die sogennanten Pythagoreer* (1930) ; Loeb *Plutarch, Lives* vi (1918), transl. B. Perrin ; K. Ziegler, *Ploutarchos* (1949) ; Pauly-Wissowa, *Realencyclopädie d. Klass. Alterthumswissenschaft* (cited as P–W).

Chapters 17–23 record some incidents of Dion's years of exile in Greece, where he studied under Plato at the Academy. Plutarch also refers to Plato's experiences at Syracuse. In hope of effecting a settlement between Dionysius and Dion, Plato, after some years, paid a third visit to Syracuse. But his loyalty to Dion offended the tyrant, and it was only after an appeal from Archytas of Tarentum that he was permitted to return home. (Summer, 360, B.C.).

When Dion met Plato at the Olympian games he had already made up his mind to levy war against Dionysius. He had learnt of the confiscation of his property, and how his wife had been forced by the tyrant to marry one of the courtiers.

Plato, while refusing to co-operate in measures of war, allowed him to enrol volunteers from the Academy.

In addition, Dion recruited mercenaries in Peloponnesus.

[For these chapters, Plutarch consulted the Platonic Epistles with other authorities which cannot be identified.]

Chapters 23–53 treat of Dion's liberation of Syracuse and his conflicts with the democratic leader, Heracleides.

Embarking at Zacynthus after a lunar eclipse (Aug. 9, 357), Dion ultimately landed at the Punic outpost of Minoa on the South Coast of Sicily. The governor, Synalos, when he discovered that Dion was in command of the expedition gave the troops—800 in number—a friendly reception.

On the way from Minoa to Syracuse Dion was joined by contingents from the Greek cities. Dionysius at the moment was engaged in visiting his Italian possessions.

By a ruse Dion caused the tyrant's mercenaries occupying Epipolae to disperse, and thus was able to enter Syracuse without a conflict. He was elected *strategos autokrator* by a meeting of citizens. The ' island ' of Ortygia, however, was still held for Dionysius by a garrison of mercenaries. Dion accordingly built a wall across the isthmus connecting it with the mainland.

In a few days Dionysius returned to the castle on Ortygia. A period followed of futile fighting combined with futile negotiation ; which produced a distrust of Dion in the minds of the Syracusan populace.

Then a new body of liberators arrived, led by Heracleides, a Syracusan exile who, like Dion, had formerly been in the service of the tyrants. This expedition was an independent one, for Heracleides had quarrelled with Dion when in Peloponnesus. Heracleides was elected *nauarchos* by the Syracusans, but the appointment was declared *ultra vires* by Dion, who then nominated him on his own authority. When Philistus, commanding the tyrant's navy, appeared in the Great Harbour he was met by the Syracusan fleet under Heracleides. He was defeated and took his own life,—or else (as Timonides asserted), was put to death. After this Dionysius eluding Heracleides sailed away to Italy, leaving the garrison on Ortygia in charge of his son, Apollocrates.

Heracleides, to retrieve his reputation, caused a partisan to propose a decree for the redistribution of landed property. It was carried in spite of Dion's opposition. When midsummer came the Syracusans proceeded to hold an election for *strategoi*. Among those chosen was Heracleides. Dion and his mercenaries now withdrew to Leontini.

Dionysius next sent re-inforcements, under the command of Nypsius, a Neapolitan, to his garrison on Ortygia. Nypsius' men breached Dion's cross-wall and devastated a portion of the city.

On the third day Dion was unanimously recalled : he forced the raiders back into the fortress. Heracleides appealed to Dion's forbearance ; Dion took no action against him or any other of his political opponents. On the motion of Heracleides, Dion was, for the second time, elected *strategos autokrator*. He allowed the Assembly to re-elect Heracleides to the command of the fleet. But he annulled the ' Land Act ' which the Assembly had recently passed, and thus drove Heracleides into opposition once again.

When commanding the fleet at Messene, Heracleides made speeches to the sailors in which he accused Dion of aiming at a tyranny. He also engaged in secret negotiations with a Spartan named Pharax, and later with another Spartan, Gaesylus, who told him that he had come to take supreme command of the Greek forces in Sicily (like Gylippus formerly). In the end, however, Gaesylus took Dion's side, reconciled the opponents, and caused Heracleides to take an oath to be loyal to Dion in future. The Syracusans next disbanded the fleet, and shortly afterwards Apollocrates surrendered the fortress on Ortygia.

After this Dion offered Heracleides a seat on his ' synedrion ' (' privy council '). It was declined, Heracleides insisting that his place was with his fellow-citizens in the Ecclesia, while he denounced Dion for his failure to demolish the fortress ; for checking the people when they started to desecrate the tomb of the elder Dionysius ; and finally for sending to Corinth for counsellors and colleagues.

Dion, at last convinced that the political reforms which he desired to carry out would find in Heracleides an uncompromising opponent, authorised certain of his followers to put him out of the way ; and they accordingly assassinated him. Dion gave the victim a state funeral, and in an address to the people of Syracuse ' satisfied them that it had been impossible for the city to enjoy tranquillity while Dion and Heracleides were in public life together.'

[For these chapters Plutarch's authority is generally held to have been Timonides, a volunteer in Dion's army, writing to Plato's nephew, Speusippus.—See section 3.]

Chapters 54–58 describe how the Athenian Callippus, Dion's intimate friend, conspired against him in hope of becoming Tyrant ; how, when the conspirators were completing their preparations, Dion was alarmed by the apparition of a Fury, which was followed by the suicide of his son ; and finally, how Dion was murdered in his own home by some Zacynthians on the festival of Persephone.

[The source of these chapters was evidently Timaeus.]

SECTION II.—*Plutarch's point of view in Biography and in Politics.*

To the modern student the *Dion* is valuable mainly as a source of historical information. But Plutarch wrote his Lives to *depict character*. As he remarks in introducing his *Alexander* : ' I am a writer not of histories but of biographies. As painters produce a likeness by representing . . . the features which reveal character . . . so I, too, must be allowed to delineate the external signs of character, and so to portray the life of each person ' : and again in the *Nicias* : ' My object has been to provide a record for the study of human character.'

Yet the distinction between Biographer and Historian cannot be sharply defined. To portray aright the character of some historical personage the biographer must first take due care that, where authorities disagree about matters of fact, the version he has adopted is the true, or at least the most probable one. This duty Plutarch in the *Dion* has not taken seriously. His criticism of authorities is rare, and concerned with trivialities.

Further, we must bear in mind Plutarch's amiable habit of idealising his heroes, and ignoring or extenuating their mis-deeds.

In *Cimon* 2 he tries to justify this practice :

Portrait painters, he remarks, when depicting handsome and gracious forms, should neither omit entirely nor reproduce with absolute precision an unpleasing feature in their subjects.

" So our biographers,—since it is hard if not impossible to present a human life free from blemish—should, when treating of noble actions, reproduce the truth in its fulness, but where we find a life marked by failings due to passion or political necessity, we should regard these shortcomings as deficiencies in some particular virtue rather than as the crimes of a vicious disposition ; and hence . . . instead of going out of our way to bring such defects into prominence, we should treat them with compassion for poor human nature which produces no character which is without alloy or whose claim to virtue is beyond question."

Thus in the *Dion* Plutarch mentions the assassination of Heracleides without one word of comment (ch. 50), merely suggesting (ch. 53) that later on Dion came to regard the deed as a stain on his career.

Neither has Plutarch a word to say on the extortions to which, according to Nepos following Timaeus, Dion resorted after the death of Heracleides in his endeavour to meet expenses.

It is true that in the *Comparison* Plutarch allows himself a little more freedom, when he observes that Dion's reason for driving Dionysius from power was that the tyrant had exiled him, and adds that since Dion made war on Dionysius only when he had lost Dionysius' confidence many even of his friends suspected that he was seeking power for himself. For the rest, Plutarch's only criticism of Dion is that ' he perished when he confided in wicked men (Callippus and his like) whether he misjudged their character or turned them from good to bad.' (In the Biography from start to finish, there is nothing that can help to explain the point of this remark).

The date of the *Dion* appears to fall between 116 and 120 A.D. In *Sulla* 21 Plutarch notes that almost 200 years had elapsed since the battle of Orchomenos—fought in 83 B.C. The *Sulla*, however, belonged to one of the earlier *books* of the Parallel Lives, for its companion Life, the *Lysander*, is cited in the *Pericles*, and the *Pericles* is part of Book 10, whereas the *Dion* and *Brutus* formed the twelfth Book.

Plutarch, who was born in 46 A.D., was at least seventy when he wrote the *Dion*. He had been a notable figure in the public life of Greece :—Boeotarch ; honorary citizen of Athens ; for more than twenty years a priest of the Delphian Apollo. He had also become a Roman citizen, ' Mestrios Ploutarchos,' as he is named on a Delphian inscription.[1] In Suidas the state-

---

[1] Dittenberger, Syll. Inscr.³ 842 : *Mestrius* Florus was one of Plutarch's intimate friends at Rome.

ment is actually found that Trajan gave Plutarch consular rank ; while Eusebius records that in his old age he was appointed *procurator* (finance minister) of Achaea by Hadrian :— and though some modern critics have found reason to reject these statements, the tradition they embody implies that under these emperors Plutarch was ' well in ' with the governing class at Rome.

Trajan and Hadrian were among the five ' good emperors ' in whose time, according to Gibbon, the human race was at its happiest.

Obviously, however, the political situation with which Plutarch was familiar could not help him to understand the public lives of men who lived in the days before the Roman conquest.

' How could Plutarch,' asks A. W. Gomme, —' born in a politically unimportant province of an Empire . . . ruled by a careful bureaucracy and an autocratic Prince, enjoying a profound peace—understand the political conditions of the Greek states in the fifth and fourth centuries B.C.? ' [2]

Only, we may reply, if he had been a ' researcher ' in the modern sense : but in fact Plutarch was not a ' researcher ' but a masterly populariser.

Among his writings there has come down to us a short and highly rhetorical tract of uncertain date, on *Monarchy, Oligarchy and Democracy.* Though it cannot be regarded as a contribution to the subject an extract may serve to illustrate Plutarch's political standpoint.

At the end of the tract (*Mor.* 827) he suggests that, just as a master of musical theory—although by his science he can produce melody from any instrument—will soon, like Plato, come to prefer a simple lyre or cithara, so the statesman,— while he will handle skilfully a Laconian oligarchy, adapting to his use men who are equal in power and honour, by quietly exerting pressure upon them ; and while he will skilfully co-operate with a democracy of many sounds and strings, relaxing the constitution here and tightening it there,—yet, if granted choice of constitutions, would, in obedience to Plato, select none but *Monarchy, the only constitution with the capacity to produce that perfect, clear-ringing note which is the note of true efficiency.* Other constitutions, while controlled by the Statesman, in turn exercise control over him, and while under *his* direction, at the same time direct *him*, because he has no steadfast power which he can employ against the persons from whom he derives his power.

---

[2] *Commentary on Thucydides* I, p. 59.

It is not surprising that Plutarch, with his admiration for Plato, his predilection for Monarchy and his somewhat limited conception of the duty of a biographer, should have based his account of the crucial years of Dion's life on the narrative of one of Dion's partisans ignoring what the historians had urged in criticism of Dion or in defence of his democratic opponents.

SECTION III.—*The Principal Sources of the Dion.*

IN a monograph (now unobtainable) published in 1884 on the sources of the *Dion* and the *Timoleon*, W. Biedenweg argued that Plutarch's principal sources for the *Dion* were (1) the Platonic Epistles, (2) the Narrative of Timonides, (3) the History of Timaeus.

This view has been generally accepted ; but F. Leo, *Die griechisch-römische Biographie* (1901), held that the *Dion* was ' based on the Platonic Epistles and the historians, but the material had already been put together by a biographer before Cornelius Nepos ' (1 cent. B.C.).

The notion that Plutarch *habitually* based his biographies on ' intermediate sources ' has been effectively criticised by A. W. Gomme, *op. cit.* p. 82 :

> " I do not in fact believe that a man universally declared to be widely read, and universally declared to be honest, used only one or two books for an Essay or a Life, keeping close to their form and content, using all their learning (which also may be second or third hand), pretending to quote from so many authors, criticising some of them, and suppressing the name of one author in particular, the one from whom he took nearly everything he knew."

In its application to the *Dion* the doctrine of the ' intermediate source ' seems to be refuted by the constant references we find there to the letters of Plato. That Plutarch, who was a lifelong student and admirer of Plato, would be content to quote him at second hand is out of the question.

Among the topics to be discussed here the most important are :

(1) How far was Plutarch indebted to Timaeus?

(2) What can be inferred as to the character of Timonides' narrative, its use by Plutarch and its authenticity ?

(3) Are the five Platonic Epistles cited by Plutarch genuine?

A.—*The Historian Timaeus* (356–260 B.C.).

Timaeus' History, as Beloch has remarked, overshadowed the writings of his predecessors, ' and to him we indirectly owe most of our knowledge of Sicilian affairs in the fourth century B.C.'

The work perished in the fourth century A.D. and our acquaintance with its contents is derived from the reproduction of parts of it by later authors, and from the criticisms which were levelled against it. The criticisms were largely caused by Timaeus' unwillingness ' to tell the thing just as it happened.' His judgement of persons and events was coloured with prejudice due partly to his own experiences in early manhood, partly to a preconception he had formed about the working of divine providence.

Timaeus was the son of Andromachus, ' dynast ' of Tauromenium (*mod.* Taormina), who had established there the surviving citizens of Naxos, destroyed in 403 by Dionysius I. Andromachus later on was one of the first Sicilians to assist Timoleon.

Timaeus had reasons of his own for adopting a hostile attitude to tyrants. In the year 317 (or somewhat later) he was banished by the then tyrant of Syracuse, Agathocles. He retired to Athens where he did most of his historical work. He is said to have returned to Sicily in his old age and to have died there at 96.

There are four peculiarities for which Timaeus was notorious :

1. *Animosity to tyrants.* This appears in his references to Theron, Thrasybulus, Hiero and the Dionysii, as well as to Agathocles.

2. *Partiality towards Gelon.* To Timaeus Gelon was no tyrant but saviour of Sicily and benefactor of Syracuse. Polybius blames Timaeus for exaggerating the happiness of the city in Gelon's time.

3. *Superstition.* Timaeus was credulous of fables and marvels. ' He sought to show that to every sinner punishment, unmistakable as such, is meted out. He was ever on the watch for the revelation of mysterious or daemonic influences on human affairs.'[3]

---

[3] J. B. Bury, *Ancient Greek Historians*, p. 169 : cf. Polyb. 12, 24, 5. On Timaeus see Diod. 16, 17 ; 21 frag. 17 (from Polybius) : Marcellinus, *Vita Thucydidis* 27 : Plut. *Mor.* 605 : Lucian, *Macrob.* 22.

4. *Interest in trivialities.* He was nicknamed 'old gossip-hunter', 'from his fondness for reporting casual occurrences.' (Suidas).

Plutarch was not unaware of Timaeus' shortcomings. In the *Nicias* he stigmatises him as an amateur in history with the mind of an adolescent. We may infer that he used Timaeus in the *Dion* because he found in his pages more *biographical* material than in the earlier historians.[4]

When Plutarch wrote of Dion's life at the court of the Dionysii and of Callippus' conspiracy Timaeus was his principal authority. In the remainder of the Life there is no indication of his influence.

Evidence. Comparing Plutarch's *Dion* with the *Dion* of Cornelius Nepos we find a number of passages where the treatment is so similar as to point to a common source.

In two of these Plutarch cites Timaeus as his authority. The first is the account of the death of Dionysius the Elder, which is said to have followed upon a sleeping-draught administered by his physicians. The same story is told in Nepos' *Dion* 2.[5]

Plutarch cites Timaeus also in connexion with the deportation of Dion (14–15). The account in Nepos although less detailed is almost identical, except that Nepos represents Dion as 'conveyed to Corinth in a trireme,' Plutarch, as carried 'to Italy in a small boat.' Here evidently Plutarch has corrected Timaeus by reference to Plato's Seventh Epistle.

If we assume that Nepos' very short biography is throughout derived (immediately or ultimately) from Timaeus it may be inferred that the passages in Plutarch's *Dion* which correspond *in substance* to passages in the *Dion* of Nepos have likewise been drawn from Timaeus. Further, in association with material found also in Nepos' *Dion*, there occur in Plutarch's a number of passages exhibiting one of the idiosyncrasies of Timaeus already mentioned,—prejudice against Tyrants ; admiration for Gelon ; interest in trivialities ; insistence on supernatural manifestations. Such passages are confined to chapters 3–16 and 54–58.

On one or other of these grounds the following topics [for which see *Notes*] may be ascribed to the authority of Timaeus :

Domestic life of Dionysius I : acts of cruelty to Plato and

---

[4] i.e., Ephorus whose history (so far as concerned Sicily) was continued by Diyllus : Philistus' history continued by Athanis : and the *Philippica* of Theopompus.

[5] There was a different tradition that D. died after a supper (at which he had imbibed too freely). [Diod. 15, 74.]

others : relations with Dion : ridicule of Gelon : banishment of Philistus : last illness and death : the younger Dionysius' invitation to Plato, recall of Philistus and deportation of Dion : the circumstances of Callippus' conspiracy (c. 54 ff.) : the Apparition seen by Dion : his son's suicide : murder of Dion.

It has been suggested by G. R. Morrow that Timaeus was acquainted with Plato's Seventh Epistle.

It is true that the following topics are found both in his representative Nepos, and in Epistle 7:—

(1) Dionysius II was urged by Plato to restore liberty to the Syracusans :

(2) Plato (in 367–6 B.C.) visited Sicily a second time at the entreaty of Dion : .

(3) Dionysius was well-intentioned but misled by Philistus.

But Nepos has two statements about Plato which are not to be found in the Epistle, that he was (1) invited to Syracuse by the *Elder* Dionysius at Dion's request, and (2) sold into slavery at Dionysius' instigation.

It is quite possible that Timaeus' source for these last two statements was also his source for the first three.

In one passage (already referred to) a statement in Nepos contradicts the Seventh Epistle. Plato states that Dionysius put Dion on a small boat and expelled him from Syracuse : Nepos, that he gave him a trireme to convey him to Corinth.

B.—*The Narrative of Timonides.*

THIS appears to have been Plutarch's source for his account of Dion's invasion of Sicily and proceedings at Syracuse down to and including the murder of Heracleides (ch. 53).

In chapters 22, 28, 31, 35 Plutarch writes of Timonides as a statesman and philosopher who accompanied Dion to Sicily ; on one occasion took his place as leader in a battle ; reported to Plato's nephew, Speusippus, that Philistus was slain by the Syracusans (whereas Ephorus stated that he committed suicide); and being a friend and comrade of Dion was more likely than Timaeus to know the true name of Dion's son.

Elsewhere Timonides is mentioned only once in an ancient writer, Diogenes Laertius, *Lives of the Philosophers* 4, 5, but Diogenes (who lived in the 3rd cent. A.D.) appears to have taken his information from Plutarch. (See note on *Dion* 28).

Timonides' narrative apparently consisted of a number of Letters.

Speusippus had been largely responsible for Dion's expedition. In 361-60 while staying at Syracuse with Plato, and, therefore, as a guest of the Tyrant, he made an enquiry into the state of popular feeling, and sent Dion an encouraging report. It may indeed have been due to his uncle's scruples that Speusippus did not himself take part in Dion's expedition.

From chapter 22, 8 to 48, 6, Plutarch's story is remarkably well told. Throughout there is a uniform bias against ' the Syracusans ' and in favour of Dion's mercenaries.

If, by contrast, in chapters 48-9 the incidents in which Pharax and Gaesylus make their appearance are obscurely treated, the explanation may be simply that Timonides was ill-informed about these transactions.

That Timonides was Plutarch's source for the account of the death and funeral of Heracleides (ch. 53) may be inferred from the statement at the end of the chapter that after having listened to a speech from Dion *the Syracusans came to recognise* that the city had been unable to escape disorder while he and Heracleides were in public life together. This statement with its implication that all was now going well with Dion and his cause is evidence that the document in which Plutarch found it was written very shortly after the delivery of Dion's oration. There are also in chapter 53 implicit references to chapters 31 and 47, where we are told that friends of Dion (some months previously) demanded the ' liquidation ' of Heracleides.

Beloch (3, 2, 105), holding as he did that the Seventh Platonic Epistle was actually written by a member of the Academy at a time when Timoleon's victory had awakened interest in Dion's career, was naturally disposed to regard the narrative of Timonides as a forgery composed to meet the demand for inside information. He seeks to justify his attitude by pointing out that whereas Timaeus spoke of Dion's son as ' Aretaeus ' (a name derived from that of his mother Arete) Timonides, as we learn in *Dion* 31, referred to him as ' Hipparinus.'

Beloch insists that ' Aretaeus ' was the correct name, because Arete, daughter of the elder Dionysius, was superior in rank to Dion.

But Polyaenus, 5, 2, 8, gives the youth's name as *Hipparion*. When we find three names, Hipparinus, Hipparion and Aretaeus, attributed to one whose paternal grandfather was named Hipparinus, and whose first cousin (a son of Dionysius I) was also Hipparinus, it is a fair inference that Hipparinus was his real name, Aretaeus and Hipparion being ' nicknames ' in use at Syracuse to distinguish him from his cousin. (A similar explanation has been given by Tarn of the name Chryseis, applied to Phthia, mother of Philip V of Macedon).

Evidence for authenticity of Timonides' Narrative. In chapters 22–53 of Plutarch's *Dion* we find numerous descriptive touches which suggest that it is based on the work of a memoir writer rather than an arm-chair historian,—just as the appearance of similar *minutiae* in the *Anabasis* points to its author being in fact not Themistogenes of Syracuse but Xenophon. In both cases we feel that we are reading the account of an eye-witness who found pleasure in recalling persons and occurrences of little significance in themselves.

Thus we are told that Dion's mercenaries were encouraged to face the perils of a war with Dionysius by a speech from Alcimenes, a leading man among the Achaeans ; the same mercenaries are much impressed by the magnificence of Dion's dinner-service, but alarmed by an eclipse of the moon (which actually occurred on Aug. 9, 357) ; at C. Pachynus, Dion's pilot, Protus, wanted the party to land because the weather was threatening, but was overruled by Dion for strategic reasons ; Sosis is convicted of mischief-making by medical testimony ; the wounded Heracleides sends first his brother, then his uncle to entreat Dion to return and relieve Syracuse.

We may note further that there is only one allusion to Timonides as man of action,—his taking command of the troops when Dion was wounded. A forger would have given him something interesting to do !

Again, the Carthaginian governor of Minoa is named by Plutarch *Synalos*, which appears to be a Semitic name (see on 25, 12) ; whereas in Diod. 16, 9, 4, he is called Paralos, which is pure Greek. (It was the name of a son of Pericles).

Finally, Plutarch's account seems to be based on an authority well acquainted with the topography of Syracuse, who was writing for a reader equally well equipped. In ch. 30 we learn that an ox ran wild and scattered the crowd in the *theatre*, after which it careered frantically over " as much of the city as the enemy afterwards occupied." As the theatre lay west of the Temenites quarter, the statement implies that Temenites was the scene of Nypsius' raids : a conclusion which —through an obviously undesigned coincidence—is confirmed by a statement eight chapters further on, where there is a reference to ' the danger now *approaching* Achradina ' [42, 1, where see note].

It has been suggested by Harward that Timonides' communications were preserved among the epistles of Speusippus . and thus became accessible to Plutarch.

3.—*Platonic Epistles*, 3, 4, 7, 8, 13.

PLUTARCH refers to Epistle 7 in about twenty places : to Epistle 3 in about ten ; and occasionally to 4, to 8, and to 13.

Thirteen epistles are found in our MSS. of Plato, and these are cited by Diogenes Laertius as having been included in the Platonic canon of Thrasylus who flourished in the first century A.D. The earliest writer to mention any of them is Cicero.

At the present day there is a general willingness to admit the authenticity of Epistles 7 and 8 : as to the others, authorities differ. In my opinion the weight of evidence is in favour of all the five cited by Plutarch.

Beloch, writing in 1923, was the last critic of eminence to reject all the ' Sicilian ' epistles. As he has done so mainly on historical grounds I examine his arguments later on.

The contents of the five letters cited by Plutarch may be thus summarised :—

Epistle 13 (which, if genuine, appears to have been composed about B.C. 364) is a friendly letter to Dionysius II. It is mainly occupied with personal topics. Helicon, the astronomer, is commended and there is an obscure reference to Dion [see Plut. *Dion* 21, 2, f. *and note*]. The request that follows for financial assistance in discharging certain domestic obligations has been thought unworthy of Plato by some critics, who have, therefore, condemned the Epistle as spurious.

Epistle 3 is conceived in a very different spirit. It is an ' open letter ' to Dionysius, who is blamed for having told some ambassadors at his court that he had been dissuaded by Plato from turning the *tyrannis* into a constitutional monarchy. It is further alleged that ' other persons ' had criticised Plato for exercising a bad influence on Syracusan politics.

Dionysius is also censured for having broken his promises to Plato, (1) by confiscating Dion's property, and (2) by his treatment of Dion's friend, Heracleides, who had been accused —wrongfully—of fomenting a mutiny.

In *Dion*, 16–19, *Epistle* 3 is cited (or referred to) four times. Its contents suggest a date in the latter part of 357 B.C.

Epistle 4, addressed to Dion, combines congratulations on his victory ; an exhortation to provide a constitution for Syracuse which shall surpass the achievements of the famous legislators of tradition ; and a warning against dissension among the ' Notables '. Plutarch attributes this epistle to the time when news of the surrender of Ortygia to Dion had reached Athens,—the late summer or autumn of 355.

Epistle 7—on every ground the most important in the collection—is about three quarters as long as Plutarch's *Dion.*

If genuine, it was written about the end of the year 354, for it implies that Callippus was still in power at Syracuse.

Its professed object is to advise the 'intimates and companions' of the deceased Dion. (They are stated to have invoked Plato's co-operation, assuring him that their aims were the same as Dion's had been).

In fact, however, only a fraction of the Epistle is devoted to advice. Its main themes are :

Plato's reasons for having held aloof from Athenian politics :

The nature of the teaching he had given Dion a generation before :

The purpose of his two visits to the court of Dionysius II :

The treatment he had received from the tyrant (here the story of their quarrel over the 'Heracleides affair' is brought up again).

Included in the Epistle is a long philosophical digression.

The writer's sympathy with Dion's aims is clearly indicated.[6]

Epistle 8 (which purports to have been written about the time when Callippus lost Syracuse—Aug., 353) contains proposals for a political settlement at Syracuse of the kind which, according to Plutarch, *Dion* 53, had been contemplated by Dion.

Plutarch refers to *Epistle* 8 in chapters 3 and 53 of the *Dion*, but he takes no notice of the passages where the *Epistle* represents Dion's son as having survived his father.

In the second edition of his History, which appeared after Wilamowitz had published his reasons for accepting as genuine *Epistles* 6, 7, and 8, Beloch writes (3, 2, p. 45):

"Among extant authorities the Platonic Epistles are the oldest. I am not satisfied as to their authenticity in which Antiquity believed, and which has recently found distinguished advocates.

The Academy on every ground had reason to defend its founder against the reproach of having entangled himself with the tyrants Dionysius and Dion, and to shake off Callippus from its coat-tails. For this purpose the Seventh Epistle was written ; its author, I think,

---

[6] There are a few inconsistencies between statements in the *Dion* and Epistle 7 (see on chapters 11, 2 : 18, 1 : 20, 2). These inconsistencies are due to oversight.

was one of Plato's pupils—perhaps Xenocrates—and he wrote about the time when Timoleon had succeeded where Plato and Dion had failed. The epistle bears the same relation to Plato as Plato's dialogues to Socrates. But it contains good material and may be used with caution as a source.

In connexion with this epistle the remaining ' Sicilian Letters ' were forged, some of them at a quite early date, for Aristophanes of Byzantium included them in his edition."

The main reason why in Beloch's opinion *Plato* cannot be the author of the Seventh Epistle is that the epistle contains references to the ' ruined cities of Sicily ', and to the resettlement of the island as a main point in Dion's programme [332 e, 336 a *and* d : also Epist. 8, 357a].

" This suits Timoleon's time but not the time of Dion's return to Sicily, for then Sicily was economically prosperous and there were no ruined Greek towns. Some like Tyndaris and Adranon had been newly founded. Naxos was restored under the name of Tauromenion."

But, as Holm (2, 446) had remarked :

" Selinous and Himera had been destroyed by the Carthaginians in 409 ; the former recovered slightly, the latter not at all. Acragas from its destruction in 406 till Timoleon's time scarcely existed as an independent state ; Gela, destroyed in 405 (Diod. 13, 11), was again inhabited in 387 (Id. 14, 47), but on a small scale (Id. 14, 68). We hear of it in Dion's time (Id. 16, 9) but it was not of importance till re-colonised in 338 (Plut. Tim. 35). Leontini was captured by Dionysius I and given to his mercenaries (Diod. 14, 15 ; cf. 13, 113 ; 14, 14). Camarina lost her citizens by their removal to Syracuse in 405 (Id. 13 ; 111–113) ; it was but scantily repeopled (Id. 14 ; 47, 48) and did not recover till the time of Timoleon (Id. 16, 82). Catana in 403 was given by Dionysius to Campanian mercenaries (Id. 14, 15 ; cf. 14 ; 66, 88). Messana was destroyed in 396 and repeopled with foreigners by Dionysius (Id. 14, 78)."

In the light of the facts here recorded with dates and references to ancient authorities Beloch's charge against the Seventh Epistle must be reduced from anachronism to over-emphasis or exaggeration.

This argument of Beloch's, therefore, cannot be said to establish his case.

Beloch's *second* argument against the Epistle is thus stated :

'*Why should Plato have addressed a lengthy disquisition to Dion's friends* to tell them something they had long known,— namely, what Plato had been doing in Sicily and what had been Dion's policy ? '

But if it is absurd to suppose that Plato would have ' addressed a long disquisition to Dion's friends to tell them what they knew already,' why should we be asked to believe that one of Plato's followers, ' perhaps Xenocrates ',[8] tried to persuade contemporaries that Plato had committed this ' absurdity '—and, what is more, *did* persuade them?

Should we not rather hold—with Bury,—that the Epistle is the work of Plato, ' who indulged in a literary fiction which enabled him to publish in epistolary form what is at once a history, an apology and a manifesto ' ? . . . ' It was the public opinion of his own countrymen, that Plato was chiefly con- cerned to influence '.[9]

Epistle 8. Here Beloch objects to four statements :—

(1) The appointment of Dion's father, Hipparinus, as a *colleague* of Dionysius in 406 : Diodorus says nothing of a col- league (see on *Dion*, 3, 4).

(2) The strategoi of 407–6 ' were stoned to death ' : (Diod. says ' were cashiered ').

(3) Dion's son ' survived his father ' ; but Plutarch, Nepos, Aelian, say he died before him.

(4) The phraseology attributed to the Syracusans, who are said to have named Dionysius and Hipparinus " *tyrannoi autokratores*, as they say."

But since Plato was not a ' professed historian ' objections 1 and 2 are not in Beloch's view fundamental.

As to (3) he remarks : In view of Plato's intimacy with Dion, he is unlikely to have remained ignorant of the fact that ' the son ' died before his father.

There is, however, no evidence that Dion was closely associated with Plato after their meeting at Olympia in 360. Plato is represented as having disapproved of Dion's attack on Dionysius. (There would be no point in a forger's inventing

---

[8] Xenocrates, we may note, is stated by Diogenes Laertius, to have accompanied Plato on his final visit to Sicily. He had presumably as good information about the Sicilian cities as his master !

[9] Loeb *Plato*, VII, p. 473.

this, even if Epistle 7 is not the work of Plato). If Dion did not write to ask Plato for advice in reference to Heracleides, why need we assume that he informed Plato of ' the son's ' death?

(4) Beloch holds that the title ' tyrants with full powers ' would not have been applied by Plato to Dionysius and Hipparinus (Dion's father). He ignores the qualifying clause, ' as they phrase it ' (i.e., the Syracusans).

The difficulty disappears if we assume that the title *tyrannos* was popularly used of the Dionysii without invidious implication. For this there is sufficient evidence :—

Epistle 13 begins, ' Plato to Dionysius *tyrannos* of Syracuse '.

At the beginning of *Epistle* 3 the writer rebukes Dionysius for addressing the Delphian Apollo in the hexameter line :

' Hail ! secure the *tyrannos* a life of joys never ending '.

Aristoxenus, Aristotle's pupil, is cited in Athen. 12, 545 A, for an account of how Polyarchus, an envoy of Dionysius II, declared at Tarentum, ' Our *tyrannos* is second in happiness to the Persian king alone.'

In *Dion* 13 a herald prays in the *tyranneion* for the perpetuity of the *tyrannis*. The passage may be based on Timaeus, but the anecdote belonged to the tradition of Plato's visit.

Beloch's assumption that in Plato's time the word *tyrannos* would not have been used without the offensive implication of unlawful authority is quite arbitrary. In fact the time when the *colourless* use of the word might be expected to be in vogue at Syracuse was during the reigns of the Dionysii.

Again, it is hard to accept Beloch's rejection of Epistle 3 on the ground that Philistus appears in it as Philistides, in view of the fact that a similar use of the patronymic is found in Aristophanes *Clouds* 134 (cf. 65) and *Frogs* 1511 (where see B. B. Rogers' notes).

Beloch's attitude to the Seventh Epistle and to the Narrative of Timonides is, naturally enough, reflected in his History. For example, if he had accepted the Epistle as Plato's he would have been less inclined to maintain that Dion was aiming at tyranny all along : if he had admitted the *Narrative* as authentic he would (like E. Meyer) have accepted Plutarch's statement that Heracleides' expedition to Syracuse was independent of Dion's, rather than Diodorus' account, which represents Heracleides as *left behind* by Dion as commander of the fleet (see on *Dion* 32).

ADDENDUM : *Diodorus' source for Book* 16, *chapters* 5 ; 9–13 ; 16–20—the ' Dion chapters.'

The commonly accepted view is that for these chapters—which deal with Dion's proceedings during the years 357 and 356.—Diodorus' source was Ephorus. To this view I adhere.

Laqueur's hypothesis [P.—W. Timaeus]—that Diodorus made use of Ephorus but introduced additions and qualifications derived from Timaeus—is open to the objection that it assumes Diodorus to have changed his source eighteen times in four chapters. (Hammond *C. Quart.* xxxii, 1938, p. 137).

Hammond's own view is that these ' Dion chapters ' were based on the *Philippica* of Theopompus. But the impartial treatment of leading characters—Philistus, Nypsius, Heracleides, Dion, Dionysius—which Hammond finds in these chapters, suggests rather the conscientious chronicler Ephorus than Theopompus. Nepos (*Alcib.* II) actually speaks of Theopompus and Timaeus as *duo maledicentissimi*.

Again, Hammond himself proved (*C. Quart.* xxxi (1937), p. 86) that Ephorus' narrative of Sicilian affairs stopped with the year 356 B.C. This suggests that the absence of any account in Diodorus of such remarkable occurrences as the surrender of Ortygia to Dion, the murder of Heracleides, the conspiracy of Callippus, is simply due to his source having dried up.

Finally we may note that in Diod. 16 ; 16 there occur two statements which Plutarch in *Dion* 35 and 36 attributes to Ephorus.

Hammond, however, in maintaining Theopompus to be Diodorus' *sole* authority for the Sicilian events related in the first seventy chapters of his sixteenth book, remarks, ' a consideration of the style and of the choice of vivid incidents leads to the exclusion of Ephorus.'

But the year 357–6 was full of ' vivid incidents ' which *every* historian was bound to record.

It remains to ask : what conclusion as to Diodorus' authority is to be drawn from a comparison of his remarks in 16, 5 ; 16, 9 ; 16, 70 ?

In 16, 5 he writes :

' Dionysius who had inherited the largest Empire in Europe lost the Monarchy, which his father had described as ' bound with fetters of adamant,' in a manner almost incredible, through lack of spirit. I shall try to explain the causes of his overthrow.'

Is Diodorus here alluding to Dionysius' overthrow by Dion in 357–5 or to his surrender to Timoleon in 344?

His overthrow by Dion was obviously the more surprising of the two events.

Hammond, however, thinks that chapter 5 is to be interpreted in the light of chapter 70, where, in writing of Dionysius' *subsequent surrender to Timoleon*, Diodorus adds : ' thus in the manner indicated, from want of spirit he surrendered the far-famed monarchy bound, as people said, with fetters of adamant.'

Both of these statements (in Hammond's view) were found by Diodorus in his source. In chapter 5 his authority announced the subject to be treated ; in chapter 70, the fulfilment of the task. In that case his authority cannot have been Ephorus whose narrative stopped with the year 356.

But there is also to be taken into account a statement which occurs in chapter 9 : ' *Dion* landed in Sicily . . . and . . . overthrew the largest empire in Europe.'

Alike in chapter 5 (as we have seen) and in chapter 9, the Empire of the Dionysii is described as the largest in Europe : and we observe that in the latter passage *Dion* is said to have overthrown it.

On the other hand, chapters 5 and 70 alike characterise the dominion of the elder Dionysius as *bound with fetters of adamant*.

It may fairly be maintained that, if we regard the use of the same phraseology in chapters 5 and 9 as evidence that these two passages come from a common source, that common source was Ephorus. In that case we may suppose the passage cited from chapter 70 to have been written by Diodorus ' on his own', simply for the purpose of giving a semblance of unity to the Sicilian material in the first 70 chapters.

Observe, too, that the phrase, ' bound in fetters of adamant ' is in chapter 70 attributed to ' common talk', whereas in chapter 5 it had been assigned (as by Plutarch in *Dion* 9) to the elder Dionysius. Such carelessness points to Diodorus as the ' sole begetter' of the passage in chapter 70.

It would seem then that in the Dion chapters of Diodorus we have (however imperfectly transmitted) the ' Ephorus ' tradition of Dion's career ; while in Nepos and Plutarch we have the ' Timaeus ' tradition.

Section IV.—*Note on the Manuscripts.*

[See Ziegler, *Plut. Vitae* II, i, Preface.]

Codex Laurentianus conv. suppr. 206, copied early in the 10th century from a MS. which appears to belong to the 4th or 5th. Ziegler denotes this MS. as L.

Copies of L :—

> H = Codex Parisinus 1678 (11th or 12th century).
>
> A ,, ,, ,, 1671 (Date, A.D. 1296).
>
> D ,, ,, ,, 1674.

Ziegler denotes the agreement of L with its copies by the symbol Λ.

P = Palatinus Heidelburgensis $168 + 169$ (about the 11th century).

L^2, P^2, corrections in L and P, respectively.

L and P are 'the most ancient and leasti nterpolated MSS." In addition to them Ziegler occasionally cites C (= Paris, 1673), B (= Paris, 1672), M (= Monacensis, 85), V^b (= Vindobonensis, 60).

Q denotes the consensus of these four MSS. or of the majority.

The MS. C 'has been emended by a scholar drawing partly on readings he had found in other MSS., partly on his own conjectures.'

There is a fourth class comprised of

> M^b = Marcianus 385 ;
>
> F^a = Parisinus 1676,

the consensus of which is denoted by Ziegler as Z.

AVOIDANCE OF HIATUS IN THE LIVES.

It is accepted that Plutarch avoided writing a word beginning with a vowel after a word ending with a long vowel or diphthong or a short vowel incapable of elision. Hiatus, however, is found (1) after the article, (2) after the words και and η and μη, (3) after prepositions and numerals, (4) with words expressing a single notion, and (5) after a pause, as in *Dion* 5, 8 : 16, 4 : 56, 1.

In nearly all instances where *illicit* hiatus occurs in the MSS. of the Dion an adscript appears to have become incorporated with the text ; but in 30, 2 the hiatus is due to the mistake of a copyist.

THE Text here presented is that of Ziegler, *Plutarchi Vitae*, 2, 1 (Teubner) except that in seven passages manuscript readings discarded by Ziegler have been retained ; in six I have introduced conjectures of my own, and in twenty-three have adopted readings cited by Ziegler in his critical Notes. See the commentary for a discussion of the problems involved.

SYMBOLS.

[   ] enclosing words or letters presumed to have been erroneously added to the Text.

<   > enclosing words or letters presumed to have been omitted in error.

When a passage contains an emendation not indicated by either of these symbols it is distinguished by the addition of an asterisk in the margin.

ΔΙΩΝ

1. Ἀρά γ᾽, ὥσπερ ὁ Σιμωνίδης φησίν, ὦ Σόσσιε Σενεκίων, τοῖς Κορινθίοις οὐ μηνίειν τὸ Ἴλιον ἐπιστρατεύσασι μετὰ τῶν Ἀχαιῶν, ὅτι κἀκείνοις οἱ περὶ Γλαῦκον ἐξ ἀρχῆς Κορίνθιοι γεγονότες συνεμάχουν προθύμως, οὕτως εἰκὸς τῇ Ἀκαδημείᾳ μήτε Ῥωμαίους μήθ᾽ Ἕλληνας ἐγκαλεῖν, ἴσον φερομένους ἐκ τῆς γραφῆς ταύτης, ἢ τὸν τε Βρούτου περιέχει βίον καὶ τὸν Δίωνος ; ὧν ὁ μὲν αὐτῷ 2 Πλάτωνι πλησιάσας, ὁ δὲ τοῖς λόγοις ἐντραφεὶς τοῖς Πλάτωνος, ὥσπερ ἐκ μιᾶς ὥρμησαν ἀμφότεροι παλαίστρας ἐπὶ τοὺς μεγίστους ἀγῶνας. καὶ τὸ μὲν ὅμοια 3 πολλὰ καὶ ἀδελφὰ πράξαντας μαρτυρῆσαι τῷ καθηγεμόνι τῆς ἀρετῆς, ὅτι δεῖ φρονήσει καὶ δικαιοσύνῃ δύναμιν ἐπὶ τὸ αὐτὸ καὶ τύχην συνελθεῖν, ἵνα κάλλος ἅμα καὶ μέγεθος αἱ πολιτικαὶ πράξεις λάβωσιν, οὐ θαυμαστόν ἐστιν. Ὡς γὰρ Ἱππόμαχος ὁ ἀλείπτης ἔλεγε τοὺς 4 γεγυμνασμένους παρ᾽ αὐτῷ κἂν κρέας ἐξ ἀγορᾶς ἰδὼν * φέροντας ἐπιγνῶναι πόρρωθεν, οὕτω τὸν λόγον ἐστὶν εἰκὸς τῶν πεπαιδευμένων ὁμοίως ἕπεσθαι ταῖς πράξεσιν, ἐμμέλειάν τινα καὶ ῥυθμὸν ἐπιφέροντα μετὰ τοῦ πρέποντος.

2. Αἱ δὲ τύχαι, τοῖς συμπτώμασι μᾶλλον ἢ ταῖς προαιρέσεσιν [οὖσαι αἱ αὐταί] συνάγουσι τῶν ἀνδρῶν τοὺς βίους εἰς ὁμοιότητα. Προανῃρέθησαν γὰρ ἀμφό- 2 τεροι τοῦ τέλους, εἰς ὃ προὔθεντο τὰς πράξεις ἐκ πολλῶν καὶ μεγάλων ἀγώνων καταθέσθαι, <τυχεῖν> μὴ δυνηθέντες. Ὃ δὲ πάντων θαυμασιώτατον, ὅτι καὶ τὸ 3 δαιμόνιον ἀμφοτέροις ὑπεδήλωσε τὴν τελευτήν, ὁμοίως ἑκατέρῳ φάσματος εἰς ὄψιν οὐκ εὐμενοῦς παραγενομένου. Καίτοι λόγος τίς ἐστι τῶν ἀναιρούντων τὰ τοιαῦτα, 4 μηδενὶ [ἂν] νοῦν ἔχοντι προσπεσεῖν <ἂν> φάντασμα δαίμονος μηδ᾽ εἴδωλον, ἀλλὰ παιδάρια καὶ γύναια καὶ παραφόρους δι᾽ ἀσθένειαν ἀνθρώπους, ἔν τινι πλάνῳ

ψυχῆς ἢ δυσκρασίᾳ σώματος γενομένους, δόξας ἐφέλ-
κεσθαι κενὰς καὶ ἀλλοκότους, δαίμονα πονηρὸν ἐν αὑτοῖς
5 [εἶναι] Δεισιδαιμονίαν ἔχοντας. Εἰ δὲ Δίων καὶ Βροῦτος,
ἄνδρες ἐμβριθεῖς καὶ φιλόσοφοι, καὶ πρὸς οὐδὲν ἀκρο-
σφαλεῖς οὐδ᾽ εὐάλωτοι πάθος, οὕτως ὑπὸ φάσματος
διετέθησαν, ὥστε καὶ φράσαι πρὸς ἑτέρους, οὐκ οἶδα μὴ
τῶν πάνυ παλαιῶν τὸν ἀτοπώτατον ἀναγκασθῶμεν
6 προσδέχεσθαι λόγον, ὡς τὰ φαῦλα δαιμόνια καὶ
βάσκανα, προσφθονοῦντα τοῖς ἀγαθοῖς ἀνδράσι, καὶ
ταῖς πράξεσιν ἐνιστάμενα, ταραχὰς καὶ φόβους ἐπάγει,
σείοντα καὶ σφάλλοντα τὴν ἀρετήν, ὡς μὴ διαμείναντες
ἄπτωτες ἐν τῷ καλῷ καὶ ἀκέραιοι βελτίονος ἐκείνων
μοίρας μετὰ τὴν τελευτὴν τύχωσιν. Ἀλλὰ ταῦτα μὲν εἰς
ἄλλον ἀνακείσθω λόγον. Ἐν τούτῳ δέ, δωδεκάτῳ τῶν
παραλλήλων ὄντι βίων, τὸν τοῦ πρεσβυτέρου προεισ-
αγάγωμεν.

3. Διονύσιος ὁ πρεσβύτερος εἰς τὴν ἀρχὴν καταστὰς
εὐθὺς ἔγημε τὴν Ἑρμοκράτους τοῦ Συρακοσίου θυγατέρα.
2 Ταύτην, οὔπω τῆς τυραννίδος ἱδρυμένης βεβαίως,
ἀποστάντες οἱ Συρακόσιοι δεινὰς καὶ παρανόμους
ὕβρεις εἰς τὸ σῶμα καθύβρισαν, ἐφ᾽ αἷς προήκατο τὸν
3 βίον ἑκουσίως. Διονύσιος δὲ τὴν ἀρχὴν ἀναλαβὼν καὶ
κρατυνάμενος, αὖθις ἄγεται δύο γυναῖκας ἅμα, τὴν μὲν
ἐκ Λοκρῶν ὄνομα Δωρίδα, τὴν δ᾽ ἐπιχώριον Ἀριστομάχην, θυγατέρα Ἱππαρίνου, πρωτεύσαντος ἀνδρὸς
Συρακοσίων καὶ Διονυσίῳ συνάρξαντος, ὅτε πρῶτον
4 αὐτοκράτωρ ἐπὶ τὸν πόλεμον ᾑρέθη στρατηγός. Λέγεται
δ᾽ ἡμέρᾳ μὲν ἀμφοτέρας ἀγαγέσθαι μιᾷ, καὶ μηδενὶ
γενέσθαι φανερὸς ἀνθρώπων, ὁποτέρᾳ προτέρᾳ συνέλθοι,
τὸν δ᾽ ἄλλον χρόνον ἴσον νέμων ἑαυτὸν διατελεῖν
ἑκατέρᾳ, κοινῇ μὲν εἰθισμένων δειπνεῖν μετ᾽ αὐτοῦ, παρὰ
5 νύκτα δ᾽ ἐν μέρει συναναπαυομένων. Καίτοι τῶν
Συρακοσίων ἐβούλετο τὸ πλῆθος τὴν ἐγγενῆ πλέον ἔχειν
τῆς ξένης· ἀλλ᾽ ἐκείνη προτέρᾳ [ὑπῆρχε] τεκούσῃ τὸν
πρεσβεύοντα τῆς Διονυσίου γενεᾶς υἱὸν <ὑπῆρχεν> αὐτῇ
6 βοηθεῖν πρὸς τὸ γένος. Ἡ δ᾽ Ἀριστομάχη πολὺν χρόνον
ἄπαις συνῴκει τῷ Διονυσίῳ, καίπερ σπουδάζοντι περὶ

τὴν ἐκ ταύτης τέκνωσιν, ὅς γε καὶ τὴν μητέρα τῆς
Λοκρίδος, αἰτιασάμενος καταφαρμακεύειν τὴν 'Αριστο-
μάχην, ἀπέκτεινε.

4. Ταύτης ἀδελφὸς ὢν ὁ Δίων, ἐν ἀρχῇ μὲν εἶχε τιμὴν
ἀπὸ τῆς ἀδελφῆς, ὕστερον δὲ τοῦ φρονεῖν διδοὺς πεῖραν,
ἤδη καθ' ἑαυτὸν ἠγαπᾶτο παρὰ τῷ τυράννῳ. Καὶ πρὸς 2
ἅπασι τοῖς ἄλλοις εἴρητο τοῖς ταμίαις, ὅ τι ἂν αἰτῇ Δίων
διδόναι, [δι]δόντας δὲ πρὸς αὐτὸν αὐθημερὸν φράζειν.
*Ων δὲ καὶ πρότερον ὑψηλὸς τῷ ἤθει καὶ μεγαλόφρων καὶ 3
ἀνδρώδης, ἔτι μᾶλλον ἐπέδωκε πρὸς ταῦτα, θείᾳ τινὶ
τύχῃ Πλάτωνος εἰς Σικελίαν παραβαλόντος κατ' οὐδένα
λογισμὸν ἀνθρώπινον· ἀλλὰ δαίμων τις, ὡς ἔοικε, 4
πόρρωθεν ἀρχὴν ἐλευθερίας [παρα]βαλλόμενος Συρακοσίοις, καὶ τυραννίδος κατάλυσιν μηχανώμενος, ἐκόμισεν
ἐξ 'Ιταλίας εἰς Συρακούσας Πλάτωνα, καὶ Δίωνα
συνήγαγεν εἰς λόγους αὐτῷ, νέον μὲν ὄντα κομιδῇ, 5
πολὺ δ' εὐμαθέστατον ἁπάντων τῶν Πλάτωνι συγγε-
γονότων καὶ ὀξύτατον ὑπακοῦσαι πρὸς ἀρετήν, ὡς αὐτὸς
γέγραφε Πλάτων καὶ τὰ πράγματα μαρτυρεῖ. Τραφεὶς 6
γὰρ ἐν ἤθεσιν ὑπὸ τυράννῳ ταπεινοῖς, καὶ βίου μὲν
ἀνίσου καὶ καταφόβου, θεραπείας δὲ νεοπλούτου καὶ
τρυφῆς ἀπειροκάλου καὶ διαίτης ἐν ἡδοναῖς καὶ πλεονε-
ξίαις τιθεμένης τὸ καλὸν ἐθὰς καὶ μεστὸς γενόμενος, ὡς 7
πρῶτον ἐγεύσατο λόγου καὶ φιλοσοφίας ἡγεμονικῆς πρὸς
ἀρετήν, ἀνεφλέχθη τὴν ψυχὴν ταχύ, καὶ τῇ περὶ αὐτὸν
εὐπειθείᾳ τῶν καλῶν ἀκάκως πάνυ καὶ νεωτερικῶς
προσδοκήσας ὑπὸ τῶν αὐτῶν λόγων ὅμοια πείσεσθαι
Διονύσιον, ἐσπούδασε καὶ διεπράξατο ποιησάμενος
σχολὴν αὐτὸν ἐντυχεῖν Πλάτωνι καὶ ἀκοῦσαι.

5. Γενομένης δὲ τῆς συνουσίας αὐτοῖς τὸ μὲν ὅλον
περὶ [ἀνδρὸς] ἀρετῆς, πλείστων δὲ περὶ ἀνδρείας
διαπορηθέντων, ὡς πάντα<ς> μᾶλλον ὁ Πλάτων ἢ τοὺς
τυράννους ἀπέφαινεν ἀνδρείους, ἐκ δὲ τούτου τραπόμενος
περὶ δικαιοσύνης ἐδίδασκεν, ὡς μακάριος μὲν ὁ τῶν
δικαίων, ἄθλιος δὲ ὁ τῶν ἀδίκων βίος, οὔτε τοὺς λόγους 2
ἔφερεν ὁ τύραννος, ὥσπερ ἐξελεγχόμενος, ἤχθετό τε τοῖς
παροῦσι θαυμαστῶς ἀποδεχομένοις τὸν ἄνδρα καὶ

3 κηλουμένοις ὑπὸ τῶν λεγομένων. Τέλος δὲ θυμωθεὶς καὶ παροξυνθεὶς, ἠρώτησεν αὐτόν, ὅ τι δὴ βουλόμενος εἰς
4 Σικελίαν παραγένοιτο. Τοῦ δὲ φήσαντος ἀγαθὸν ἄνδρα ζητεῖν, ὑπολαβὼν ἐκεῖνος " Ἀλλὰ νὴ τοὺς θεούς " εἶπε
5 " καὶ φαίνῃ μήπω τοιοῦτον εὑρηκώς." Οἱ μὲν οὖν περὶ τὸν Δίωνα τοῦτ᾽ <οὔπω> τέλος ᾤοντο τῆς ὀργῆς
* γεγονέναι, καὶ τὸν Πλάτωνα σπεύδοντες συνεξέπεμπον ἐπὶ τριήρους, ᾗ Πόλλιν ἐκόμιζεν εἰς τὴν Ἑλλάδα τὸν
6 Σπαρτιάτην· ὁ δὲ Διονύσιος κρύφα τοῦ Πόλλιδος ἐποιήσατο δέησιν, μάλιστα μὲν ἀποκτεῖναι τὸν ἄνδρα κατὰ πλοῦν, εἰ δὲ μή, πάντως ἀποδόσθαι· βλαβήσεσθαι γὰρ οὐδέν, ἀλλ᾽ εὐδαιμονήσειν ὁμοίως δίκαιον ὄντα, κἂν
7 δοῦλος γένηται. Διὸ καὶ λέγεται Πόλλις εἰς Αἴγιναν φέρων ἀποδόσθαι Πλάτωνα, πολέμου πρὸς Ἀθηναίους ὄντος αὐτοῖς καὶ ψηφίσματος, ὅπως ὁ ληφθεὶς Ἀθηναίων
8 ἐν Αἰγίνῃ πιπράσκηται. Οὐ μὴν ὅ γε Δίων ἔλαττον εἶχε παρὰ τῷ Διονυσίῳ τιμῆς ἢ πίστεως, ἀλλὰ πρεσβείας τε τὰς μεγίστας διῴκει <καὶ> πεμπόμενος πρὸς Καρχηδονίους ἐθαυμάσθη [τε] διαφερόντως· καὶ τὴν παρρησίαν ἔφερεν αὐτοῦ μόνου σχεδόν, ἀδεῶς λέγοντος τὸ παριστά-
9 μενον, ὡς καὶ τὴν περὶ Γέλωνος ἐπίπληξιν. Χλευαζομένης
* γάρ, ὡς ἔοικε, τῆς Γέλωνος ἀρχῆς, αὐτοῦ τε τὸν Γέλωνα τοῦ Διονυσίου γέλωτα τῆς Σικελίας γεγονέναι φήσαντος, οἱ μὲν ἄλλοι τὸ σκῶμμα προσεποιοῦντο θαυμάζειν, ὁ δὲ Δίων δυσχεράνας " Καὶ μὴν " ἔφη " σὺ τυραννεῖς διὰ Γέλωνα πιστευθείς· διὰ σὲ δ᾽ οὐδεὶς ἕτερος πιστευθή-
10 σεται." Τῷ γὰρ ὄντι φαίνεται κάλλιστον μὲν Γέλων ἐπιδειξάμενος θέαμα μοναρχουμένην πόλιν, αἴσχιστον δὲ Διονύσιος.

6. Ὄντων δὲ Διονυσίῳ παίδων τριῶν μὲν ἐκ τῆς Λοκρίδος, τεττάρων δ᾽ ἐξ Ἀριστομάχης, ὧν δύο ἦσαν
* θυγατέρες, Σωφροσύνη καὶ Ἀρετή, Σωφροσύνην μὲν Διονυσίῳ τῷ υἱῷ συνῴκισεν, Ἀρετὴν δὲ Θεαρίδῃ τῷ ἀδελφῷ. Τελευτήσαντος δὲ τοῦ [ἀδελφοῦ] Θεαρίδου,
2 Δίων ἔλαβε τὴν Ἀρετήν, ἀδελφιδῆν οὖσαν. Ἐπεὶ δὲ νοσῶν ἔδοξεν ὁ Διονύσιος ἀβιώτως ἔχειν, ἐπεχείρησεν αὐτῷ διαλέγεσθαι περὶ τῶν ἐκ τῆς Ἀριστομάχης τέκνων

ὁ Δίων. Οἱ δ' ἰατροὶ τῷ μέλλοντι τὴν ἀρχὴν διαδέχεσθαι 3 χαριζόμενοι, καιρὸν οὐ παρέσχον· ὡς δὲ Τίμαιός φησι, καὶ φάρμακον ὑπνωτικὸν αἰτοῦντι δόντες ἀφείλοντο τὴν αἴσθησιν αὐτοῦ, θανάτῳ συνάψαντες τὸν ὕπνον. Οὐ μὴν 4 ἀλλὰ συλλόγου πρώτου τῶν φίλων γενομένου παρὰ τὸν νέον Διονύσιον, οὕτω διελέχθη περὶ τῶν συμφερόντων πρὸς τὸν καιρὸν ὁ Δίων, ὥστε τοὺς ἄλλους ἅπαντας τῇ μὲν φρονήσει παῖδας ἀποδεῖξαι, τῇ δὲ παρρησίᾳ δούλους τῆς τυραννίδος, ἀγεννῶς καὶ περιφόβως τὰ πολλὰ πρὸς χάριν τῷ μειρακίῳ συμβουλεύοντας. Μάλιστα δ' αὐτοὺς 5 ἐξέπληξε, τὸν ἀπὸ Καρχηδόνος κίνδυνον ἐπικρεμάμενον τῇ ἀρχῇ δεδοικότας, ὑποσχόμενος, εἰ μὲν εἰρήνης δέοιτο Διονύσιος, πλεύσας εὐθὺς εἰς Λιβύην ὡς ἄριστα διαθήσεσθαι τὸν πόλεμον· εἰ δὲ πολεμεῖν προθυμοῖτο, θρέψειν αὐτὸς ἰδίοις τέλεσι καὶ παρέξειν εἰς τὸν πόλεμον αὐτῷ πεντήκοντα τριήρεις πλεούσας.

7. Ὁ μὲν οὖν Διονύσιος ὑπερφυῶς τὴν μεγαλοψυχίαν ἐθαύμασε καὶ τὴν προθυμίαν ἠγάπησεν· οἱ δ' ἐλέγχε- 2 σθαι τῇ λαμπρότητι καὶ ταπεινοῦσθαι τῇ δυνάμει τοῦ Δίωνος οἰόμενοι, ταύτην εὐθὺς ἀρχὴν λαβόντες, οὐδεμιᾶς ἐφείδοντο φωνῆς, ᾗ τὸ μειράκιον ἐξαγριαίνειν ἔμελλον πρὸς αὐτόν, ὡς ὑπερχόμενον διὰ τῆς θαλάττης τυραννίδα, καὶ περισπῶντα ταῖς ναυσὶ τὴν δύναμιν εἰς τοὺς Ἀριστομάχης παῖδας, ἀδελφιδοῦς ὄντας αὐτῷ. Φανερώταται δὲ 3 καὶ μέγισται τῶν εἰς φθόνον καὶ μῖσος αἰτιῶν ὑπῆρχον ἡ τοῦ βίου διαφορὰ καὶ τὸ τῆς διαίτης ἄμεικτον. Οἱ 4 μὲν γὰρ εὐθὺς ἐξ ἀρχῆς νέου τυράννου καὶ τεθραμμένου φαύλως ὁμιλίαν καὶ συνήθειαν ἡδοναῖς καὶ κολακείαις καταλαμβάνοντες, ἀεί τινας ἔρωτας καὶ διατριβὰς ἐμηχανῶντο ῥεμβώδεις περὶ πότους καὶ γυναῖκας καὶ παιδιὰς ἑτέρας ἀσχήμονας· ὑφ' ὧν ἡ τυραννίς, ὥσπερ σίδηρος, 5 μαλασσομένη τοῖς μὲν ἀρχομένοις ἐφάνη φιλάνθρωπος, καὶ τὸ λίαν ἀπάνθρωπον ὑπανῆκεν, οὐκ ἐπιεικείᾳ τινὶ μᾶλλον ἢ ῥαθυμίᾳ τοῦ κρατοῦντος ἀμβλυνομένη· ἐκ δὲ 6 τούτου προϊοῦσα καὶ νεμομένη κατὰ μικρὸν ἡ περὶ τὸ μειράκιον ἄνεσις τοὺς ἀδαμαντίνους δεσμοὺς ἐκείνους, οἷς ὁ πρεσβύτερος Διονύσιος ἔφη δεδεμένην ἀπολείπειν

7 τὴν μοναρχίαν, ἐξέτηξε καὶ διέφθειρεν. Ἡμέρας γάρ,
ὥς φασιν, ἐνενήκοντα συνεχῶς ἔπινεν ἀρξάμενος, καὶ τὴν
αὐλὴν ἐν τῷ χρόνῳ τούτῳ σπουδαίοις ἀνδράσι καὶ
λόγοις ἄβατον καὶ ἀνείσοδον οὖσαν, μέθαι καὶ σκώμ-
ματα καὶ ψαλμοὶ καὶ ὀρχήσεις καὶ βωμολοχίαι κατεῖχον.

8. Ἦν οὖν, ὡς εἰκός, ὁ Δίων ἐπαχθής, εἰς οὐδὲν ἡδὺ
καὶ νεωτερικὸν ἐνδιδοὺς ἑαυτόν. Διὸ καὶ πιθανὰ κακιῶν
προσρήματα ταῖς ἀρεταῖς ἐπιφέροντες αὐτοῦ, διέβαλλον,
ὑπεροψίαν τὴν σεμνότητα καὶ τὴν παρρησίαν αὐθάδειαν
2 ἀποκαλοῦντες· καὶ νουθετῶν κατηγορεῖν ἐδόκει, καὶ μὴ
συνεξαμαρτάνων καταφρονεῖν. Ἀμέλει δὲ καὶ φύσει
τινὰ τὸ ἦθος ὄγκον εἶχεν αὐτοῦ καὶ τραχύτητα δυσπρό-
3 σοδον ἐντεύξει καὶ δυσξύμβολον. Οὐ γὰρ μόνον ἀνδρὶ
νέῳ καὶ διατεθρυμμένῳ τὰ ὦτα κολακείαις ἄχαρις ἦν
συγγενέσθαι καὶ προσάντης, πολλοὶ δὲ καὶ τῶν πάνυ
χρωμένων αὐτῷ, καὶ τὴν ἁπλότητα καὶ τὸ γενναῖον
ἀγαπώντων τοῦ τρόπου, κατεμέμφοντο τῆς ὁμιλίας, ὡς
ἀγροικότερον καὶ βαρύτερον πολιτικῶν χρειῶν τοῖς δεο-
4 μένοις συναλλάσσοντα. Περὶ ὧν καὶ Πλάτων ὕστερον
ὥσπερ ἀποθεσπίζων ἔγραψε πρὸς αὐτόν, ἐξευλαβεῖσθαι
5 τὴν αὐθάδειαν, ὡς ἐρημίᾳ συνοικοῦσαν. Οὐ μὴν ἀλλὰ
τότε πλείστου δοκῶν ἄξιος ὑπάρχειν διὰ τὰ πράγματα,
⁎ καὶ μόνος ἢ μάλιστα τὴν τυραννίδα σαλεύουσαν ἂν
ὀρθοῦν καὶ διαφυλάττειν, ἐγίνωσκεν οὐ πρὸς χάριν, ἀλλ'
ἄκοντος ὑπὸ χρείας τοῦ τυράννου πρῶτος ὢν καὶ μέγιστος.

9. Αἰτίαν δὲ τούτου τὴν ἀπαιδευσίαν εἶναι νομίζων,
ἐμβαλεῖν αὐτὸν εἰς διατριβὰς ἐλευθερίους ἐφιλοτιμεῖτο,
καὶ γεῦσαι λόγων καὶ μαθημάτων ἠθοποιῶν, ὡς ἀρετήν
τε παύσαιτο δεδιώς, καὶ τοῖς καλοῖς χαίρειν ἐθισθείη.
2 Φύσει γὰρ οὐ γεγόνει τῶν φαυλοτάτων τυράννων ὁ Διονύσιος, ἀλλ' ὁ πατὴρ δεδοικὼς μὴ φρονήματος μεταλαβὼν
καὶ συγγενόμενος νοῦν ἔχουσιν ἀνθρώποις ἐπιβουλεύσειεν
αὐτῷ καὶ παρέλοιτο τὴν ἀρχήν, ἐφρούρει κατάκλειστον
οἴκοι, δι' ἐρημίαν ὁμιλίας ἑτέρας καὶ ἀπειρίᾳ πραγμάτων.
ὥς φασιν, ἁμάξια καὶ λυχνίας καὶ δίφρους ξυλίνους καὶ
3 τραπέζας τεκταινόμενον. Οὕτω γὰρ ἦν ἄπιστος **καὶ**

πρὸς ἅπαντας ἀνθρώπους ὕποπτος καὶ προβεβλημένος διὰ φόβον ὁ πρεσβύτερος Διονύσιος, ὥστε μηδὲ τῆς κεφαλῆς τὰς τρίχας ἀφελεῖν <ἐᾶν> κουρικαῖς μαχαίραις, ἀλλὰ τῶν πλαστῶν τις ἐπιφοιτῶν ἄνθρακι τὴν κόμην περιέκαιεν. Εἰσήει δὲ πρὸς αὐτὸν εἰς τὸ δωμάτιον οὔτ' 4 ἀδελφὸς οὔθ' υἱὸς ὡς ἔτυχεν ἠμφιεσμένος, ἀλλ' ἔδει πρὶν εἰσελθεῖν ἀποδύντα τὴν ἑαυτοῦ στολὴν ἕκαστον ἑτέραν ἀναλαβεῖν, ὁραθέντα γυμνὸν ὑπὸ τῶν φυλαττόντων. Ἐπεὶ 5 δὲ Λεπτίνης ὁ ἀδελφὸς αὐτῷ ποτε χωρίου φύσιν ἐξηγούμενος, λαβὼν λόγχην παρά τινος τῶν δορυφόρων ὑπέγραψε τὸν τόπον, ἐκείνῳ μὲν ἰσχυρῶς ἐχαλέπηνε, τὸν δὲ δόντα τὴν λόγχην ἀπέκτεινεν. Ἔλεγε δὲ τοὺς φίλους φυλάτ- 6 τεσθαι, νοῦν ἔχοντας εἰδὼς καὶ βουλομένους μᾶλλον τυραννεῖν ἢ τυραννεῖσθαι. Καὶ Μαρσύαν δέ τινα τῶν 7 προηγμένων ὑπ' αὐτοῦ καὶ τεταγμένων ἐφ' ἡγεμονίας ἀνεῖλε δόξαντα κατὰ τοὺς ὕπνους σφάττειν αὐτόν, ὡς ἀπ' ἐννοίας μεθημερινῆς καὶ διαλογισμοῦ τῆς ὄψεως ταύτης εἰς τὸν ὕπνον αὐτῷ παραγενομένης. Ὁ μὲν 8 δὴ Πλάτωνι θυμωθείς, ὅτι μὴ πάντων αὐτὸν ἀνθρώπων ἀνδρειότατον [ὄντα] ἀπέφηνεν, οὕτω περίφοβον καὶ τοσούτων ὑπὸ δειλίας κακῶν μεστὴν εἶχε τὴν ψυχήν.

10. Τὸν δ' υἱὸν αὐτοῦ, καθάπερ εἴρηται, διαλελωβημένον ἀπαιδευσίᾳ καὶ συντετριμμένον τὸ ἦθος ὁ Δίων ὁρῶν, παρεκάλει πρὸς παιδείαν τραπέσθαι, καὶ δεηθῆναι τοῦ πρώτου τῶν φιλοσόφων πᾶσαν δέησιν, ἐλθεῖν εἰς Σικελίαν· ἐλθόντι δὲ παρασχεῖν αὐτόν, ὅπως διακοσμηθεὶς 2 τὸ ἦθος εἰς ἀρετὴν λόγῳ, καὶ πρὸς τὸ θειότατον * ἀφομοιωθεὶς παράδειγμα τῶν ὄντων καὶ κάλλιστον, ᾧ τὸ πᾶν ἡγουμένῳ πειθόμενον ἐξ ἀκοσμίας κόσμος ἐστί, πολλὴν μὲν εὐδαιμονίαν ἑαυτῷ μηχανήσεται, πολλὴν δὲ * τοῖς πολίταις, ὅσα νῦν ἐν ἀθυμίᾳ διοικοῦσι πρὸς ἀνάγκην 3 τῆς ἀρχῆς, ταῦτα σωφροσύνῃ καὶ δικαιοσύνῃ μετ' εὐμενείας πατρονομούμενα παρασχών, καὶ γενόμενος βασιλεὺς ἐκ τυράννου. Τοὺς γὰρ ἀδαμαντίνους δεσμοὺς 4 οὐχ, ὥσπερ ὁ πατὴρ ἔλεγεν αὐτοῦ, φόβον καὶ βίαν καὶ νεῶν πλῆθος εἶναι καὶ βαρβάρων μυρίανδρον φυλακήν, εὔνοιαν δὲ καὶ προθυμίαν καὶ χάριν ἐγγενομένην ὑπ'

ἀρετῆς καὶ δικαιοσύνης, ἃ καίπερ ὄντα μαλακώτερα τῶν
συντόνων καὶ σκληρῶν ἐκείνων, ἰσχυρότερα πρὸς
5 διαμονὴν ἡγεμονίας ὑπάρχειν. Χωρὶς δὲ τούτων ἀφιλό-
τιμον εἶναι καὶ ἄζηλον τὸν ἄρχοντα, τῷ μὲν σώματι
περιττῶς ἀμπεχόμενον καὶ τῇ περὶ τὴν οἴκησιν ἁβρότητι
καὶ κατασκευῇ λαμπρυνόμενον, ὁμιλίᾳ δὲ καὶ λόγῳ μηδὲν
ὄντα τοῦ προστυχόντος σεμνότερον, μηδὲ τῆς ψυχῆς τὸ
βασίλειον ἀξιοῦντα κεκοσμημένον ἔχειν βασιλικῶς καὶ
πρεπόντως.

11. Ταῦτα πολλάκις τοῦ Δίωνος παραινοῦντος, καὶ
τῶν λόγων τοῦ Πλάτωνος ἔστιν οὕστινας ὑποσπείροντος,
ἔσχεν ἔρως τὸν Διονύσιον ὀξὺς καὶ περιμανὴς τῶν τε
2 λόγων καὶ τῆς συνουσίας τοῦ Πλάτωνος. Εὐθὺς οὖν
Ἀθήναζε πολλὰ μὲν ἐφοίτα γράμματα παρὰ τοῦ
Διονυσίου, πολλαὶ δ' ἐπισκήψεις παρὰ τοῦ Δίωνος, ἄλλα
δ' ἐξ Ἰταλίας παρὰ τῶν Πυθαγορικῶν, διακελευομένων
παραγενέσθαι καὶ νέας ψυχῆς ἐξουσίᾳ μεγάλῃ καὶ
δυνάμει περιφερομένης ἐπιλαβέσθαι, καὶ κατασχεῖν
3 ἐμβριθεστέροις λογισμοῖς. Πλάτων μὲν οὖν, ὥς φησιν
* αὐτός, ἑαυτὸν αἰσχυνθεὶς μάλιστα, μὴ δόξειε λόγος εἶναι
μόνον, ἔργου δ' ἑκὼν οὐδενὸς ἂν ἅψασθαι, καὶ προσδοκήσας δι' ἑνὸς ἀνδρὸς ὥσπερ ἡγεμονικοῦ μέρους
ἐκκαθαρθέντος ὅλην ἰατρεύσειν Σικελίαν νοσοῦσαν, ὑπή-
4 κουσεν. Οἱ δὲ τῷ Δίωνι πολεμοῦντες, φοβούμενοι τὴν
τοῦ Διονυσίου μεταβολήν, ἔπεισαν αὐτὸν ἀπὸ τῆς φυγῆς
μεταπέμπεσθαι Φίλιστον, ἄνδρα καὶ πεπαιδευμένον περὶ
λόγους καὶ τυραννικῶν ἠθῶν ἐμπειρότατον, ὡς ἀντίταγμα
5 πρὸς Πλάτωνα καὶ φιλοσοφίαν ἐκεῖνον ἕξοντες. Ὁ γὰρ
δὴ Φίλιστος ἐξ ἀρχῆς τε τῇ τυραννίδι καθισταμένῃ
προθυμότατον ἑαυτὸν παρέσχε, καὶ τὴν ἄκραν διεφύλαξε
φρουραρχῶν ἐπὶ πολὺν χρόνον. Ἦν δὲ λόγος, ὡς καὶ τῇ
μητρὶ πλησιάζοι τοῦ πρεσβυτέρου Διονυσίου, τοῦ
6 τυράννου μὴ παντάπασιν ἀγνοοῦντος. Ἐπεὶ δὲ Λεπτίνης
ἐκ γυναικός, ἣν διαφθείρας ἑτέρῳ συνοικοῦσαν ἔσχε,
γενομένων αὐτῷ δυοῖν θυγατέρων, τὴν ἑτέραν ἔδωκε
Φιλίστῳ, μηδὲ φράσας πρὸς Διονύσιον, ὀργισθεὶς
ἐκεῖνος τὴν μὲν γυναῖκα [τοῦ Λεπτίνου] δήσας ἐν πέδαις

καθεῖρξε, τὸν δὲ Φίλιστον ἐξήλασε Σικελίας, φυγόντα παρὰ ξένους τινὰς εἰς τὸν Ἀδρίαν, ὅπου καὶ δοκεῖ τὰ πλεῖστα συνθεῖναι τῆς ἱστορίας σχολάζων. Οὐ γὰρ 7 ἐπανῆλθε τοῦ πρεσβυτέρου ζῶντος, ἀλλὰ μετὰ τὴν ἐκείνου τελευτήν, ὥσπερ εἴρηται, κατήγαγεν αὐτὸν ὁ πρὸς Δίωνα τῶν ἄλλων φθόνος, ὡς αὐτοῖς τε μᾶλλον ἐπιτήδειον ὄντα καὶ τῇ τυραννίδι βεβαιότερον.

12. Οὗτος μὲν οὖν εὐθὺς κατελθὼν διεπεφύκει τῆς τυραννίδος· τῷ δὲ Δίωνι καὶ παρ' ἄλλων ἐτύγχανον οὖσαι διαβολαὶ καὶ κατηγορίαι πρὸς τὸν τύραννον, ὡς διειλεγμένῳ περὶ καταλύσεως τῆς ἀρχῆς πρός τε Θεοδότην καὶ πρὸς Ἡρακλείδην. Ἤλπιζε μὲν γάρ, ὡς 2 ἔοικε, διὰ Πλάτωνος παραγενομένου τὸ δεσποτικὸν καὶ λίαν ἄκρατον ἀφελὼν τῆς τυραννίδος, ἐμμελῆ τινα καὶ νόμιμον ἄρχοντα τὸν Διονύσιον καταστήσειν· εἰ δ' 3 ἀντιβαίνοι καὶ μὴ μαλάσσοιτο, καταλύσας ἐκεῖνον ἐγνώκει τὴν πολιτείαν ἀποδιδόναι Συρακοσίοις, οὐκ ἐπαινῶν μὲν δημοκρατίαν, πάντως δὲ βελτίω τυραννίδος ἡγούμενος τοῖς διαμαρτάνουσιν ὑγιαινούσης ἀριστοκρατίας.

13. Ἐν τοιαύτῃ δὲ καταστάσει τῶν πραγμάτων ὄντων, Πλάτων εἰς Σικελίαν ἀφικόμενος, περὶ μὲν τὰς πρώτας ἀπαντήσεις θαυμαστῆς ἐτύγχανε φιλοφροσύνης καὶ τιμῆς. Καὶ γὰρ ἅρμα τῶν βασιλικῶν αὐτῷ παρέστη 2 κεκοσμημένον διαπρεπῶς ἀποβάντι τῆς τριήρους, καὶ θυσίαν ἔθυσεν ὁ τύραννος, ὡς εὐτυχήματος μεγάλου τῇ ἀρχῇ προσγεγονότος. Αἰδὼς δὲ συμποσίων καὶ σχημα- 3 τισμὸς αὐλῆς καὶ πρᾳότης αὐτοῦ τοῦ τυράννου περὶ ἕκαστα τῶν χρηματιζομένων θαυμαστὰς ἐνέδωκεν ἐλπίδας μεταβολῆς τοῖς πολίταις. Φορὰ δέ τις ἦν ἐπὶ λόγους καὶ 4 φιλοσοφίαν ἁπάντων, καὶ τὸ τυραννεῖον, ὥς φασι, κονιορτὸς ὑπὸ πλήθους τῶν γεωμετρούντων κατεῖχεν. Ἡμερῶν δ' ὀλίγων διαγενομένων, θυσία μὲν ἦν πάτριος 5 ἐν τοῖς τυραννείοις· τοῦ δὲ κήρυκος, ὥσπερ εἰώθει, κατευξαμένου διαμένειν τὴν τυραννίδα ἀσάλευτον πολλοὺς χρόνους, ὁ Διονύσιος λέγεται παρεστὼς "Οὐ παύσῃ"

6 φάναι "καταρώμενος ἡμῖν;". Τοῦτο κομιδῇ τοὺς περὶ τὸν Φίλιστον ἐλύπησεν, ἄμαχόν τινα τοῦ Πλάτωνος ἡγουμένους ἔσεσθαι χρόνῳ καὶ συνηθείᾳ τὴν δύναμιν, εἰ νῦν ἐκ συνουσίας ὀλίγης ἠλλοίωκεν οὕτω καὶ μεταβέβληκε τὴν γνώμην τὸ μειράκιον.

14. Οὐκέτ᾽ οὖν καθ᾽ ἕνα καὶ λαθραίως, ἀλλὰ πάντες ἀναφανδὸν ἐλοιδόρουν τὸν Δίωνα, λέγοντες ὡς οὐ λέληθε κατεπάδων καὶ καταφαρμάσσων τῷ Πλάτωνος λόγῳ Διονύσιον, ὅπως ἀφέντος ἑκουσίως αὐτοῦ καὶ προεμένου τὴν ἀρχήν, ὑπολαβὼν εἰς τοὺς Ἀριστομάχης περιστήσῃ 2 παῖδας, ὧν θεῖός ἐστιν. Ἔνιοι δὲ προσεποιοῦντο δυσχεραίνειν, εἰ πρότερον μὲν Ἀθηναῖοι ναυτικαῖς καὶ πεζικαῖς δυνάμεσι μεγάλαις δεῦρο πλεύσαντες, ἀπώλοντο 3 καὶ διεφθάρησαν πρότερον ἢ λαβεῖν Συρακούσας, νυνὶ δὲ δι᾽ ἑνὸς σοφιστοῦ καταλύσουσι τὴν Διονυσίου τυραννίδα, συμπείσαντες αὐτὸν ἐκ τῶν μυρίων δορυφόρων ἀποδράντα, καὶ καταλιπόντα τὰς τετρακοσίας τριήρεις καὶ τοὺς μυρίους ἱππεῖς καὶ τοὺς πολλάκις τοσούτους ὁπλίτας, ἐν Ἀκαδημείᾳ τὸ σιωπώμενον ἀγαθὸν ζητεῖν καὶ διὰ γεωμετρίας εὐδαίμονα γενέσθαι, τὴν ἐν ἀρχῇ καὶ χρήμασι καὶ τρυφαῖς εὐδαιμονίαν Δίωνι καὶ 4 τοῖς Δίωνος ἀδελφιδοῖς προέμενον. Ἐκ τούτων ὑποψίας πρῶτον, εἶτα καὶ φανερωτέρας ὀργῆς καὶ διαφορᾶς γενομένης, ἐκομίσθη τις ἐπιστολὴ κρύφα πρὸς Διονύσιον, ἣν ἐγεγράφει Δίων πρὸς τοὺς Καρχηδονίων ἐπιμελητάς, κελεύων, ὅταν Διονυσίῳ περὶ τῆς εἰρήνης διαλέγωνται, μὴ χωρὶς αὐτοῦ ποιήσασθαι τὴν ἔντευξιν, ὡς πάντα 5 θησομένους ἀμεταπτώτως δι᾽ αὐτοῦ. Ταύτην ἀναγνοὺς Διονύσιος Φιλίστῳ, καὶ μετ᾽ ἐκείνου βουλευσάμενος, ὥς φησι Τίμαιος, ὑπῆλθε τὸν Δίωνα πεπλασμέναις διαλύ- 6 σεσι· καὶ μέτρια σκηψάμενος, διαλλάττεσθαί τε φήσας, μόνον τ᾽ ἀπαγαγὼν ὑπὸ τὴν ἀκρόπολιν πρὸς τὴν θάλασσαν, ἔδειξε τὴν ἐπιστολὴν καὶ κατηγόρησεν, ὡς 7 συνισταμένου μετὰ Καρχηδονίων ἐπ᾽ αὐτόν. Ἀπολογεῖσθαι δὲ βουλομένου τοῦ Δίωνος οὐκ ἀνασχόμενος, ἀλλ᾽ εὐθύς, ὡς εἶχεν, ἐνθέμενος εἰς ἀκάτιον, προσέταξε τοῖς ναύταις κομίζοντας αὐτὸν ἐκθεῖναι πρὸς τὴν Ἰταλίαν.

15. Γενομένου δὲ τούτου, καὶ φανέντος ὠμοῦ τοῖς ἀνθρώποις, τὴν μὲν οἰκίαν τοῦ τυράννου πένθος εἶχε διὰ τὰς γυναῖκας, ἡ δὲ πόλις ἡ τῶν Συρακοσίων ἐπῆρτο, πράγματα νεώτερα καὶ μεταβολὴν προσδεχομένη ταχεῖαν ἐκ τοῦ περὶ Δίωνα θορύβου καὶ τῆς πρὸς τὸν τύραννον ἀπιστίας τῶν ἄλλων. Ἃ δὴ συνορῶν ὁ Διονύσιος καὶ 2 δεδοικώς, τοὺς μὲν φίλους παρεμυθεῖτο καὶ τὰς γυναῖκας, ὡς οὐ φυγῆς, ἀλλ' ἀποδημίας τῷ Δίωνι γεγενημένης, ὡς μή τι χεῖρον ὀργῇ πρὸς τὴν αὐθάδειαν αὐτοῦ παρόντος ἁμαρτεῖν βιασθείη· δύο δὲ ναῦς παραδοὺς τοῖς Δίωνος 3 οἰκείοις, ἐκέλευσεν ἐνθεμένοις ὅσα βούλοιντο τῶν ἐκείνου χρήματα καὶ θεράποντας, ἀπάγειν πρὸς αὐτὸν εἰς Πελοπόννησον. Ἦν δ' οὐσία μεγάλη τῷ Δίωνι καὶ 4 σχεδόν τι τυραννικὴ πομπὴ καὶ κατασκευὴ περὶ τὴν δίαιταν, ἣν οἱ φίλοι συλλαβόντες ἐκόμιζον. Ἄλλα δ' 5 ἐπέμπετο πολλὰ παρὰ τῶν γυναικῶν καὶ τῶν ἑταίρων, ὥστε χρημάτων ἕνεκα καὶ πλούτου λαμπρὸν ἐν τοῖς Ἕλλησιν εἶναι, καὶ διαφανῆναι τῇ τοῦ φυγάδος εὐπορίᾳ τὴν τῆς τυραννίδος δύναμιν.

16. Πλάτωνα δὲ Διονύσιος εὐθὺς μὲν εἰς τὴν ἀκρόπολιν μετέστησεν, ἔντιμον αὐτῷ σχήματι ξενίας φιλανθρώπου φρουρὰν μηχανησάμενος, ὡς μὴ συμπλέοι Δίωνι μάρτυς ὧν ἠδίκητο. Χρόνῳ δὲ καὶ συνδιαιτήσει, 2 καθάπερ ψαῦσιν ἀνθρώπου θηρίον, ἐθισθεὶς ὑπομένειν * τε τὴν ὁμιλίαν αὐτοῦ καὶ τὸν λόγον, ἠράσθη τυραννικὸν ἔρωτα, μόνος ἀξιῶν ὑπὸ Πλάτωνος ἀντερᾶσθαι, καὶ θαυμάζεσθαι μάλιστα πάντων, ἕτοιμος ὢν ἐπιτρέπειν τὰ πράγματα καὶ τὴν τυραννίδα μὴ προτιμῶντι τὴν πρὸς Δίωνα φιλίαν τῆς πρὸς αὐτόν. Ἦν οὖν τῷ Πλάτωνι 3 συμφορὰ τὸ πάθος αὐτοῦ τοῦτο, μαινομένου καθάπερ οἱ δυσέρωτες ὑπὸ ζηλοτυπίας, καὶ πολλὰς μὲν ὀργὰς ἐν ὀλίγῳ χρόνῳ, πολλὰς δὲ διαλλαγὰς καὶ δεήσεις ποιου- μένου πρὸς αὐτόν, ἀκροᾶσθαι δὲ τῶν λόγων καὶ κοινωνεῖν τῆς περὶ φιλοσοφίαν πραγματείας σπουδάζοντος μὲν ὑπερφυῶς, αἰδουμένου δὲ τοὺς ἀποτρέποντας ὡς διαφ- θαρησομένου. Ἐν τούτῳ δὲ πολέμου τινὸς ἐμπεσόντος, 4 ἀποπέμπει τὸν Πλάτωνα, συνθέμενος εἰς ὥραν ἔτους

5 μεταπέμψασθαι Δίωνα. Καὶ τοῦτο μὲν εὐθὺς ἐψεύσατο,
τὰς δὲ προσόδους τῶν κτημάτων ἀπέπεμπεν [αὐτῷ] ἀξιῶν
Πλάτωνα συγγνῶναι περὶ τοῦ χρόνου διὰ τὸν πόλεμον
* 6 (εἰρήνης γὰρ γενομένης, τάχιστα μεταπέμψεσθαι τὸν
Δίωνα) καὶ ἀξιοῦν αὐτὸν ἡσυχίαν ἄγειν καὶ μηδὲν
νεωτερίζειν μηδὲ βλασφημεῖν κατ' αὐτοῦ πρὸς τοὺς
Ἕλληνας.

17. Ταῦτ' ἐπειρᾶτο ποιεῖν Πλάτων, καὶ Δίωνα τρέψας
2 ἐπὶ φιλοσοφίαν ἐν Ἀκαδημείᾳ συνεῖχεν.. Ὤικει μὲν οὖν
ἐν ἄστει παρὰ Καλλίππῳ τινὶ τῶν γνωρίμων, ἀγρὸν δὲ
διαγωγῆς χάριν ἐκτήσατο, καὶ τοῦτον ὕστερον εἰς
3 Σικελίαν πλέων Σπευσίππῳ δωρεὰν ἔδωκεν, ᾧ μάλιστα
τῶν Ἀθήνησι φίλων ἐχρῆτο καὶ συνδιῃτᾶτο, βουλομένου
τοῦ Πλάτωνος ὁμιλίᾳ χάριν ἐχούσῃ καὶ παιδιᾶς ἐμμελοῦς
* κατὰ καιρὸν ἁπτομένῃ κεραννύμενον ἐφηδύνεσθαι τοῦ
4 Δίωνος τὸ ἦθος. Τοιοῦτος δέ τις ὁ Σπεύσιππος ἦν· ᾗ
καὶ ' σκῶψαι ἀγαθὸν' αὐτὸν ἐν τοῖς Σίλλοις ὁ Τίμων
5 προσηγόρευσεν. Αὐτῷ δὲ Πλάτωνι χορηγοῦντι παίδων
χορῷ τόν τε χορὸν ἤσκησεν ὁ Δίων, καὶ τὸ δαπάνημα
πᾶν ἐτέλεσε παρ' ἑαυτοῦ, συγχωροῦντος τοῦ Πλάτωνος
τὴν τοιαύτην φιλοτιμίαν πρὸς τοὺς Ἀθηναίους, ὡς ἐκείνῳ
6 μᾶλλον εὔνοιαν ἢ δόξαν αὐτῷ φέρουσαν. Ἐπεφοίτα δὲ
καὶ ταῖς ἄλλαις πόλεσιν ὁ Δίων, καὶ συνεσχόλαζε καὶ
συνεπανηγύριζε τοῖς ἀρίστοις καὶ πολιτικωτάτοις ἀν-
* δράσιν, οὐδὲν ἐν τῇ διαίτῃ σόλοικον ἐπιδεικνύμενος οὐδὲ
τυραννικὸν οὐδὲ διατεθρυμμένον, ἀλλὰ σωφροσύνην καὶ
ἀρετὴν καὶ ἀνδρείαν καὶ περὶ λόγους καὶ περὶ φιλοσοφίαν
7 εὐσχήμονας διατριβάς. Ἐφ' οἷς εὔνοια παρὰ πάντων
ἐγίνετο καὶ ζῆλος αὐτῷ, τιμαί τε δημόσιαι καὶ ψηφίσματα
8 παρὰ τῶν πόλεων. Λακεδαιμόνιοι δὲ καὶ Σπαρτιάτην
αὐτὸν ἐποιήσαντο, τῆς Διονυσίου καταφρονήσαντες
ὀργῆς, καίπερ αὐτοῖς τότε προθύμως ἐπὶ τοὺς Θηβαίους
9 συμμαχοῦντος. Λέγεται δέ ποτε τὸν Δίωνα τοῦ Με-
γαρέως Πτοιοδώρου δεόμενον ἐπὶ τὴν οἰκίαν ἐλθεῖν·
ἦν δ', ὡς ἔοικε, τῶν πλουσίων τις καὶ δυνατῶν ὁ Πτοιό-
10 δωρος· ὄχλον οὖν ἐπὶ θύραις ἰδὼν ὁ Δίων καὶ πλῆθος
ἀσχολιῶν, καὶ δυσέντευκτον αὐτὸν καὶ δυσπρόσοδον,

ἀπιδὼν πρὸς τοὺς φίλους, δυσχεραίνοντας καὶ ἀγανακτοῦντας, " Τί τοῦτον" ἔφη " μεμφόμεθα ; καὶ γὰρ αὐτοὶ πάντως ἐν Συρακούσαις ὅμοια τούτοις ἐποιοῦμεν ".

18. Χρόνου δὲ προιόντος, ὁ Διονύσιος ζηλοτυπῶν καὶ δεδοικὼς τοῦ Δίωνος τὴν παρὰ τοῖς Ἕλλησιν εὔνοιαν, ἐπαύσατο τὰς προσόδους ἀποστέλλων, καὶ τὴν οὐσίαν παρέδωκεν ἰδίοις ἐπιτρόποις. Βουλόμενος δὲ καὶ τὴν εἰς 2 τοὺς φιλοσόφους διὰ Πλάτωνα κακοδοξίαν ἀναμάχεσθαι, πολλοὺς συνῆγε τῶν πεπαιδεῦσθαι δοκούντων. Φιλο- 3 τιμούμενος δ᾽ <ἐν> τῷ διαλέγεσθαι περιεῖναι πάντων, ἠναγκάζετο τοῖς Πλάτωνος παρακούσμασι κακῶς χρῆσθαι. Καὶ πάλιν ἐκεῖνον ἐπόθει, καὶ κατεγίνωσκει 4 αὐτὸς αὑτοῦ, μὴ χρησάμενος παρόντι, μηδὲ διακούσας ὅσα καλῶς εἶχεν. Οἷα δὲ τύραννος ἔμπληκτος ἀεὶ ταῖς 5 ἐπιθυμίαις καὶ πρὸς πᾶσαν ὀξύρροπος σπουδήν, εὐθὺς ὥρμησεν ἐπὶ τὸν Πλάτωνα, καὶ πᾶσαν μηχανὴν αἴρων συνέπεισε τοὺς περὶ Ἀρχύταν Πυθαγορικούς, τῶν ὁμολογουμένων ἀναδόχους γενομένους καλεῖν Πλάτωνα· δι᾽ 6 ἐκείνου γὰρ αὐτοῖς ἐγεγόνει φιλία καὶ ξενία τὸ πρῶτον. Οἱ δ᾽ ἔπεμψαν Ἀρχέδημον παρ᾽ αὐτόν· ἔπεμψε δὲ καὶ Διονύσιος τριήρη καὶ φίλους δεησομένους τοῦ Πλάτωνος· * αὐτός τε σαφῶς καὶ διαρρήδην ἔγραψεν, ὡς οὐδὲν ἂν 7 γένοιτο τῶν μετρίων Δίωνι, μὴ πεισθέντος Πλάτωνος ἐλθεῖν εἰς Σικελίαν, πεισθέντος δὲ πάντα. Πολλαὶ δ᾽ 8 ἀφίκοντο πρὸς Δίωνα παρὰ τῆς ἀδελφῆς καὶ γυναικὸς ἐπισκήψεις, δεῖσθαι Πλάτωνος ὑπακοῦσαι Διονυσίῳ καὶ μὴ πρόφασιν παρασχεῖν. Οὕτω μὲν δή φησιν ὁ Πλάτων 9 ἐλθεῖν τὸ τρίτον εἰς τὸν πορθμὸν τὸν περὶ Σκύλλαν, *

ὄφρ᾽ ἔτι τὴν ὀλοὴν ἀναμετρήσειε Χάρυβδιν.

19. Ἐλθὼν δὲ μεγάλης μὲν αὐτὸν ἐνέπλησε χαρᾶς, μεγάλης δὲ πάλιν ἐλπίδος Σικελίαν, συνευχομένην καὶ συμφιλοτιμουμένην Πλάτωνα μὲν Φιλίστου περιγενέσθαι, φιλοσοφίαν δὲ τυραννίδος. Ἦν δὲ πολλὴ μὲν τῶν γυναι- 2 κῶν σπουδὴ περὶ αὐτόν, ἐξαίρετος δὲ παρὰ τῷ Διονυσίῳ πίστις, ἣν οὐδεὶς ἄλλος εἶχεν, ἀδιερεύνητον αὐτῷ πλησιάζειν. Δωρεὰς δὲ χρημάτων πολλῶν καὶ πολλάκις, τοῦ 3

14 ΠΛΟΥΤΑΡΧΟΥ

μὲν διδόντος, τοῦ δὲ μὴ δεχομένου, παρὼν Ἀρίστιππος ὁ
Κυρηναῖος ἀσφαλῶς ἔφη μεγαλόψυχον εἶναι Διονύσιον,
αὐτοῖς μὲν γὰρ μικρὰ διδόναι πλειόνων δεομένοις, Πλά-
4 τωνι δὲ πολλὰ μηδὲν λαμβάνοντι. Μετὰ δὲ τὰς πρώτας
φιλοφροσύνας ἀρξαμένου Πλάτωνος ἐντυγχάνειν περὶ
5 Δίωνος, ὑπερθέσεις τὸ πρῶτον ἦσαν, εἶτα μέμψεις καὶ
διαφοραὶ λανθάνουσαι τοὺς ἐκτός, ἐπικρυπτομένου Διονυσίου, καὶ ταῖς ἄλλαις τὸν Πλάτωνα θεραπείαις καὶ τιμαῖς
πειρωμένου παράγειν ἀπὸ τῆς Δίωνος εὐνοίας, οὐδ᾽ αὐτὸν
ἔν γε τοῖς πρώτοις χρόνοις ἀποκαλύπτοντα τὴν ἀπιστίαν
αὐτοῦ καὶ ψευδολογίαν, ἀλλ᾽ ἐγκαρτεροῦντα καὶ σχημα-
6 τιζόμενον. Οὕτω δὲ διακειμένων πρὸς ἀλλήλους καὶ
λανθάνειν πάντας οἰομένων, Ἕλικων ὁ Κυζικηνός, εἷς
τῶν Πλάτωνος συνήθων, ἡλίου προεῖπεν ἔκλειψιν· καὶ
γενομένης ὡς προεῖπε, θαυμασθεὶς ὑπὸ τοῦ τυράννου,
7 δωρεὰν ἔλαβεν ἀργυρίου τάλαντον. Ἀρίστιππος δὲ
παίζων πρὸς τοὺς ἄλλους φιλοσόφους ἔφη τι καὶ αὐτὸς
ἔχειν τῶν παραδόξων προειπεῖν. Ἐκείνων δὲ φράσαι
δεομένων "Προλέγω τοίνυν" εἶπεν "ὀλίγου χρόνου
8 Πλάτωνα καὶ Διονύσιον ἐχθροὺς γενησομένους". Τέλος
δὲ τὴν μὲν οὐσίαν τοῦ Δίωνος ὁ Διονύσιος ἐπώλει, καὶ
τὰ χρήματα κατεῖχε, Πλάτωνα δ᾽ ἐν τῷ περὶ τὴν οἰκίαν
κήπῳ διαιτώμενον εἰς τοὺς μισθοφόρους μετέστησε,
πάλαι μισοῦντας αὐτὸν καὶ ζητοῦντας ἀνελεῖν, ὡς
πείθοντα Διονύσιον ἀφεῖναι τὴν τυραννίδα καὶ ζῆν
ἀδορυφόρητον.

20. Ἐν τοιούτῳ δὲ κινδύνῳ γενομένου τοῦ Πλάτωνος,
οἱ περὶ Ἀρχύταν πυθόμενοι ταχὺ πέμπουσι πρεσβείαν
καὶ τριακόντορον, ἀπαιτοῦντες τὸν ἄνδρα παρὰ Διονυσίου
καὶ λέγοντες, ὡς αὐτοὺς λαβὼν ἀναδόχους τῆς ἀσφαλείας
2 πλεύσειεν εἰς Συρακούσας. Ἀπολεγομένου δὲ τοῦ Διονυσίου τὴν ἔχθραν ἑστιάσεσι καὶ φιλοφροσύναις περὶ
τὴν προπομπήν, ἐν δέ τι προαχθέντος πρὸς αὐτὸν τοιοῦτον
εἰπεῖν· "Ἦ που, Πλάτων, πολλὰ καὶ δεινὰ κατηγορή-
σεις ἡμῶν πρὸς τοὺς συμφιλοσοφοῦντας," ὑπομειδιάσας
3 ἐκεῖνος ἀπεκρίνατο· "Μὴ τοσαύτη λόγων ἐν Ἀκαδημείᾳ
4 γένοιτο σπάνις, ὥστε σοῦ τινα μνημονεῦσαι". Τοιαύτην

μὲν τὴν ἀποστολὴν τοῦ Πλάτωνος γενέσθαι λέγουσιν·
οὐ μέντοι τὰ Πλάτωνος αὐτοῦ πάνυ τούτοις συνᾴδει.

21. Δίων δὲ καὶ τούτοις ἐχαλέπαινε, καὶ μετ᾽ ὀλίγον
χρόνον ἐξεπολεμώθη παντάπασι, πυθόμενος τὸ περὶ τὴν
γυναῖκα, περὶ οὗ καὶ Πλάτων ᾐνίξατο γράφων πρὸς
Διονύσιον. Ἦν δὲ τοιοῦτον. Μετὰ τὴν ἐκβολὴν τοῦ 2
Δίωνος ἀποπέμπων Πλάτωνα Διονύσιος ἐκέλευσεν αὐτοῦ
δι᾽ ἀπορρήτων πυθέσθαι, μή τι κωλύοι τὴν γυναῖκα πρὸς
γάμον ἑτέρῳ δοθῆναι· καὶ γὰρ ἦν λόγος εἴτ᾽ ἀληθὴς εἴτε 3
συντεθεὶς ὑπὸ τῶν Δίωνα μισούντων, ὡς οὐ καθ᾽ ἡδονὴν ὁ
γάμος εἴη Δίωνι γεγονώς, οὐδ᾽ εὐάρμοστος ἡ πρὸς τὴν
γυναῖκα συμβίωσις. Ὡς οὖν ἧκεν ὁ Πλάτων Ἀθήναζε, 4
καὶ τῷ Δίωνι περὶ πάντων ἐνέτυχε, γράφει πρὸς τὸν
τύραννον ἐπιστολήν, τὰ μὲν ἄλλα σαφῶς πᾶσιν, αὐτὸ
δὲ τοῦτο μόνῳ γνώριμον ἐκείνῳ φράζουσαν, ὡς διαλεχθείη   *
Δίωνι περὶ τοῦ πράγματος ἐκείνου, καὶ σφόδρα δῆλος εἴη
χαλεπαίνων <ἂν> εἰ τοῦτο Διονύσιος ἐξεργάσαιτο. Καὶ 5
τότε μὲν ἔτι πολλῶν ἐλπίδων οὐσῶν πρὸς τὰς διαλύσεις,
οὐδὲν ἔπραξε περὶ τὴν ἀδελφὴν νεώτερον, ἀλλ᾽ εἴα μένειν
αὐτὴν μετὰ τοῦ παιδίου τοῦ Δίωνος οἰκοῦσαν. Ἐπεὶ δὲ 6
παντάπασιν ἀσυμβάτως εἶχε, καὶ Πλάτων αὖθις ἐλθὼν
ἀπεπέμφθη πρὸς ἀπέχθειαν, οὕτω τὴν Ἀρετὴν ἄκουσαν
ἑνὶ τῶν φίλων Τιμοκράτει, δίδωσιν, οὐ μιμησάμενος τὴν
κατά γε τοῦτο τοῦ πατρὸς ἐπιείκειαν. Ἐγεγόνει γάρ, ὡς 7
ἔοικε, κἀκείνῳ Πολύξενος ὁ τὴν ἀδελφὴν ἔχων αὐτοῦ
Θέστην πολέμιος· ἀποδράντος οὖν αὐτοῦ διὰ φόβον καὶ
φυγόντος ἐκ Σικελίας μεταπεμψάμενος ᾐτιᾶτο τὴν
ἀδελφήν, ὅτι συνειδυῖα τὴν φυγὴν τοῦ ἀνδρὸς οὐ κατεῖπε
πρὸς αὐτόν. Ἡ δ᾽ ἀνεκπλήκτως καὶ νὴ Δί᾽ ἀφόβως 8
" Εἶθ᾽ οὕτω σοι δοκῶ, Διονύσιε, φαύλη γυνὴ γεγονέναι
καὶ ἄνανδρος, ὥστε προγνοῦσα τὴν φυγὴν τοῦ ἀνδρὸς
οὐκ ἂν συνεκπλεῦσαι καὶ μετασχεῖν τῆς αὐτῆς τύχης;
ἀλλ᾽ οὐ προέγνων· ἐπεὶ καλῶς εἶχέ μοι μᾶλλον Πολυξένου
γυναῖκα φεύγοντος ἢ σοῦ τυραννοῦντος ἀδελφὴν λέγεσθαι." ταῦτα τῆς Θέστης παρρησιασαμένης, θαυμάσαι 9
λέγουσι τὸν τύραννον. Ἐθαύμασαν δὲ καὶ οἱ Συρακόσιοι
τὴν ἀρετὴν τῆς γυναικός, ὥστε καὶ μετὰ τὴν κατάλυσιν

τῆς τυραννίδος ἐκείνῃ τιμὴν καὶ θεραπείαν βασιλικὴν
ὑπάρχειν, ἀποθανούσης δὲ δημοσίᾳ πρὸς τὴν ταφὴν
ἐπακολουθῆσαι τοὺς πολίτας. Ταῦτα μὲν οὖν οὐκ
ἄχρηστον ἔχει τὴν παρέκβασιν.

22. Ὁ δὲ Δίων ἐντεῦθεν ἤδη τρέπεται πρὸς πόλεμον,
αὐτοῦ μὲν Πλάτωνος ἐκποδὼν ἱσταμένου δι' αἰδῶ τῆς
πρὸς Διονύσιον ξενίας καὶ γήρας, Σπευσίππου δὲ καὶ τῶν
ἄλλων ἑταίρων τῷ Δίωνι συλλαμβανόντων καὶ παρακελευομένων ἐλευθεροῦν Σικελίαν, χεῖρας ὀρέγουσαν αὐτῷ
2 καὶ προθύμως ὑποδεχομένην. Ὅτε γὰρ ἐν Συρακούσαις
Πλάτων διέτριβεν, οἱ περὶ Σπεύσιππον, ὡς ἔοικε, μᾶλλον
ἀναμειγνύμενοι τοῖς ἀνθρώποις, κατεμάνθανον τὴν
3 διάνοιαν αὐτῶν. Καὶ τὸ μὲν πρῶτον ἐφοβοῦντο τὴν
παρρησίαν, ὡς διάπειραν οὖσαν ὑπὸ τοῦ τυράννου, χρόνῳ
δ' ἐπίστευσαν. Ὁ γὰρ αὐτὸς ἦν παρὰ πάντων λόγος,
δεομένων καὶ παρακελευομένων ἐλθεῖν Δίωνα μὴ ναῦς
ἔχοντα μηδ' ὁπλίτας μηδ' ἵππους, ἀλλ' αὐτὸν εἰς ὑπηρε-
τικὸν ἐμβάντα χρῆσαι τὸ σῶμα καὶ τοὔνομα Σικελιώταις
4 ἐπὶ τὸν Διονύσιον. Ταῦτα τῶν περὶ Σπεύσιππον
ἀγγελλόντων, ἐπιρρωσθεὶς ἐξενολόγει κρύφα καὶ δι'
5 ἑτέρων, ἐπικρυπτόμενος τὴν διάνοιαν. Συνέπραττον δὲ
καὶ τῶν πολιτικῶν πολλοὶ καὶ τῶν φιλοσόφων, ὅ τε
Κύπριος Εὔδημος, εἰς ὃν Ἀριστοτέλης ἀποθανόντα τὸν
περὶ ψυχῆς διάλογον ἐποίησε, καὶ Τιμωνίδης ὁ Λευκάδιος.
6 Συνέστησαν δὲ καὶ Μιλτᾶν αὐτῷ τὸν Θεσσαλόν, ἄνδρα
μάντιν καὶ μετεσχηκότα τῆς ἐν Ἀκαδημείᾳ διατριβῆς.
7 Τῶν δ' ὑπὸ τοῦ τυράννου πεφυγαδευμένων, οὐ μεῖον ἢ
χιλίων ὄντων, πέντε καὶ εἴκοσι μόνοι τῆς στρατείας
ἐκοινώνησαν, οἱ δ' ἄλλοι προὔδοσαν ἀποδειλιάσαντες.
8 Ὁρμητήριον δ' ἦν ἡ Ζακυνθίων νῆσος, εἰς ἣν οἱ
στρατιῶται συνελέγησαν, ὀκτακοσίων ἐλάττους γενόμενοι
γνώριμοι δὲ πάντες ἐκ πολλῶν καὶ μεγάλων στρατ[ε]ιῶν,
καὶ τοῖς σώμασιν ἠσκημένοι διαφερόντως, ἐμπειρίᾳ δὲ
καὶ τόλμῃ πολὺ πάντων κράτιστοι, καὶ δυνάμενοι πλῆθος
ὅσον ἤλπιζεν ἕξειν ἐν Σικελίᾳ Δίων ὑπεκκαῦσαι καὶ
συνεξορμῆσαι πρὸς ἀλκήν.

23. Οὗτοι τὸ μὲν πρῶτον ἀκούσαντες ἐπὶ Διονύσιον καὶ Σικελίαν αἴρεσθαι τὸν στόλον, ἐξεπλάγησαν καὶ κατέγνωσαν, ὡς ὀργῆς τινος παραφροσύνῃ καὶ μανίᾳ τοῦ Δίωνος ἢ χρηστῶν ἐλπίδων ἀπορίᾳ ῥιπτοῦντος ἑαυτὸν εἰς ἀπεγνωσμένας πράξεις, καὶ τοῖς ἑαυτῶν ἡγεμόσι καὶ ξενολόγοις ὠργίζοντο μὴ προειποῦσιν εὐθὺς ἐξ ἀρχῆς τὸν πολέμ<ι>ον. Ἐπεὶ δὲ Δίων τῷ λόγῳ τὰ σαθρὰ τῆς 2 τυραννίδος ἐπεξιὼν ἐδίδασκεν, ὡς οὐ στρατιώτας, ἀλλὰ μᾶλλον ἡγεμόνας αὐτοὺς κομίζοι Συρακοσίων καὶ τῶν ἄλλων Σικελιωτῶν, πάλαι πρὸς ἀπόστασιν ἑτοίμων ὑπαρχόντων, μετὰ δὲ τὸν Δίωνα διαλεχθέντος αὐτοῖς Ἀλκιμένους, ὃς πρῶτος ὢν Ἀχαιῶν δόξῃ καὶ γένει συνεστράτευεν, ἐπείσθησαν. Ἦν μὲν οὖν θέρους ἀκμή, 3 καὶ κατεῖχον ἐτησίαι τὸ πέλαγος, ἡ δὲ σελήνη διχομηνίαν ἦγε· τῷ δ' Ἀπόλλωνι θυσίαν μεγαλοπρεπῆ παρασκευάσας ὁ Δίων ἐπόμπευσε μετὰ τῶν στρατιωτῶν, κεκοσμημένων ταῖς πανοπλίαις πρὸς τὸ ἱερόν· καὶ μετὰ τὴν θυσίαν ἐν τῷ σταδίῳ τῶν Ζακυνθίων κατακλιθέντας 4 αὐτοὺς εἱστία, θαυμάζοντας ἀργυρῶν καὶ χρυσῶν ἐκπωμάτων καὶ τραπεζῶν ὑπερβάλλουσαν ἰδιωτικὸν πλοῦτον λαμπρότητα, καὶ λογιζομένους, ὅτι παρηκμακὼς ἀνὴρ ἤδη καὶ τοσαύτης εὐπορίας κύριος οὐκ ἂν ἐπιχειροίη παραβόλοις πράγμασι χωρὶς ἐλπίδος βεβαίου καὶ φίλων ἐνδιδόντων ἐκεῖθεν αὐτῷ τὰς πλείστας καὶ μεγίστας ἀφορμάς.

24. Μετὰ δὲ τὰς σπονδὰς καὶ τὰς νενομισμένας κατευχὰς ἐξέλιπεν ἡ σελήνη. Καὶ τοῖς μὲν περὶ τὸν Δίωνα θαυμαστὸν οὐδὲν ἦν, λογιζομένοις τὰς ἐκλειπτικὰς περιόδους καὶ τὴν γινομένην τοῦ σκιάσματος ἀπάντησιν πρὸς τὴν σελήνην, καὶ τῆς γῆς τὴν ἀντίφραξιν πρὸς τὸν ἥλιον. Ἐπεὶ δὲ τοῖς στρατιώταις διαταραχθεῖσιν ἔδει 2 τινὸς παρηγορίας, Μιλτᾶς ὁ μάντις ἐν μέσῳ καταστὰς ἐκέλευε θαρρεῖν αὐτοὺς καὶ προσδοκᾶν τὰ κράτιστα· σημαίνειν γὰρ τὸ δαιμόνιον ἔκλειψίν τινος τῶν νῦν 3 ἐπιφανῶν· ἐπιφανέστερον δὲ μηδὲν εἶναι τῆς Διονυσίου τυραννίδος, ἧς τὸ λαμπρὸν ἀποσβέσειν ἐκείνους εὐθὺς ἁψαμένους Σικελίας. Τοῦτο μὲν οὖν ὁ Μιλτᾶς εἰς μέσον 4

B

ἐξέθηκε πᾶσι· τὸ δὲ τῶν μελισσῶν, αἳ περὶ τὰ πλοῖα τοῦ
Δίωνος ὤφθησαν ἑσμὸν λαμβάνουσαι κατὰ πρύμναν, ἰδίᾳ
πρὸς αὐτὸν καὶ τοὺς φίλους ἔφραζε δεδιέναι, μὴ καλαὶ
μὲν αἱ πράξεις αὐτοῦ γένωνται, χρόνον δ' ὀλίγον
5 ἀνθήσασαι μαρανθῶσι. Λέγεται δὲ καὶ τῷ Διονυσίῳ
πολλὰ τερατώδη παρὰ τοῦ δαιμονίου γενέσθαι σημεῖα.
6 Ἀετὸς μὲν γὰρ ἁρπάσας δοράτιόν τινος τῶν δορυφόρων,
7 ἀράμενος ὑψοῦ καὶ φέρων ἀφῆκεν εἰς τὸν βυθόν· ἡ δὲ
προσκλύζουσα πρὸς τὴν ἀκρόπολιν θάλασσα μίαν
ἡμέραν τὸ ὕδωρ γλυκὺ καὶ πότιμον παρέσχεν, ὥστε
8 γευσαμένοις πᾶσι κατάδηλον εἶναι. Χοῖροι δ' ἐτέχθησαν
αὐτῷ, τῶν μὲν ἄλλων οὐδενὸς ἐνδεεῖς μορίων, ὦτα δ' οὐκ
9 ἔχοντες. Ἀπεφαίνοντο δ' οἱ μάντεις, τοῦτο μὲν ἀποστά-
σεως καὶ ἀπειθείας εἶναι σημεῖον, ὡς οὐκέτι τῶν πολιτῶν
ἀκουσομένων τῆς τυραννίδος, τὴν δὲ γλυκύτητα τῆς
θαλάσσης μεταβολὴν καιρῶν ἀνιαρῶν καὶ πονηρῶν εἰς
πράγματα χρηστὰ φέρειν Συρακοσίοις. Ἀετὸς δὲ
10 θεράπων Διός, λόγχη δὲ παράσημον ἀρχῆς καὶ δυνα-
στείας· ἀφανισμὸν οὖν καὶ κατάλυσιν τῇ τυραννίδι
δηλοῦν τὸν τῶν θεῶν μέγιστον. Ταῦτα μὲν οὖν
Θεόπομπος ἱστόρηκε.

25. Τοὺς δὲ στρατιώτας τοὺς Δίωνος ἐξεδέξαντο
στρογγύλαι δύο ναῦς, τρίτον δὲ πλοῖον οὐ μέγα καὶ δύο
2 τριακόντοροι παρηκολούθουν. Ὅπλα δέ, χωρὶς ὧν εἶχον
οἱ στρατιῶται, δισχιλίας μὲν ἐκόμιζεν ἀσπίδας, βέλη δὲ
καὶ δόρατα πολλὰ καὶ πλῆθος ἐφοδίων ἄφθονον, ὅπως
ἐπιλίπῃ μηδὲν αὐτοὺς ποντοπορούντας, ἅτε δὴ τὸ σύμπαν
ἐπὶ πνεύμασι καὶ θαλάσσῃ πεποιημένους τὸν πλοῦν, διὰ
τὸ τὴν γῆν φοβεῖσθαι καὶ πυνθάνεσθαι Φίλιστον ἐν
3 Ἰαπυγίᾳ ναυλοχοῦντα παραφυλάττειν. Ἀραιῷ δὲ καὶ
μαλακῷ πνεύματι πλεύσαντες ἡμέρας δώδεκα, τῇ τρισ-
καιδεκάτῃ κατὰ Πάχυνον ἦσαν, ἄκραν τῆς Σικελίας.
4 Καὶ Πρῶτος μὲν ὁ κυβερνήτης κατὰ τάχος ἐκέλευσεν
ἀποβαίνειν, ὡς, ἂν ἀποσπάσ[θ]ωσι τῆς γῆς καὶ τὴν
ἄκραν ἑκόντες ἀφῶσι, πολλὰς ἡμέρας καὶ νύκτας ἐν τῷ
πελάγει τριβησομένους, ὥρᾳ θέρους νότον περιμένοντας.
5 Δίων δὲ τὴν ἐγγὺς τῶν πολεμίων ἀπόβασιν δεδιώς, καὶ

τῶν πρόσω μᾶλλον ἅψασθαι βουλόμενος, παρέπλευσε
τὸν Πάχυνον. Ἐκ δὲ τούτου τραχὺς μὲν ἀπαρκτίας 6
ἐπιπεσών, ἤλαυνε πολλῷ κλύδωνι τὰς ναῦς ἀπὸ τῆς
Σικελίας, ἀστραπαὶ δὲ καὶ βρονταὶ φανέντος Ἀρκτούρου
συμπεσοῦσαι, πολὺν ἐξ οὐρανοῦ χειμῶνα καὶ ῥαγδαῖον
ὄμβρον ἐξέχεαν· ᾧ τῶν ναυτῶν συνταραχθέντων, καὶ 7
πλάνης γενομένης, καθορῶσιν αἰφνίδιον ὑπὸ τοῦ κύματος
ὠθουμένας τὰς ναῦς ἐπὶ τὴν πρὸς Λιβύῃ Κέρκιναν, ᾗ
μάλιστα κρημνώδης ἀπήντα καὶ τραχεῖα προσφερομένοις
αὐτοῖς ἡ νῆσος. Μικρὸν οὖν δεήσαντες ἐκριφῆναι καὶ 8
συντριβῆναι περὶ τὰς πέτρας, ἐβιάζοντο πρὸς κοντὸν
παραφερόμενοι μόλις, ἕως ὁ χειμὼν ἐλώφησε, καὶ πλοίῳ
συντυχόντες ἔγνωσαν ἐπὶ ταῖς καλουμέναις Κεφαλαῖς τῆς
μεγάλης Σύρτεως ὄντες. Ἀθυμοῦσι δ' αὐτοῖς πρὸς τὴν 9
γαλήνην καὶ διαφερομένοις, αὔραν τινὰ κατέσπειρεν ἡ
χώρα νότιον, οὐ πάνυ προσδεχομένοις νότον οὐδὲ πιστεύ-
ουσι τῇ μεταβολῇ. Κατὰ μικρὸν δὲ ῥωννυμένου τοῦ 10
πνεύματος καὶ μέγεθος λαμβάνοντος, ἐκτείναντες ὅσον
ἦν ἱστίων, καὶ προσευξάμενοι τοῖς θεοῖς, πελάγιοι πρὸς
τὴν Σικελίαν ἔφευγον ἀπὸ τῆς Λιβύης· καὶ θέοντες 11
ἐλαφρῶς, πεμπταῖοι κατὰ Μίνῳαν ὡρμίσαντο, πολισ-
μάτιον ἐν τῇ Σικελίᾳ τῆς Καρχηδονίων ἐπικρατείας.
Ἔτυχε δὲ παρὼν ὁ Καρχηδόνιος ἄρχων Σύναλος ἐν τῷ 12
χωρίῳ, ξένος ὢν καὶ φίλος Δίωνος. Ἀγνοῶν δὲ τὴν
παρουσίαν αὐτοῦ καὶ τὸν στόλον, ἐπειρᾶτο κωλύειν τοὺς
στρατιώτας ἀποβαίνοντας. Οἱ δὲ μετὰ τῶν ὅπλων ἐκδρα- 13
μόντες, ἀπέκτειναν μὲν οὐδένα, ἀπειρήκει γὰρ ὁ Δίων
διὰ τὴν οὖσαν αὐτῷ φιλίαν πρὸς τὸν Καρχηδόνιον,
φεύγουσι δὲ συνεισπεσόντες, αἱροῦσι τὸ χωρίον. Ὡς 14
δ' ἀπήντησαν ἀλλήλοις οἱ ἡγεμόνες καὶ ἠσπάσαντο,
Δίων μὲν ἀπέδωκε τὴν πόλιν, [Συνάλῳ] οὐδὲν ἀδικήσας,
Σύναλος δὲ τοὺς στρατιώτας ἐξένιζε, καὶ συμπαρεσκεύ-
αζεν ὧν Δίων ἐδεῖτο.

26. Μάλιστα δ' αὐτοὺς ἐθάρρυνε τὸ συμβεβηκὸς
αὐτομάτως περὶ τὴν ἀποδημίαν τοῦ Διονυσίου· νεωστὶ
γὰρ ἐκπεπλευκὼς ἐτύγχανεν ὀγδοήκοντα ναυσὶν εἰς τὴν
Ἰταλίαν. Διὸ καὶ τοῦ Δίωνος παρακαλοῦντος ἐνταῦθα 2

τοὺς στρατιώτας ἀναλαμβάνειν, πολὺν χρόνον ἐν τῇ
θαλάσσῃ κεκακωμένους, οὐχ ὑπέμειναν, αὐτοὶ σπεύδοντες
ἁρπάσαι τὸν καιρόν, ἀλλ᾽ ἐκέλευον ἡγεῖσθαι τὸν Δίωνα
3 πρὸς τὰς Συρακούσας. Ἀποσκευασάμενος οὖν τὰ πε-
ριόντα τῶν ὅπλων καὶ τῶν φορτίων ἐκεῖ, καὶ τοῦ Συνάλου
δεηθείς, ὅταν ᾖ καιρός, ἀποστεῖλαι πρὸς αὐτόν, ἐβάδιζεν
4 ἐπὶ τὰς Συρακούσας. Πορευομένῳ δ᾽ αὐτῷ πρῶτον μὲν
Ἀκραγαντίνων προσεχώρησαν ἱππεῖς διακόσιοι τῶν περὶ
5 τὸ Ἔκνομον οἰκούντων, μετὰ δὲ τούτους Γελῷοι. Ταχὺ
δὲ τῆς φήμης διαδραμούσης εἰς Συρακούσας Τιμοκράτης,
ὁ τῇ Δίωνος γυναικὶ συνοικῶν [Διονυσίου ἀδελφῇ], τῶν
ἀπολελειμμένων ἐν τῇ πόλει φίλων προεστώς, ἐκπέμπει
κατὰ τάχος ἄγγελον τῷ Διονυσίῳ, γράμματα κομίζοντα
6 περὶ τῆς Δίωνος ἀφίξεως. Αὐτὸς δὲ τοῖς κατὰ τὴν
πόλιν προσεῖχε θορύβοις καὶ κινήμασιν, ἐπηρμένων μὲν
πάντων, διὰ δ᾽ ἀπιστίαν ἔτι καὶ φόβον ἡσυχαζόντων.
Τῷ δὲ πεμφθέντι γραμματοφόρῳ τύχῃ τις συμπίπτει
7 παράλογος. Διαπλεύσας γὰρ εἰς τὴν Ἰταλίαν, καὶ τὴν
Ῥηγίνην διελθών, ἐπειγόμενος εἰς Καυλωνίαν πρὸς Διονύσιον, ἀπήντησέ τινι τῶν συνήθων ἱερεῖον νεωστὶ τεθυ-
μένον κομίζοντι· καὶ λαβὼν παρ᾽ αὐτοῦ μοῖραν τῶν
8 κρεῶν, ἐχώρει σπουδῇ. Τῆς δὲ νυκτὸς μέρος ὁδεύσας,
καὶ μικρὸν ἀποδαρθεῖν ὑπὸ κόπου βιασθείς, ὡς εἶχε,
9 παρὰ τὴν ὁδὸν ἐν ὕλῃ τινὶ κατέκλινεν ἑαυτόν. Πρὸς
δὲ τὴν ὀσμὴν λύκος ἐπελθών, καὶ λαβόμενος τῶν κρεῶν
ἀναδεδεμένων ἐκ τῆς πήρας, ᾤχετο φέρων ἅμα σὺν αὐτοῖς
τὴν πήραν, ἐν ᾗ τὰς ἐπιστολὰς ὁ ἄνθρωπος εἶχεν. Ὡς
10 δὲ διεγερθεὶς ᾔσθετο, καὶ πολλὰ μάτην πλανηθεὶς καὶ
διώξας οὐχ εὗρεν, ἔγνω μὴ πορεύεσθαι δίχα τῶν
γραμμάτων πρὸς τὸν τύραννον, ἀλλ᾽ ἀποδρὰς ἐκποδὼν
γενέσθαι.

27. Διονύσιος μὲν οὖν ὀψὲ καὶ παρ᾽ ἑτέρων ἔμελλε
πυνθάνεσθαι τὸν ἐν Σικελίᾳ πόλεμον, Δίωνι δὲ πορευομένῳ Καμαριναῖοί τε προσέθεντο, καὶ τῶν κατ᾽ ἀγροὺς
Συρακοσίων ἀνισταμένων ἐπέρρει πλῆθος οὐκ ὀλίγον.
2 Οἱ δὲ μετὰ Τιμοκράτους τὰς Ἐπιπολὰς φυλάσσοντες
Λεοντῖνοι καὶ Καμπανοί, λόγον ψευδῆ προσπέμψαντος

εἰς αὐτοὺς τοῦ Δίωνος, ὡς ἐπὶ τὰς πόλεις πρῶτον τρέποιτο τὰς ἐκείνων, ἀπολιπόντες ᾤχοντο τὸν Τιμοκράτην, τοῖς οἰκείοις βοηθήσοντες. Ὡς δ᾽ ἀπηγγέλη ταῦτα πρὸς 3 τὸν Δίωνα περὶ τὰς [μ]Ἄκρας στρατοπεδεύοντα, νυκτὸς ἔτι τοὺς στρατιώτας ἀναστήσας, πρὸς τὸν Ἄναπον ποταμὸν ἧκεν, ἀπέχοντα τῆς πόλεως δέκα σταδίους. Ἐνταῦθα 4 δὲ τὴν πορείαν ἐπιστήσας, ἐσφαγιάζετο πρὸς τὸν ποταμόν, ἀνατέλλοντι τῷ ἡλίῳ προσευξάμενος· ἅμα δ᾽ οἱ μάντεις παρὰ τῶν θεῶν νίκην ἔφραζον αὐτῷ. Καὶ θεασάμενοι τὸν Δίωνα διὰ τὴν θυσίαν ἐστεφανωμένον οἱ παρόντες, ἀπὸ μιᾶς ὁρμῆς ἐστεφανοῦντο πάντες. Ἦσαν δὲ πεντακισχιλίων οὐκ ἐλάττους <οἱ> προσγεγο- 5 νότες κατὰ τὴν ὁδόν· ὡπλισμένοι δὲ φαύλως ἐκ τοῦ προστυχόντος, ἀνεπλήρουν τῇ προθυμίᾳ τὴν τῆς παρασκευῆς ἔνδειαν, ὥστε κινήσαντος τοῦ Δίωνος δρόμῳ χωρεῖν, μετὰ χαρᾶς καὶ βοῆς ἀλλήλους παρακαλοῦντας ἐπὶ τὴν ἐλευθερίαν.

28. Τῶν δ᾽ ἐν τῇ πόλει Συρακοσίων, οἱ μὲν γνώριμοι καὶ χαρίεντες ἐσθῆτα καθαρὰν ἔχοντες ἀπήντων ἐπὶ τὰς πύλας, οἱ δὲ πολλοὶ τοῖς <τοῦ> τυράννου φίλοις ἐπετίθεντο, καὶ συνήρπαζον τοὺς καλουμένους προσαγωγίδας, ἀνθρώπους ἀνοσίους καὶ θεοῖς ἐχθρούς, οἳ περιενόστουν ἐν τῇ πόλει καταμεμειγμένοι τοῖς Συρακοσίοις, πολυπραγμονοῦντες καὶ διαγγέλλοντες τῷ τυράννῳ τάς τε διανοίας καὶ τὰς φωνὰς ἑκάστων. Οὗτοι μὲν οὖν πρῶτοι δίκην 2 ἐδίδοσαν, ὑπὸ τῶν προστυγχανόντων ἀποτυμπανιζόμενοι. Τιμοκράτης δὲ συμμεῖξαι τοῖς φρουροῦσι τὴν ἀκρόπολιν μὴ δυνηθείς, ἵππον λαβὼν διεξέπεσε τῆς πόλεως, καὶ πάντα φεύγων ἐνέπλησε φόβου καὶ ταραχῆς, ἐπὶ μεῖζον αἴρων τὰ τοῦ Δίωνος, ὡς μὴ δοκοίη μέτριόν τι δείσας ἀποβεβληκέναι τὴν πόλιν. Ἐν τούτῳ δὲ καὶ Δίων προσ- 3 ερχόμενος ἤδη καταφανὴς ἦν πρῶτος αὐτὸς ὡπλισμένος λαμπρῶς, καὶ παρ᾽ αὐτὸν ἔνθεν μὲν ὁ ἀδελφὸς Μεγακλῆς, ἔνθεν δὲ Κάλλιππος ὁ Ἀθηναῖος, ἐστεφανωμένοι. Τῶν 4 δὲ ξένων ἑκατὸν μὲν εἵποντο φύλακες περὶ τὸν Δίωνα, τοὺς δ᾽ ἄλλους ἦγον οἱ λοχαγοὶ διακεκοσμημένους, θεωμένων τῶν Συρακοσίων καὶ δεχομένων ὥσπερ ἱεράν τινα

καὶ θεοπρεπῆ πομπὴν Ἐλευθερίας καὶ Δημοκρατίας, δι'
ἐτῶν ὀκτὼ καὶ τετταράκοντα κατιούσης εἰς τὴν πόλιν.

29. Ἐπεὶ δ' εἰσῆλθεν ὁ Δίων κατὰ τὰς Τεμενίτιδας
πύλας, τῇ σάλπιγγι καταπαύσας τὸν θόρυβον ἐκήρυξεν,
ὅτι Δίων καὶ Μεγακλῆς ἥκοντες ἐπὶ καταλύσει τῆς
τυραννίδος ἐλευθεροῦσι Συρακοσίους καὶ τοὺς ἄλλους
2 Σικελιώτας ἀπὸ τοῦ τυράννου. Βουλόμενος δὲ καὶ δι'
ἑαυτοῦ προσαγορεῦσαι τοὺς ἀνθρώπους, ἀνῄει διὰ τῆς
Ἀχραδινῆς, ἑκατέρωθεν παρὰ τὴν ὁδὸν τῶν Συρακοσίων
ἱερεῖα καὶ τραπέζας καὶ κρατῆρας ἱστάντων, καὶ καθ' οὓς
γένοιτο προχύταις τε βαλλόντων καὶ προ<σ>τρεπομένων
3 ὥσπερ θεὸν κατευχαῖς. Ἦν δ' ὑπὸ τὴν ἀκρόπολιν καὶ τὰ
Πεντάπυλα, Διονυσίου κατασκευάσαντος, ἡλιοτρόπιον
καταφανὲς καὶ ὑψηλόν. Ἐπὶ τοῦτο προβὰς ἐδημη-
γόρησε, καὶ παρώρμησε τοὺς πολίτας ἀντέχεσθαι τῆς
4 ἐλευθερίας. Οἱ δὲ χαίροντες καὶ φιλοφρονούμενοι
κατέστησαν ἀμφοτέρους αὐτοκράτορας στρατηγούς, καὶ
προσείλοντο, βουλομένων καὶ δεομένων ἐκείνων, αὐτοῖς
συνάρχοντας εἴκοσιν, ὧν ἡμίσεις ἦσαν ἐκ τῶν μετὰ
Δίωνος ἀπὸ τῆς φυγῆς συγκατερχομένων. Τοῖς δὲ
5 μάντεσιν αὖθις ἐδόκει τὸ μὲν ὑπὸ πόδας λαβεῖν τὸν
Δίωνα δημηγοροῦντα τὴν φιλοτιμίαν καὶ τὸ ἀνάθημα τοῦ
τυράννου λαμπρὸν εἶναι σημεῖον· ὅτι δ' ἡλιοτρόπιον ἦν,
ἐφ' οὗ βεβηκὼς ᾑρέθη στρατηγός, ὠρρώδουν, μὴ τροπήν
τινα τῆς τύχης αἱ πράξεις ταχεῖαν λάβωσιν. Ἐκ τούτου
6 τὰς μὲν Ἐπιπολὰς ἑλών, τοὺς καθειργμένους τῶν πολιτῶν
7 ἔλυσε, τὴν δ' ἀκρόπολιν ἀπετείχισεν. Ἑβδόμῃ δ' ἡμέρᾳ
Διονύσιος κατέπλευσεν εἰς τὴν ἀκρόπολιν, καὶ Δίωνι
προσῆγον ἅμαξαι <τὰς> πανοπλίας ἃς Συνάλῳ κατέλιπε.
Ταύτας διένειμε τοῖς πολίταις, τῶν δ' ἄλλων ἕκαστος
ἑαυτόν, ὡς δυνατὸν ἦν, ἐκόσμει καὶ παρεῖχεν ὁπλίτην
πρόθυμον.

30. Διονύσιος δὲ πρῶτον ἰδίᾳ πρὸς Δίωνα πρέσβεις
ἔπεμπεν ἀποπειρώμενος· ἔπειτα κελεύσαντος ἐκείνου
διαλέγεσθαι κοινῇ Συρακοσίοις ὡς ἐλευθέροις οὖσιν,
ἐγένοντο λόγοι διὰ τῶν πρέσβεων παρὰ τοῦ τυράννου

φιλάνθρωποι, φόρων ὑπισχνουμένου μετριότητα καὶ
ῥᾳστώνην στρατειῶν, ὧν <ἂν μὴ> αὐτοὶ σύμψηφοι *
γένωνται. Ταῦτ᾽ ἐχλεύαζον οἱ Συρακόσιοι. Δίων δ᾽ 2
ἀπεκρίνατο τοῖς πρέσβεσι, μὴ διαλέγεσθαι πρὸς αὐτοὺς
Διονύσιον, εἰ μὴ τὴν ἀρχὴν ἀφίησιν· ἀφέντι δὲ
συμπράξειν ἄδειαν αὐτός, κἂν ἄλλο τι τῶν μετρίων
δύνηται. μεμνημένος τῆς οἰκειότητος. Ταῦτα Διονύσιος 3
ἐπῄνει, καὶ πάλιν ἔπεμπε πρέσβεις, κελεύων ἥκειν τινὰς
εἰς τὴν ἀκρόπολιν τῶν Συρακοσίων, οἷς τὰ μὲν πείθων, τὰ
δὲ πειθόμενος διαλέξεται περὶ τῶν κοινῇ συμφερόντων.
Ἐπέμφθησαν οὖν ἄνδρες πρὸς αὐτόν, οὓς Δίων ἐδοκί- 4
μασε. Καὶ λόγος πολὺς ἐκ τῆς ἄκρας εἰς τοὺς
Συρακοσίους κατῄει, Διονύσιον ἀφήσειν τὴν τυραννίδα
καὶ μᾶλλον ἑαυτοῦ ποιήσεσθαι χάριν ἢ Δίωνος. Ἦν δὲ 5 *
δόλος ἡ προσποίησις αὕτη τοῦ τυράννου καὶ σκευωρία
κατὰ τῶν Συρακοσίων. Τοὺς μὲν γὰρ ἐλθόντας πρὸς
αὐτὸν ἐκ τῆς πόλεως συγκλείσας εἶχε, τοὺς δὲ μισθοφόρους πρὸς ὄρθρον ἐμπλήσας ἀκράτου, δρόμῳ πρὸς τὸ
περιτείχισμα τῶν Συρακοσίων ἀφῆκε, γενομένης δὲ τῆς 6
προσβολῆς ἀνελπίστου, καὶ τῶν βαρβάρων θράσει
πολλῷ καὶ θορύβῳ καθαιρούντων τὸ διατείχισμα, καὶ
τοῖς Συρακοσίοις ἐπιφερομένων, οὐδεὶς ἐτόλμα μένων
ἀμύνεσθαι, πλὴν τῶν ξένων τῶν Δίωνος, οἳ πρῶτον *
αἰσθόμενοι τὸν θόρυβον ἐξεβοήθησαν. Οὐδ᾽ οὗτοι δὲ 7
τῆς βοηθείας τὸν τρόπον συνεφρόνουν οὐδ᾽ εἰσήκουον
ὑπὸ κραυγῆς καὶ πλάνης τῶν φευγόντων Συρακοσίων
ἀναπεφυρμένων αὐτοῖς καὶ διεκθεόντων, πρίν γε δὴ Δίων,
ἐπεὶ λέγοντος οὐδεὶς κατήκουεν, ἔργῳ τὸ πρακτέον
ὑφηγήσασθαι βουλόμενος ἐμβάλλει πρῶτος εἰς τοὺς
βαρβάρους. Καὶ γίνεται περὶ αὐτὸν ὀξεῖα καὶ δεινὴ 8
μάχη, γινωσκόμενον οὐχ ἧττον ὑπὸ τῶν πολεμίων ἢ τῶν
φίλων· ὥρμησαν γὰρ ἅμα πάντες ἐμβοήσαντες. Ὁ δ᾽ 9
ἦν μὲν ἤδη βαρύτερος δι᾽ ἡλικίαν ἢ κατὰ τοιούτους
ἀγῶνας, ἀλκῇ δὲ καὶ θυμῷ <τοὺς> προσφερομένους
ὑφιστάμενος καὶ ἀνακόπτων, τιτρώσκεται λόγχῃ τὴν
χεῖρα, πρὸς δὲ τὰ ἄλλα βέλη καὶ τὰς ἐκ χειρὸς πληγὰς
μόλις ὁ θώραξ ἤρκεσε, διὰ τῆς ἀσπίδος δόρασι πολλοῖς
καὶ λόγχαις τυπτόμενος· ὧν κατακλασθέντων κατέ-

10 πεσεν ὁ Δίων. Εἶτ᾽ ἀναρπασθεὶς ὑπὸ τῶν στρατιωτῶν,
ἐκείνοις μὲν ἡγεμόνα Τιμωνίδην ἐπέστησεν, αὐτὸς
δὲ τὴν πόλιν ἵππῳ περιελαύνων, τούς τε Συρακοσίους
ἔπαυε φυγῆς, καὶ τῶν ξένων τοὺς φυλάττοντας τὴν
Ἀχραδινὴν ἀναστήσας ἐπῆγε τοῖς βαρβάροις, ἀκμῆτας
ἐκπεπονημένοις καὶ προθύμους ἀπαυδῶσιν ἤδη πρὸς τὴν
11 πεῖραν. Ἐλπίσαντες γὰρ ἅμα τῇ πρώτῃ ῥύμῃ τὴν πόλιν
ἅπασαν ἐξ ἐπιδρομῆς καθέξειν, εἶτα παρὰ δόξαν ἐντυγ-
χάνοντες ἀνδράσι πλήκταις καὶ μαχίμοις, ἀνεστέλλοντο
12 πρὸς τὴν ἀκρόπολιν. Ἔτι δὲ μᾶλλον, ὡς ἐνέδωκαν,
ἐπικειμένων τῶν Ἑλλήνων, τραπόμενοι κατεκλείσθησαν
εἰς τὸ τεῖχος, ἑβδομήκοντα μὲν καὶ τέσσαρας ἀποκτεί-
ναντες τῶν μετὰ Δίωνος, ἑαυτῶν δὲ πολλ<ῷ πλεί>ους
ἀποβαλόντες.

31. Γενομένης δὲ λαμπρᾶς τῆς νίκης, οἱ μὲν
Συρακόσιοι τοὺς ξένους ἑκατὸν μναῖς ἐστεφάνωσαν,
2 οἱ δὲ ξένοι Δίωνα χρυσῷ στεφάνῳ. Κήρυκες δὲ παρὰ
τοῦ Διονυσίου κατέβαινον, ἐπιστολὰς πρὸς Δίωνα παρὰ
τῶν οἰκείων κομίζοντες. Μία δ᾽ ἦν ἔξωθεν ἐπιγεγραμμένη
"Τῷ πατρὶ παρ᾽ Ἱππαρίνου" · Τοῦτο γὰρ ἦν ὄνομα τῷ
3 Δίωνος υἱῷ. Καίτοι φησὶ Τίμαιος Ἀρεταῖον αὐτὸν ἀπὸ
τῆς μητρὸς Ἀρετῆς καλεῖσθαι. Τιμωνίδῃ δὲ μᾶλλον, ὡς
οἴομαι, περί γε τούτων πιστευτέον, ἀνδρὶ φίλῳ καὶ
4 συστρατιώτῃ Δίωνος. Αἱ μὲν οὖν ἄλλαι τοῖς Συρακοσίοις
ἀνεγνώσθησαν ἐπιστολαὶ πολλὰς ἱκεσίας καὶ δεήσεις
ἔχουσαι παρὰ τῶν γυναικῶν, τὴν δὲ παρὰ τοῦ παιδὸς
εἶναι δοκοῦσαν οὐκ ἐώντων φανερῶς λυθῆναι, βιασάμενος
5 ὁ Δίων ἔλυσεν. Ἦν δὲ παρὰ τοῦ Διονυσίου, τοῖς μὲν
γράμμασι πρὸς τὸν Δίωνα, τοῖς δὲ πράγμασι πρὸς τοὺς
Συρακοσίους διαλεγομένου, σχῆμα μὲν ἔχουσα δεήσεως
καὶ δικαιολογίας, συγκειμένη δὲ πρὸς διαβολὴν τοῦ
6 Δίωνος. Ὑπομνήσεις τε γὰρ ἦσαν, ὧν ὑπὲρ τῆς τυραννίδος ἔπραξε προθύμως, καὶ κατὰ τῶν φιλτάτων ἀπειλαὶ
σωμάτων, ἀδελφῆς καὶ τέκνου καὶ γυναικός, ἐπισκήψεις
τε δειναὶ μετ᾽ ὀλοφυρμῶν καί, τὸ μάλιστ᾽ <ἂν> κινῆσαν
* αὐτούς, <ἀξιώσεις>, ἀξιοῦντος μὴ καθαιρεῖν, ἀλλὰ παρα-
λαμβάνειν τὴν τυραννίδα, μηδ᾽ ἐλευθεροῦν μισοῦντας

ἀνθρώπους καὶ μνησικακοῦντας, ἀλλ' αὐτὸν ἄρχειν, παρέχοντα τοῖς φίλοις καὶ οἰκείοις τὴν ἀσφάλειαν.

32. Ἀναγινωσκομένων δὲ τούτων οὐχ, ὅπερ ἦν δίκαιον, εἰσῄει τοὺς Συρακοσίους ἐκπλήττεσθαι τὴν ἀπάθειαν καὶ τὴν μεγαλοψυχίαν τοῦ Δίωνος, ὑπὲρ τῶν καλῶν καὶ δικαίων ἀπισχυριζομένου πρὸς τοιαύτας οἰκειότητας, ἀλλ' ὑποψίας καὶ φόβου λαβόντες ἀρχήν, 2 ὡς μεγάλης οὔσης ἀνάγκης ἐκείνῳ φείδεσθαι τοῦ τυράννου, πρὸς ἑτέρους ἤδη προστάτας ἀπέβλεπον, καὶ μάλιστα πυνθανόμενοι καταπλεῖν Ἡρακλείδην ἀνεπτοήθησαν. Ἦν δὲ τῶν φυγάδων Ἡρακλείδης, στρατηγικὸς 3 μὲν ἄνθρωπος καὶ γνώριμος ἀφ' ἡγεμονίας, ἣν ἔσχε παρὰ τοῖς τυράννοις, οὐκ ἀραρὼς δὲ τὴν γνώμην, ἀλλὰ πρὸς πάντα κοῦφος, ἥκιστα δὲ βέβαιος ἐν κοινωνίᾳ πραγμάτων ἀρχὴν ἐχόντων καὶ δόξαν. Οὗτος ἐν Πελοποννήσῳ 4 πρὸς Δίωνα στασιάσας, ἔγνω καθ' αὐτὸν ἰδιόστολος πλεῖν ἐπὶ τὸν τύραννον, εἴς τε Συρακούσας ἀφικόμενος ἑπτὰ τριήρεσι καὶ τρισὶ πλοίοις, Διονύσιον μὲν αὖθις εὗρε περιτετειχισμένον, ἐπηρμένους δὲ τοὺς Συρακοσίους. Εὐθὺς οὖν ὑπεδύετο τὴν τῶν πολλῶν χάριν, ἔχων μέν τι 5 καὶ φύσει πιθανὸν καὶ κινητικὸν ὄχλου θεραπεύεσθαι ζητοῦντος, ὑπολαμβάνων δὲ καὶ μετάγων ῥᾷον αὐτούς, οἳ <γε> τὸ σεμνὸν τοῦ Δίωνος ὡς βαρὺ καὶ δυσπολίτευτον ἀπεστρέφοντο, διὰ τὴν γεγενημένην ἐκ τοῦ κρατεῖν ἄνεσιν καὶ θρασύτητα, πρὸ τοῦ δῆμος εἶναι τὸ δημαγωγεῖσθαι θέλοντες.

33. Καὶ πρῶτον μὲν εἰς ἐκκλησίαν ἀφ' αὐτῶν συνδραμόντες, εἵλοντο τὸν Ἡρακλείδην ναύαρχον. Ἐπεὶ δὲ Δίων παρελθὼν ᾐτιᾶτο τὴν ἐκείνῳ διδομένην 2 ἀρχὴν ἀφαίρεσιν εἶναι τῆς πρότερον αὐτῷ δεδομένης, οὐκέτι γὰρ αὐτοκράτωρ μένειν, ἂν ἄλλος ἡγῆται τῶν κατὰ θάλασσαν, ἄκοντες οἱ Συρακόσιοι πάλιν ἀπεψηφίσαντο τὸν Ἡρακλείδην. Γενομένων δὲ τούτων, μεταπεμψάμενος αὐτὸν ὁ Δίων οἴκαδε, καὶ μικρὰ 3 μεμψάμενος, ὡς οὐ καλῶς οὐδὲ συμφερόντως ὑπὲρ δόξης στασιάζοντα πρὸς αὐτὸν ἐν καιρῷ ῥοπῆς ὀλίγης· δεομένῳ

πρὸς ἀπώλειαν, αὖθις ἐκκλησίαν αὐτὸς συναγαγών,
ναύαρχον ἀπέδειξε τὸν Ἡρακλείδην, καὶ τοῦ σώματος
ἔπεισε φυλακὴν δοῦναι τοὺς πολίτας, ὥσπερ αὐτὸς εἶχεν.
4 Ὁ δὲ τῷ μὲν λόγῳ καὶ τῷ σχήματι τὸν Δίωνα θεραπεύων,
καὶ χάριν ὁμολογῶν ἔχειν, παρηκολούθει ταπεινός,
ὑπηρετῶν τὸ κελευόμενον. κρύφα δὲ τοὺς πολλοὺς καὶ
νεωτεριστὰς διαφθείρων καὶ ὑποκινῶν, θορύβοις τὸν
Δίωνα περιέβαλλεν, εἰς ἅπασαν ἀπορίαν καθιστάμενον.
5 Εἴτε γὰρ ἀφιέναι κελεύοι Διονύσιον ὑπόσπονδον ἐκ τῆς
ἄκρας, διαβολὴν εἶχε φείδεσθαι καὶ περισώζειν ἐκεῖνον,
εἴτε λυπεῖν μὴ βουλόμενος ἐπὶ τῆς πολιορκίας ἡσυχάζοι,
διατηρεῖν ἐδόκει τὸν πόλεμον, ὡς μᾶλλον ἄρχοι καὶ
καταπλήττοιτο τοὺς πολίτας.

34. Ἦν δέ τις Σῶσις, ἄνθρωπος ἐκ πονηρίας καὶ
θρασύτητος εὐδοκιμῶν παρὰ τοῖς Συρακοσίοις, περιου-
σίαν ἡγουμένο<ι>ς ἐλευθερίας τὸ μέχρι τοιούτων ἀνεῖσθαι
2 τὴν παρρησίαν. Οὗτος ἐπιβουλεύων Δίωνι, πρῶτον μὲν
ἐκκλησίας οὔσης ἀναστὰς πολλὰ τοὺς Συρακοσίους
ἐλοιδόρησεν, εἰ μὴ συνιᾶσιν, ὡς ἐμπλήκτου καὶ
μεθυούσης ἀπηλλαγμένοι τυραννίδος, ἐγρηγορότα καὶ
3 νήφοντα δεσπότην εἰλήφασιν· ἔπειτα φανερὸν τοῦ
Δίωνος ἐχθρὸν ἀναδείξας ἑαυτόν, τότε μὲν ἐκ τῆς ἀγορᾶς
ἀπῆλθε, τῇ δ' ὑστεραίᾳ γυμνὸς ὤφθη διὰ τῆς πόλεως
θέων, ἀνάπλεως αἵματος τὴν κεφαλὴν καὶ τὸ πρόσωπον,
4 ὡς δή τινας φεύγων διώκοντας. Ἐμβαλὼν δὲ τοιοῦτος
εἰς τὴν ἀγοράν, ἔλεγεν ὑπὸ τῶν ξένων τοῦ Δίωνος
ἐπιβεβουλεῦσθαι. καὶ τὴν κεφαλὴν ἐπεδείκνυε τετρω-
μένην· καὶ πολλοὺς εἶχε τοὺς συναγανακτοῦντας καὶ
συνισταμένους κατὰ τοῦ Δίωνος, ὡς δεινὰ καὶ τυραννικὰ
πράττοντος, εἰ φόνοις καὶ κινδύνοις τῶν πολιτῶν ἀφαι-
ρεῖται τὴν παρρησίαν. Οὐ μὴν ἀλλά, καίπερ ἀκρίτου
καὶ ταραχώδους ἐκκλησίας γενομένης, παρελθὼν ὁ Δίων
ἀπελογεῖτο, καὶ τὸν Σῶσιν ἀπέφαινε τῶν Διονυσίου
δορυφόρων ἑνὸς ἀδελφὸν ὄντα καὶ δι' ἐκείνου πεπει-
σμένον στασιάσαι καὶ συνταράξαι τὴν πόλιν, οὐδεμιᾶς
Διονυσίῳ σωτηρίας οὔσης, πλὴν τῆς ἐκείνων ἀπιστίας
καὶ διαφορᾶς πρὸς αὐτούς. Ἅμα δ' οἱ μὲν ἰατροὶ τοῦ

Σώσιδος τὸ τραῦμα καταμανθάνοντες εὕρισκον ἐξ
ἐπιπολῆς μᾶλλον ἢ καταφορᾶς γεγενημένον. Αἱ μὲν γὰρ
ὑπὸ ξίφους πληγαὶ μάλιστα τὸ μέσον ὑπὸ βάρους *
πιέζουσι, τὸ δὲ τοῦ Σώσιδος λεπτὸν ἦν διόλου καὶ πολλὰς
εἶχεν ἀρχάς, ὡς εἰκός ὑπ᾿ ἀλγηδόνος ἀνιέντος, εἶτ᾿ αὖθις
ἐπάγοντος. Ἧκον δέ τινες τῶν γνωρίμων, ξυρὸν 8
κομίζοντες εἰς τὴν ἐκκλησίαν, καὶ διηγούμενοι βαδί-
ζουσιν αὐτοῖς καθ᾿ ὁδὸν ἀπαντῆσαι τὸν Σῶσιν ἡμαγμένον
καὶ λέγοντα φεύγειν τοὺς Δίωνος ξένους, ὡς ἀρτίως ὑπ᾿
ἐκείνων τετρωμένος· εὐθὺς οὖν διώκοντες, ἄνθρωπον μὲν 9
οὐδένα λαβεῖν, ὑπὸ πέτραν δὲ κοίλην κείμενον ἰδεῖν
ξυρόν, ὅθεν ἐκεῖνος ὤφθη προσερχόμενος.

35. Ἦν μὲν οὖν ἤδη μοχθηρὰ τὰ περὶ τὸν Σῶσιν·
προσγενομένων δὲ τούτοις τοῖς ἐλέγχοις οἰκετῶν κατα-
μαρτυρούντων, ὡς ἔτι νυκτὸς ἐξέλθοι μόνος ἔχων τὸ
ξυρόν, οἵ τε κατηγοροῦντες τοῦ Δίωνος ὑπεχώρησαν, ὅ τε
δῆμος καταψηφισάμενος θάνατον τοῦ Σώσιδος διηλλάσ-
σετο τῷ Δίωνι. τοὺς δὲ μισθοφόρους οὐδὲν ἧττον ἐν 2
ὑποψίαις εἶχον, καὶ μάλιστα τῶν πλείστων ἀγώνων πρὸς
τὸν τύραννον ἤδη γινομένων κατὰ θάλατταν, ἐπειδὴ
Φίλιστος ἧκεν ἐξ Ἰαπυγίας ἔχων πολλὰς τριήρεις
Διονυσίῳ βοηθήσων, καὶ τῶν ξένων ὄντων ὁπλιτῶν
οὐδεμίαν ἔτι χρῆσιν ἐνόμιζον εἶναι πρὸς τὸν πόλεμον,
ἀλλὰ κἀκείνους ὑφ᾿ ἑαυτοῖς ἔσεσθαι, ναυβάταις οὖσι καὶ
τὸ κράτος ἐκ τῶν νεῶν κτωμένοις. Ἔτι δὲ μᾶλλον 3
αὐτοὺς ἐπῆρεν εὐτυχία τις γενομένη κατὰ θάλασσαν, ἐν
ᾗ νικήσαντες τὸν Φίλιστον, ὠμῶς καὶ βαρβαρικῶς αὐτῷ
προσηνέχθησαν. Ἔφορος μὲν οὖν φησιν, ὡς ἁλισκο- 4
μένης τῆς νεὼς ἑαυτὸν ἀνέλοι, Τιμωνίδης δέ, πραττομέναις
ἐξ ἀρχῆς ταῖς πράξεσι ταύταις μετὰ Δίωνος παραγε-
νόμενος, καὶ γράφων πρὸς Σπεύσιππον τὸν φιλόσοφον,
ἱστορεῖ ζῶντα ληφθῆναι τῆς τριήρους εἰς τὴν γῆν
ἐκπεσούσης τὸν Φίλιστον· καὶ πρῶτον μὲν ἀποδύσαντας 5
αὐτοῦ τὸν θώρακα τοὺς Συρακοσίους καὶ γυμνὸν ἐπιδει-
ξαμένους τὸ σῶμα προπηλακίζειν ὄντος ἤδη γέροντος·
ἔπειτα τὴν κεφαλὴν ἀποτεμεῖν καὶ τοῖς παισὶ παρα-
δοῦναι τὸ σῶμα, κελεύσαντας ἕλκειν διὰ τῆς Ἀχραδινῆς

6 καὶ καταβαλεῖν εἰς τὰς Λατομίας. Ἔτι δὲ μᾶλλον ἐφυβρίζων ὁ Τίμαιος ἐκ τοῦ σκέλους φησὶ τοῦ χωλοῦ τὰ παιδάρια τὸν νεκρὸν ἐφαψάμενα τοῦ Φιλίστου σύρειν διὰ τῆς πόλεως, χλευαζόμενον ὑπὸ τῶν Συρακοσίων πάντων, ὁρώντων τοῦ σκέλους ἑλκόμενον τὸν εἰπόντα μὴ δεῖν ἐκ τυραννίδος φεύγειν Διονύσιον ἵππῳ ταχεῖ χρώ-7 μενον, ἀλλὰ τοῦ σκέλους ἑλκόμενον. Καίτοι τοῦτο * Φίλιστος, ὡς ὑφ᾽ ἑτέρου λεχθέν, οὐχ ὑφ᾽ αὑτοῦ, πρὸς Διονύσιον ἐξήγγελκεν.

36. Ἀλλὰ Τίμαιος οὐκ ἄδικον λαβὼν πρόφασιν τὴν ὑπὲρ τῆς τυραννίδος τοῦ Φιλίστου σπουδὴν καὶ πίστιν, ἐμπίπλαται τῶν κατ᾽ αὐτοῦ βλασφημιῶν, ᾧ τοὺς μὲν ἀδικηθέντας τότε συγγνωστόν ἐστιν ἴσως ἄχρι τῆς εἰς 2 ἀναίσθητον ὀργῆς χαλεποὺς γενέσθαι, τοὺς δ᾽ ὕστερον συγγράφοντας τὰ πεπραγμένα, καὶ τῷ μὲν βίῳ μὴ λυπηθέντας αὐτοῦ, τῷ δὲ λόγῳ χρωμένους, ἡ δόξα παραιτεῖται μὴ μεθ᾽ ὕβρεως μηδὲ μετὰ βωμολοχίας ὀνειδίζειν τὰς συμφοράς, ὧν οὐδὲν ἀπέχει καὶ τὸν ἄριστον ἀνδρῶν ἐκ τύχης μετασχεῖν. Οὐ μὴν οὐδ᾽ 3 Ἔφορος ὑγιαίνει τὸν Φίλιστον ἐγκωμιάζων, ὅς, καίπερ ὢν δεινότατος ἀδίκοις πράγμασι καὶ πονηροῖς ἤθεσιν εὐσχήμονας αἰτίας περιβαλεῖν καὶ λόγους ἔχοντας κόσμον ἐξευρεῖν, αὐτὸς αὑτὸν οὐ δύναται πάντα μηχανώμενος ἐξελέσθαι τῆς γραφῆς, ὡς οὐ φιλοτυραννότατος ἀνθρώπων γένοιτο, καὶ μάλιστα πάντων ἀεὶ ζηλώσας καὶ θαυμάσας τρυφὴν καὶ δύναμιν καὶ πλούτους καὶ 4 γάμους τοὺς τῶν τυράννων. Ἀλλὰ γὰρ Φιλίστου μὲν ὁ μήτε τὰς πράξεις ἐπαινῶν μήτε τὰς τύχας ὀνειδίζων ἐμμελέστατος.

37. Μετὰ δὲ τὴν Φιλίστου τελευτὴν Διονύσιος ἔπεμπε πρὸς Δίωνα, τὴν μὲν ἀκρόπολιν ἐκείνῳ παραδιδοὺς καὶ τὰ ὅπλα καὶ τοὺς μισθοφόρους καὶ πέντε μηνῶν ἐντελῆ τούτοις μισθόν, αὐτὸς δ᾽ ἀξιῶν ὑπόσπονδος 2 εἰς Ἰταλίαν ἀπελθεῖν, κἀκεῖ κατοικῶν καρποῦσθαι τῆς * Συρακοσίας τὸν καλούμενον Γυάροτον, πολλὴν καὶ ἀγαθὴν χώραν ἀνήκουσαν ἀπὸ θαλάττης εἰς τὴν μεσόγειον. Οὐ προσδεξαμένου δὲ τοῦ Δίωνος, ἀλλὰ 3 δεῖσθαι τῶν Συρακοσίων κελεύσαντος, οἱ μὲν Συρακόσιοι ζῶντα λήψεσθαι τὸν Διονύσιον ἐλπίσαντες, ἀπήλασαν τοὺς πρέσβεις, ἐκεῖνος δὲ τὴν μὲν ἄκραν 4 Ἀπολλοκράτει, τῷ πρεσβυτέρῳ τῶν παίδων, παρέδωκεν, αὐτὸς δὲ πνεῦμα τηρήσας ἐπίφορον, καὶ τὰ τιμιώτατα τῶν σωμάτων καὶ τῶν χρημάτων ἐνθέμενος εἰς τὰς ναῦς, λαθὼν τὸν ναύαρχον Ἡρακλείδην ἐξέπλευσεν. Ὁ δὲ 5 κακῶς ἀκούων καὶ θορυβούμενος ὑπὸ τῶν πολιτῶν, Ἱππωνά τινα τῶν δημαγωγῶν καθίησι προκαλεῖσθαι τὸν δῆμον ἐπὶ γῆς ἀναδασμόν, ὡς ἐλευθερίας ἀρχὴν οὖσαν τὴν ἰσότητα, δουλείας δὲ τὴν πενίαν τοῖς ἀκτήμοσι. Συνηγορῶν δὲ τούτῳ, καὶ τὸν Δίωνα καταστα- 6 σιάζων ἐναντιούμενον, ἔπεισε τοὺς Συρακοσίους ταῦτά <τε> ψηφίσασθαι, καὶ τῶν ξένων τὸν μισθὸν ἀποστερεῖν, καὶ στρατηγοὺς ἑτέρους ἑλέσθαι, τῆς ἐκείνου βαρύτητος ἀπαλλαγέντας. Οἱ δ᾽ ὥσπερ ἐκ μακρᾶς ἀρρωστίας τῆς 7 τυραννίδος εὐθὺς ἐπιχειροῦντες ἐξανίστασθαι, καὶ πράττειν τὰ τῶν αὐτονομουμένων παρὰ καιρόν, ἐσφάλλοντο μὲν αὐτοὶ ταῖς πράξεσιν, ἐμίσουν δὲ τὸν Δίωνα, βουλόμενον ὥσπερ ἰατρὸν ἐν ἀκριβεῖ καὶ σωφρονούσῃ διαίτῃ κατέχειν τὴν πόλιν.　　*

38. Ἐκκλησιάζουσι δ᾽ αὐτοῖς ἐπὶ νέαις ἀρχαι-<ρεσίαι>ς θέρους μεσοῦντος ἐξαίσιοι βρονταὶ καὶ διοσημίαι πονηραὶ συνέβαινον ἐφ᾽ ἡμέρας δεκαπέντε συνεχῶς, ἀνιστᾶσαι τὸν δῆμον ὑπὸ δεισιδαιμονίας κωλυόμενον ἑτέρους ἀποδεῖξαι στρατηγούς. Ἐπεὶ δὲ 2 φυλάξαντες εὐδίαν σταθερὰν οἱ δημαγωγοὶ συνετέλουν τὰς ἀρχαιρεσίας, βοῦς ἁμαξεὺς οὐκ ἀήθης οὐδ᾽ ἄπειρος ὄχλων, ἄλλως δέ πως τότε πρὸς τὸν ἐλαύνοντα θυμωθεὶς καὶ φυγὼν ἀπὸ τοῦ ζυγοῦ, δρόμῳ πρὸς τὸ θέατρον ὥρμησε· καὶ τὸν μὲν δῆμον εὐθὺς ἀνέστησε καὶ διε- 3 σκέδασεν, οὐδενὶ κόσμῳ φεύγοντα, τῆς δ᾽ ἄλλης πόλεως ἐπέδραμε σκιρτῶν καὶ ταράττων ὅσον ὕστερον οἱ πολέμιοι κατέσχον. Οὐ μὴν ἀλλὰ ταῦτα χαίρειν ἐάσαντες 4 οἱ Συρακόσιοι πέντε καὶ εἴκοσι στρατηγοὺς ἐχειροτόνησαν, ὧν εἷς ἦν Ἡρακλείδης, καὶ τοὺς ξένους ὑποπέμ-

ποντες κρύφα τοῦ Δίωνος ἀφίστασαν καὶ μετεκάλουν
πρὸς αὐτούς, ἐπαγγελλόμενοι καὶ τῆς πολιτείας ἰσο-
5 μοιρίαν. Οἱ δὲ ταῦτα μὲν οὐ προσεδέξαντο, τὸν δὲ
Δίωνα πιστῶς καὶ προθύμως μετὰ τῶν ὅπλων ἀναλαβόντες
καὶ συμφράξαντες ἀπῆγον ἐκ τῆς πόλεως, ἀδικοῦντες μὲν
οὐδένα, πολλὰ δὲ τοὺς ἐντυγχάνοντας εἰς ἀχαριστίαν καὶ
6 μοχθηρίαν ὀνειδίζοντες. Οἱ δὲ τῆς ὀλιγότητος αὐτῶν καὶ
τοῦ μὴ προεπιχειρεῖν καταφρονήσαντες, καὶ γενόμενοι
πολὺ πλείους ἐκείνων, ἐφώρμησαν, ὡς ῥᾳδίως ἐπικρατή-
σοντες ἐν τῇ πόλει καὶ πάντας αὐτοὺς κατακτενοῦντες.

39. Ἐν τούτῳ δὲ γεγονὼς ἀνάγκης καὶ τύχης ὁ Δίων,
ἢ μάχεσθαι τοῖς πολίταις ἢ μετὰ τῶν ξένων ἀποθανεῖν,
πολλὰ μὲν ἱκέτευεν ὀρέγων τὰς χεῖρας τοῖς Συρακοσίοις
καὶ τὴν ἀκρόπολιν περίπλεων πολεμίων οὖσαν ὑπερφαινο-
μένων τὰ τείχη καὶ τὰ γινόμενα καθορώντων ἐπιδεικνύ-
2 μενος· ὡς δ' ἦν ἀπαραίτητος ἡ τῶν πολλῶν φορά, καὶ
κατεῖχεν ὥσπερ ἐν πελάγει τὸ τῶν δημαγωγῶν πνεῦμα
τὴν πόλιν, ἐμβολῆς μὲν ἀποσχέσθαι τοῖς ξένοις προ-
σέταξεν, ὅσον δ' ἐπιδραμόντων μετὰ βοῆς καὶ τοῖς
ὅπλοις τιναξαμένων, οὐδεὶς ἔμεινε τῶν Συρακοσίων, ἀλλ'
ᾤχοντο φεύγοντες ἀνὰ τὰς ἀγυιάς, οὐδενὸς ἐπιδιώκοντος·
εὐθὺς γὰρ ἀπέστρεψεν ὁ Δίων τοὺς ξένους καὶ προῆγεν
3 εἰς Λεοντίνους. Οἱ δ' ἄρχοντες τῶν Συρακοσίων κατα-
γέλαστοι γεγονότες ὑπὸ τῶν γυναικῶν, καὶ τὴν αἰσχύνην
ἀναλαβεῖν ζητοῦντες, αὖθις ὁπλίσαντες τοὺς πολίτας
4 ἐδίωκον τὸν Δίωνα. Καὶ κατέλαβον μὲν ἐπὶ διαβάσει
τινὸς ποταμοῦ καὶ προσίππευσαν ἀψιμαχοῦντες· ὡς δ'
ἑώρων οὐκέτι πρᾴως οὐδὲ πατρικῶς ὑπομένοντα τὰς
ἁμαρτίας αὐτῶν, ἀλλὰ θυμῷ τοὺς ξένους ἐπιστρέφοντα
καὶ παραταττόμενον, αἰσχίονα φυγὴν τῆς προτέρας
φυγόντες ὑπεχώρησαν εἰς τὴν πόλιν, οὐ πολλῶν
ἀποθανόντων.

40. Δίωνα δὲ Λεοντῖνοι λαμπραῖς ἐδέχοντο τιμαῖς,
* καὶ τοὺς ξένους ἀνελάμβανον μισθοῖς καὶ πολιτείαις·
πρὸς δὲ τοὺς Συρακοσίους ἐπρέσβευον, ἀξιοῦντες τὰ
2 δίκαια τοῖς ξένοις ποιεῖν. Οἱ δὲ πρέσβεις ἔπεμψαν

κατηγορήσοντας Δίωνος· τῶν δὲ συμμάχων ἁπάντων
εἰς Λεοντίνους ἀθροισθέντων, καὶ γενομένων λόγων ἐν
αὐτοῖς, ἔδοξαν ἀδικεῖν οἱ Συρακόσιοι· τοῖς δὲ κριθεῖσιν 3
ὑπὸ τῶν συμμάχων οὐκ ἐνέμειναν, τρυφῶντες ἤδη καὶ
μεγαλοφρονοῦντες ἐπὶ τῷ μηδενὸς ἀκούειν, ἀλλὰ χρῆσθαι
δουλεύουσι καὶ φοβουμένοις τὸν δῆμον στρατηγοῖς.

41. Ἐκ τούτου καταπλέουσιν εἰς τὴν πόλιν παρὰ
Διονυσίου τριήρεις, Νύψιον ἄγουσαι τὸν Νεαπολίτην,
σῖτον καὶ χρήματα κομίζοντα τοῖς πολιορκουμένοις.
Γενομένης δὲ ναυμαχίας, ἐνίκων μὲν οἱ Συρακόσιοι, καὶ 2
τέσσαρας τῶν τυραννικῶν νεῶν ἔλαβον, ὑβρίσαντες δὲ
τῇ νίκῃ, καὶ δι' ἀναρχίαν τὸ χαῖρον εἰς πότους καὶ
συνουσίας μανικὰς τρέψαντες, οὕτω τῶν χρησίμων
ἠμέλησαν, ὥστε τὴν ἀκρόπολιν ἔχειν δοκοῦντες ἤδη, καὶ
τὴν πόλιν προσαπέβαλον. Ὁ γὰρ Νύψιος ὁρῶν οὐδὲν 3
ὑγιαῖνον ἐν τῇ πόλει μέρος, ἀλλὰ τὸν μὲν ὄχλον αὐλή-
μασι καὶ μέθαις εἰς νύκτα βαθεῖαν ἀφ' ἡμέρας κατεχό-
μενον, τοὺς δὲ στρατηγοὺς ἐπιτερπομένους τε τούτῳ
τῷ πανηγυρισμῷ, καὶ προσάγειν ἀνάγκην μεθύουσιν
ἀνθρώποις ὀκνοῦντας, ἄριστα τῷ καιρῷ χρησάμενος, 4
ἐπεχείρησε τῷ τειχίσματι· καὶ κρατήσας καὶ διαθρύψας,
ἀφῆκε τοὺς βαρβάρους, κελεύσας χρῆσθαι τοῖς προστυγ-
χάνουσιν ὡς βούλονται καὶ δύνανται. Ταχέως μὲν οὖν 5
οἱ Συρακόσιοι τὸ κακὸν ᾔσθοντο, βραδέως δὲ καὶ
χαλεπῶς συνεβοήθουν ἐκπεπληγμένοι. Πόρθησις γὰρ 6
ἦν τὰ γινόμενα τῆς πόλεως, τῶν μὲν ἀνδρῶν φονευομένων,
τῶν δὲ τειχῶν κατασκαπτομένων, γυναικῶν δὲ καὶ παίδων
ἀγομένων εἰς τὴν ἀκρόπολιν μετ' οἰμωγῆς, ἀπεγνωκότων
δὲ τὰ πράγματα τῶν στρατηγῶν, καὶ χρῆσθαι μὴ
δυναμένων τοῖς πολίταις πρὸς τοὺς πολεμίους, ἀναπεφυρ-
μένους καὶ συμμεμειγμένους αὐτοῖς πανταχόθεν.

42. Οὕτω δὲ τῶν κατὰ τὴν πόλιν ἐχόντων, καὶ τοῦ
κινδύνου πρὸς τὴν Ἀχραδινὴν πλησιάζοντος, εἰς ὃν
μόνον ἦν καὶ λοιπὸν ἀπερείσασθαι τὴν ἐλπίδα, πάντες
μὲν ἐφρόνουν, ἔλεγε δ' οὐδείς, αἰσχυνόμενοι τὴν ἀχαριστίαν καὶ τὴν ἀβουλίαν τὴν πρὸς Δίωνα. Πλήν γε δὴ

2 τῆς ἀνάγκης ἐκβιαζομένης, παρὰ τῶν συμμάχων καὶ τῶν
ἱππέων γίνεται φωνὴ καλεῖν Δίωνα, καὶ μεταπέμπεσθαι
τοὺς Πελοποννησίους ἐκ Λεοντίνων. Ὡς δὲ πρῶτον
3 ἠκούσθη καὶ ἀπετολμήθη τοῦτο, κραυγὴ καὶ χαρὰ καὶ
δάκρυα τοὺς Συρακοσίους κατεῖχεν, εὐχομένους ἐπιφα-
νῆναι τὸν ἄνδρα, καὶ ποθοῦντας τὴν ὄψιν αὐτοῦ, καὶ
μεμνημένους τῆς παρὰ τὰ δεινὰ ῥώμης καὶ προθυμίας, ὡς
οὐ μόνον αὐτὸς ἦν ἀνέκπληκτος, ἀλλὰ κἀκείνους παρεῖχε
θαρροῦντας καὶ ἀδεῶς τοῖς πολεμίοις συμφερομένους.
4 Εὐθὺς οὖν ἐκπέμπουσι πρὸς αὐτὸν ἀπὸ μὲν τῶν
συμμάχων Ἀρχωνίδην καὶ Τελεσίδην, ἀπὸ δὲ τῶν
5 ἱππέων πέντε τοὺς περὶ Ἑλλάνικον. Οὗτοι διελάσαντες
τὴν ὁδὸν ἵπποις ἀπὸ ῥυτῆρος, ἧκον εἰς Λεοντίνους τῆς
6 ἡμέρας ἤδη καταφερομένης. Ἀποπηδήσαντες δὲ τῶν
ἵππων, καὶ τῷ Δίωνι πρώτῳ προσπεσόντες δεδακρυμένοι,
7 τὰς συμφορὰς τῶν Συρακοσίων ἔφραζον. Ἤδη δὲ καὶ
τῶν Λεοντίνων τινὲς ἀπήντων, καὶ τῶν Πελοποννησίων
ἠθροίζοντο πρὸς τὸν Δίωνα πολλοί, τῇ σπουδῇ καὶ τῇ
δεήσει τῶν ἀνδρῶν ὑπονοοῦντες εἶναί τι καινότερον.
8 Εὐθὺς οὖν ἡγεῖτο πρὸς τὴν ἐκκλησίαν αὐτοῖς, καὶ
συνδραμόντων προθύμως οἱ περὶ τὸν Ἀρχωνίδην καὶ τὸν
Ἑλλάνικον εἰσελθόντες ἐξήγγειλάν τε βραχέως τὸ
μέγεθος τῶν κακῶν, καὶ παρεκάλουν τοὺς ξένους ἐπαμῦναι
τοῖς Συρακοσίοις, τὸ μνησικακεῖν ἀφέντας, ὡς μείζονα
δίκην δεδωκότων αὐτῶν, ἢ λαβεῖν ἂν οἱ κακῶς πεπονθότες
ἠξίωσαν.

43. Παυσαμένων δὲ τούτων, σιγὴ μὲν εἶχε πολλὴ τὸ
θέατρον· ἀναστάντος δὲ τοῦ Δίωνος, καὶ λέγειν ἀρξα-
* μένου, πολλὰ τῶν δακρύων ἐκπίπτοντα τὴν φωνὴν
ἐπέσχεν· οἱ δὲ ξένοι παρεκάλουν θαρρεῖν καὶ συνήχ-
2 θοντο. Μικρὸν οὖν ἀναλαβὼν ἐκ τοῦ πάθους ἑαυτὸν ὁ
Δίων "Ἄνδρες" ἔφη "Πελοποννήσιοι καὶ σύμμαχοι,
βουλευσομένους ὑμᾶς ἐνταῦθα περὶ ὑμῶν αὐτῶν συνή-
3 γαγον. Ἐμοὶ δὲ περὶ ἐμαυτοῦ βουλεύεσθαι καλῶς οὐκ
ἔχει Σωρακουσῶν ἀπολλυμένων, ἀλλ᾽ εἰ σῶσαι μὴ
δυναίμην, ἄπειμι τῷ πυρὶ καὶ τῷ πτώματι τῆς πατρίδος
4 ἐνταφησόμενος. Ὑμεῖς δὲ βουλόμενοι μὲν ἔτι καὶ νῦν

βοηθεῖν τοῖς ἀβουλοτάτοις ἡμῖν καὶ δυστυχεστάτοις,
ὑμέτερον ἔργον οὖσαν <ἂν>ορθοῦτε τὴν Συρακοσίων
πόλιν· εἰ δὲ μεμφόμενοι Συρακοσίοις ὑπερόψεσθε, τῆς 5
γε πρότερον ἀρετῆς καὶ προθυμίας περὶ ἐμὲ χάριν ἀξίαν
κομίζοισθε παρὰ τῶν θεῶν, μεμνημένοι Δίωνος, ὡς οὔθ'
ὑμᾶς ἀδικουμένους πρότερον οὔθ' ὕστερον τοὺς πολίτας
δυστυχοῦντας ἐγκαταλιπόντος." Ἔτι δ' αὐτοῦ λέγοντος, 6
οἱ μὲν ξένοι μετὰ κραυγῆς ἀνεπήδησαν, ἄγειν καὶ
βοηθεῖν κατὰ τάχος κελεύοντες, οἱ δὲ πρέσβεις τῶν
Συρακοσίων περιβαλόντες ἠσπάσαντο πολλὰ μὲν ἐκείνῳ,
πολλὰ δὲ τοῖς ξένοις ἀγαθὰ παρὰ τῶν θεῶν εὐχόμενοι.
Καταστάντος δὲ τοῦ θορύβου, παρήγγειλεν ὁ Δίων 7
εὐθὺς ἀπιόντας παρασκευάζεσθαι, καὶ δειπνήσαντας
ἥκειν μετὰ τῶν ὅπλων εἰς αὐτὸν ἐκεῖνον τὸν τόπον,
ἐγνωκὼς διὰ νυκτὸς βοηθεῖν.

44. Ἐν δὲ ταῖς Συρακούσαις τῶν Διονυσίου στρατηγῶν, ἄχρι μὲν ἦν ἡμέρα, πολλὰ κακὰ τὴν πόλιν
ἐργασαμένων, γενομένης δὲ νυκτὸς ἀναχωρησάντων εἰς
τὴν ἀκρόπολιν, καί τινας ἐξ ἑαυτῶν ὀλίγους ἀποβαλόν-
των, ἀναθαρρήσαντες οἱ δημαγωγοὶ τῶν Συρακοσίων,
καὶ τοὺς πολεμίους ἐλπίσαντες ἀτρεμήσειν ἐπὶ τοῖς 2
διαπεπραγμένοις, παρεκάλουν τοὺς πολίτας αὖθις ἐᾶν
Δίωνα, κἂν προσίῃ μετὰ τῶν ξένων, μὴ δέχεσθαι μηδὲ
παραχωρεῖν τῆς ἀρετῆς ἐκείνοις ὡς κρείττοσιν, ἀλλὰ
σώζειν τὴν πόλιν καὶ τὴν ἐλευθερίαν αὐτοὺς δι' ἑαυτῶν.
Πάλιν οὖν ἐπέμποντο πρὸς τὸν Δίωνα, παρὰ μὲν τῶν 3
στρατηγῶν ἀποτρέποντες, παρὰ δὲ τῶν ἱππέων καὶ τῶν
γνωρίμων πολιτῶν ἐπισπεύδοντες τὴν πορείαν. Καὶ διὰ 4
τοῦτο βραδέως ἅμα καὶ κατὰ σπουδὴν πορευόμενος ✻
προσῄει. Τῆς δὲ νυκτὸς προελθούσης, οἱ μὲν μισοῦντες 5
τὸν Δίωνα κατεῖχον τὰς πύλας ὡς ἀποκλείσοντες αὐτόν, ὁ
δὲ Νύψιος ἐκ τῆς ἄκρας αὖθις πολλῷ προθυμοτέρους
γεγονότας καὶ πλείονας ἐφιεὶς τοὺς μισθοφόρους, τὸ μὲν
προτείχισμα πᾶν εὐθὺς κατέσκαπτε, τὴν δὲ πόλιν
κατέτρεχε καὶ διήρπαζεν. Ἦν δὲ φόνος μὲν οὐκέτι μόνον 6
ἀνδρῶν, ἀλλὰ καὶ γυναικῶν καὶ παίδων, ἁρπαγαὶ δ'
ὀλίγαι, φθόρος δὲ πάντων πολύς. Ἀπεγνωκότος γὰρ 7

C

ἤδη τὰ πράγματα τοῦ <υἱοῦ τοῦ> Διονυσίου, καὶ τοὺς
Συρακοσίους δεινῶς μεμισηκότος, ὥσπερ ἐνταφιάσαι τὴν
τυραννίδα τῇ πόλει πίπτουσαν ἐβούλετο. Καὶ τοῦ
8 Δίωνος προκαταλαμβάνοντες τὴν βοήθειαν, ἐπὶ τὸν
ὀξύτατον διὰ πυρὸς πάντων ὄλεθρον καὶ ἀφανισμὸν
ἐχώρησαν, τὰ μὲν ἐγγὺς ἀπὸ χειρῶν δᾳσὶ καὶ λαμπάσιν
ὑποπιμπράντες, εἰς δὲ τὰ πρόσω διασπείροντες ἀπὸ
9 τόξων πυροβόλους. Φευγόντων δὲ τῶν Συρακοσίων, οἱ
μὲν ἐν ταῖς ὁδοῖς ἐφονεύοντο καταλαμβανόμενοι, τὸ δ' εἰς
τὰς οἰκίας καταδυόμενον αὖθις ὑπὸ τοῦ πυρὸς ἐξέπιπτε,
πολλῶν ἤδη φλεγομένων καὶ καταφερομένων ἐπὶ τοὺς
διαθέοντας.

45. Τοῦτο τὸ πάθος μάλιστα τὴν πόλιν ἀνέῳξε Δίωνι,
πάντων συμφωνησάντων. Ἔτυχε μὲν γὰρ οὐκέτι σπουδῇ
πορευόμενος, ὡς ἤκουσεν εἰς τὴν ἀκρόπολιν κατακε-
2 κλεῖσθαι τοὺς πολεμίους. Προϊούσης δὲ τῆς ἡμέρας,
πρῶτον ἱππεῖς ἀπήντησαν αὐτῷ, τὴν δευτέραν κατάληψιν
3 ἀπαγγέλλοντες· ἔπειτα καὶ τῶν ὑπεναντιουμένων ἔνιοι
παρῆσαν, ἐπείγεσθαι δεόμενοι. Συντείνοντος δὲ τοῦ
κακοῦ μᾶλλον, Ἡρακλείδης τὸν ἀδελφὸν ἐξέπεμψεν, εἶτα
Θεοδότην τὸν θεῖον, ἱκετεύων ἀρήγειν, ὡς μηδενὸς
ἀντέχοντος τοῖς πολεμίοις, αὐτοῦ δὲ τετρωμένου, τῆς
δὲ πόλεως μικρὸν ἀπεχούσης ἀνατετράφθαι καὶ κατα-
4 πεπρῆσθαι. Τοιούτων ἀγγελμάτων τῷ Δίωνι προσπε-
σόντων, ἔτι μὲν ἑξήκοντα σταδίους τῶν πυλῶν ἀπεῖχε·
φράσας δὲ τὸν κίνδυνον τοῖς ξένοις καὶ παρακελευσά-
μενος, οὐκέτι βάδην ἦγεν ἀλλὰ δρόμῳ τὸ στράτευμα
πρὸς τὴν πόλιν, ἄλλων ἐπ' ἄλλοις ἀντιαζόντων καὶ
5 δεομένων ἐπείγεσθαι. Χρησάμενος δὲ θαυμαστῷ τάχει
καὶ προθυμίᾳ τῶν ξένων, εἰσέβαλε διὰ τῶν <Ἑξα>πύλων
6 εἰς τὴν Ἑκατόμπεδον λεγομένην καὶ τοὺς μὲν ἐλαφροὺς
εὐθὺς εἰσελθὼν ἀφῆκε πρὸς τοὺς πολεμίους, ὡς ἰδοῦσι
θαρσῆσαι τοῖς Συρακοσίοις ἐγγένοιτο, τοὺς δ' ὁπλίτας
αὐτὸς συνέταττε καὶ τῶν πολιτῶν τοὺς ἐπιρρέοντας καὶ
συνισταμένους, ὀρθίους λόχους ποιῶν καὶ διαιρῶν τὰς
ἡγεμονίας, ὅπως [ὁμοῦ] πολλαχόθεν ἅμα προσφέροιτο
φοβερώτερον.

46. Ἐπεὶ δὲ ταῦτα παρασκευασάμενος, καὶ τοῖς θεοῖς προσευξάμενος, ὤφθη διὰ τῆς πόλεως ἄγων ἐπὶ τοὺς πολεμίους, κραυγῇ καὶ χαρᾷ καὶ πολὺς ἀλαλαγμὸς εὐχαῖς ὁμοῦ καὶ παρακλήσεσι μεμειγμένος ἐγίνετο παρὰ τῶν Συρακοσίων, τὸν μὲν Δίωνα <πατέρα καὶ> σωτῆρα καὶ θεὸν ἀποκαλούντων, τοὺς δὲ ξένους ἀδελφοὺς καὶ πολίτας. Οὐδεὶς δὲ φίλαυτος <οὕτως> ἦν καὶ φιλόψυχος 2 παρὰ τὸν τότε καιρόν, ὃς οὐ μᾶλλον ὑπὲρ μόνου Δίωνος ἢ τῶν ἄλλων ἁπάντων ἀγωνιῶν ἐφαίνετο, πρώτου πρὸς τὸν κίνδυνον πορευομένου δι᾽ αἵματος καὶ πυρὸς καὶ νεκρῶν πολλῶν κειμένων ἐν ταῖς πλατείαις. Ἦν μὲν οὖν 3 καὶ τὰ παρὰ τῶν πολεμίων φοβερά, παντάπασιν ἀπηγριω- μένων καὶ παρατεταγμένων παρὰ τὸ τείχισμα, χαλεπὴν ἔχον καὶ δυσεκβίαστον τὴν πρόσοδον · ὁ δ᾽ ἐκ τοῦ πυρὸς κίνδυνος ἐτάραττε μᾶλλον τοὺς ξένους καὶ δύσεργον ἐποίει τὴν πορείαν. Κύκλῳ γὰρ ὑπὸ τῆς φλογὸς 4 περιελάμποντο, τὰς οἰκίας περινεμομένης · καὶ διαπύροις ἐπιβαίνοντες ἐρειπίοις, καὶ καταφερομένοις ἀπορρήγμασι μεγάλοις ὑποτρέχοντες ἐπισφαλῶς, καὶ πολὺν ὁμοῦ καπνῷ διαπορευόμενοι κονιορτόν, ἐπειρῶντο συνέχειν καὶ μὴ διασπᾶν τὴν τάξιν. Ὡς δὲ προσέμειξαν τοῖς πολεμίοις, 5 ἐν χερσὶ μὲν ὀλίγων πρὸς ὀλίγους ἐγίνετο μάχη διὰ τὴν στενότητα καὶ τὴν ἀνωμαλίαν τοῦ τόπου, κραυγῇ δὲ καὶ προθυμίᾳ τῶν Συρακοσίων ἐπιρρωσάντων, <ἐξ>εβιά- σθησαν οἱ περὶ τὸν Νύψιον. Καὶ τὸ μὲν πλεῖστον 6 αὐτῶν εἰς τὴν ἀκρόπολιν ἐγγὺς οὖσαν ἀναφεῦγον ἐσώζετο · τοὺς δ᾽ [εν] ἀπολειφθέντας ἔξω καὶ διασπαρ- έντας ἀνήρουν οἱ ξένοι διώκοντες. Ἀπόλαυσιν δὲ τῆς νίκης ἐν τῷ παραυτίκα καὶ χαρὰν καὶ περιβολὰς ἔργῳ 7 τηλικούτῳ πρεπούσας οὐ παρέσχεν ὁ καιρός, ἐπὶ τὰς οἰκίας τραπομένων τῶν Συρακοσίων καὶ τὸ πῦρ μόλις ἐν τῇ νυκτὶ κατασβεσάντων.

47. Ἡμέρα δ᾽ ὡς ἦν, τῶν μὲν ἄλλων οὐδεὶς ὑπέμεινε δημαγωγῶν, ἀλλὰ καταγνόντες ἑαυτῶν ἔφυγον, Ἡρα- κλείδης δὲ καὶ Θεοδότης αὐτοὶ κομίσαντες ἑαυτοὺς τῷ Δίωνι παρέδωκαν, ἀδικεῖν ὁμολογοῦντες, καὶ δεόμενοι βελτίονος ἐκείνου τυχεῖν, ἢ γεγόνασιν αὐτοὶ περὶ ἐκεῖνον·

2 πρέπειν δὲ Δίωνι, τὴν ἄλλην ἅπασαν ἀρετὴν ἀσύγκριτον
ἔχοντι, καὶ πρὸς ὀργὴν κρείττονι φανῆναι τῶν ἠγνωμο-
νηκότων, οἳ περὶ οὗ πρότερον ἐστασίασαν πρὸς αὐτόν,
νῦν ἥκουσιν ἡττᾶσθαι τῆς ἀρετῆς ὁμολογοῦντες. Ταῦτα
3 τῶν περὶ τὸν Ἡρακλείδην δεομένων, οἱ μὲν φίλοι παρεκε-
λεύοντο τῷ Δίωνι μὴ φείδεσθαι κακῶν καὶ βασκάνων
ἀνθρώπων, ἀλλὰ καὶ τοῖς στρατιώταις χαρίσασθαι τὸν
Ἡρακλείδην, καὶ τοῦ πολιτεύματος ἐξελεῖν δημοκοπίαν,
4 ἐπιμανὲς νόσημα, τυραννίδος οὐκ ἔλαττον. Ὁ δὲ Δίων
παραμυθούμενος αὐτοὺς ἔλεγεν, ὡς τοῖς μὲν ἄλλοις
στρατηγοῖς πρὸς ὅπλα καὶ πόλεμον ἡ πλείστη τῆς
ἀσκήσεώς ἐστιν, αὐτῷ δὲ πολὺν χρόνον ἐν Ἀκαδημείᾳ
μεμελέτηται θυμοῦ περιεῖναι καὶ φθόνου καὶ φιλονικίας
5 πάσης· ὧν ἐπίδειξίς ἐστιν οὐχ ἡ προς φίλους καὶ
χρηστοὺς μετριότης, ἀλλ᾽ εἴ τις ἀδικούμενος εὐπαραίτητος
6 εἴη καὶ πρᾷος τοῖς ἁμαρτάνουσι· βούλεσθαι δ᾽ Ἡρακλείδου μὴ τοσοῦτον δυνάμει καὶ φρονήσει κρατῶν, ὅσον
7 χρηστότητι καὶ δικαιοσύνῃ φανῆναι. Τὸ γὰρ ἀληθῶς
βέλτιον ἐν τούτοις· αἱ δὲ τοῦ πολέμου κατορθώσεις, εἰ
καὶ ἀνθρώπων μηδένα, τήν γε τύχην διαμφισβητοῦσαν
8 ἔχουσιν. Εἰ δ᾽ Ἡρακλείδης ἄπιστος καὶ κακὸς διὰ
φθόνον, οὔ τοι καὶ Δίωνα δεῖ θυμῷ διαφθεῖραι τὴν
ἀρετήν· τὸ γὰρ ἀντιτιμωρεῖσθαι τοῦ προαδικεῖν νόμῳ
δικαιότερον ὡρίσθαι, φύσει γινόνενον ἀπὸ μιᾶς ἀσθε-
9 νείας. Ἀνθρώπου δὲ κακίαν, εἰ καὶ χαλεπόν ἐστιν, οὐχ
οὕτως ἄγριον εἶναι παντάπασι καὶ δύσκολον, ὥστε μὴ
μεταβάλλειν χάριτι νικηθεῖσαν ὑπὸ τῶν πολλάκις εὖ
ποιούντων.

48. Τοιούτοις χρησάμενος λογισμοῖς ὁ Δίων ἀφῆκε
2 τοὺς περὶ τὸν Ἡρακλείδην. Τραπόμενος δὲ πρὸς τὸ
διατείχισμα, τῶν μὲν Συρακοσίων ἕκαστον ἐκέλευσεν ἕνα
* κόψαντα σταυρὸν ἐγγὺς καταβάλλειν, τοὺς δὲ ξένους
ἐπιστήσας διὰ νυκτός, ἀναπαυομένων τῶν Συρακοσίων,
ἔλαθεν ἀποσταυρώσας τὴν ἀκρόπολιν, ὥστε μεθ᾽ ἡμέραν
τὸ τάχος καὶ τὴν ἐργασίαν θεασαμένους ὁμοίως θαυμά-
3 ζειν τοὺς πολίτας καὶ τοὺς πολεμίους. Θάψας δὲ τοὺς
τεθνηκότας τῶν Συρακοσίων, καὶ λυσάμενος τοὺς ἑαλω-

κότας, δισχιλίων οὐκ ἐλάττονας ὄντας, ἐκκλησίαν συνήγαγε. Καὶ παρελθὼν Ἡρακλείδης εἰσηγήσατο 4 γνώμην, αὐτοκράτορα στρατηγὸν ἐλέσθαι Δίωνα κατὰ γῆν καὶ θάλασσαν. Ἀποδεξαμένων δὲ τῶν ἀρίστων καὶ 5 χειροτονεῖν κελευόντων, ἐθορύβησεν ὁ ναυτικὸς ὄχλος καὶ βάναυσος, ἀχθόμενος ἐκπίπτοντι τῆς ναυαρχίας τῷ Ἡρακλείδῃ, καὶ νομίζων αὐτόν, εἰ καὶ τἆλλα μηδενὸς ἄξιός ἐστι, δημοτικώτερόν γε πάντως εἶναι τοῦ Δίωνος καὶ μᾶλλον ὑπὸ χεῖρα τοῖς πολλοῖς. Ὁ δὲ Δίων τοῦτο 6 μὲν ἐφῆκεν αὐτοῖς, καὶ τὴν κατὰ θάλατταν ἀρχὴν ἀπέδωκε τῷ Ἡρακλείδῃ, πρὸς δὲ τῆς γῆς καὶ τῶν οἰκιῶν τὸν ἀναδασμὸν ὡρμημένοις ἐναντιωθείς, καὶ τὰ πρότερον ψηφισθέντα περὶ τούτων ἀκυρώσας, ἐλύπησεν. Ὅθεν 7 εὐθὺς ἑτέραν ἀρχὴν λαβὼν ὁ Ἡρακλείδης, τοὺς συνεκπλεύσαντας μετ᾽ αὐτοῦ στρατιώτας καὶ ναύτας ἐν Μεσσήνῃ καθήμενος ἐδημαγώγει καὶ παρώξυνε κατὰ τοῦ Δίωνος, ὡς τυραννεῖν μέλλοντος· αὐτὸς δὲ πρὸς Διονύσιον ἐποιεῖτο συνθήκας κρύφα διὰ Φάρακος τοῦ Σπαρτιάτου. Καὶ τοῦτο τῶν γνωριμωτάτων Συρακοσίων 8 ὑπονοησάντων, στάσις ἦν ἐν τῷ στρατοπέδῳ, καὶ δι᾽ αὐτὴν ἀπορία καὶ σπάνις ἐν ταῖς Συρακούσαις, ὥστε παντάπασιν ἀμηχανεῖν τὸν Δίωνα καὶ κακῶς ἀκούειν ὑπὸ 9 τῶν φίλων, οὕτω δυσμεταχείριστον ἄνθρωπον καὶ διεφθαρμένον ὑπὸ φθόνου καὶ πονηρίας αὐξήσαντα καθ᾽ αὑτοῦ τὸν Ἡρακλείδην.

49. Φάρακος δὲ πρὸς Νέᾳ πόλει τῆς Ἀκραγαντίνης στρατοπεδεύοντος, ἐξαγαγὼν τοὺς Συρακοσίους, ἐβούλετο μὲν ἐν ἑτέρῳ καιρῷ διαγωνίσασθαι πρὸς αὐτόν, Ἡρακλείδου δὲ καὶ τῶν ναυτῶν καταβοώντων, ὡς οὐ βούλεται μάχῃ κρῖναι τὸν πόλεμον Δίων, ἀλλ᾽ ἀεὶ μένοντος ἄρχειν, ἀναγκασθεὶς συνέβαλε καὶ ἡττήθη. Γενομένης δὲ τῆς 2 τροπῆς οὐ βαρείας, ἀλλὰ μᾶλλον ὑφ᾽ ἑαυτῶν καὶ τοῦ στασιάζειν ταραχθέντων, αὖθις ὁ Δίων παρεσκευάζετο μάχεσθαι, καὶ συνέταττε πείθων καὶ παραθαρρύνων. Τῆς δὲ νυκτὸς ἀρχομένης, ἀγγέλλεται πρὸς αὐτὸν 3 Ἡρακλείδην ἄραντα τὸν στόλον πλεῖν ἐπὶ Συρακουσῶν, ἐγνωκότα τὴν πόλιν καταλαβεῖν κἀκεῖνον ἀποκλεῖσαι

4 μετὰ τοῦ στρατεύματος. Εὐθὺς οὖν ἀναλαβὼν τοὺς
δυνατωτάτους καὶ προθυμοτάτους, ἱππάσατο διὰ τῆς
νυκτός· καὶ περὶ τρίτην ὥραν τῆς ἡμέρας πρὸς ταῖς
5 πύλαις ἦν, σταδίους κατηνυκὼς ἑπτακοσίους. Ἡρακλείδης δὲ ταῖς ναυσίν, ὡς ἁμιλλώμενος ὑστέρησεν,
* ἀποπλεύσας καὶ πλανώμενος ἐν κεναῖς πράξεσιν ἀσκό-
πως, ἐπιτυγχάνει Γαισύλῳ τῷ Σπαρτιάτῃ, φάσκοντι
πλεῖν ἐφ᾽ ἡγεμον<ί>ᾳ Σικελιωτῶν ἐκ Λακεδαίμονος, ὡς
6 πρότερόν ποτε Γύλιππος. Ἄσμενος οὖν ἀναλαβὼν
τοῦτον τὸν ἄνδρα, καὶ περιαψάμενος ὥσπερ ἀλεξιφάρμακον τοῦ Δίωνος, ἐπεδείκνυτο τοῖς συμμάχοις, καὶ
κήρυκα πέμπων εἰς τὰς Συρακούσας, ἐκέλευε δέχεσθαι
7 τὸν Σπαρτιάτην ἄρχοντα τοὺς πολίτας, ἀποκριναμένου
δὲ τοῦ Δίωνος ὡς εἰσὶν ἄρχοντες ἱκανοὶ τοῖς Συρακοσίοις,
εἰ δὲ πάντως δέοι Σπαρτιάτου τοῖς πράγμασιν, αὐτὸς
οὗτος εἶναι κατὰ ποίησιν γεγονὼς Σπαρτιάτης, τὴν μὲν
ἀρχὴν ὁ Γαισύλος ἀπέγνω, πλεύσας δὲ πρὸς τὸν Δίωνα
διήλλαξε τὸν Ἡρακλείδην, ὅρκους δόντα καὶ πίστεις τὰς
μεγίστας, <ἐφ᾽> αἷς αὐτὸς ὁ Γαισύλος ὤμοσε τιμωρὸς
ἔσεσθαι Δίωνι καὶ κολαστὴς Ἡρακλείδου κακοπραγμο-
νοῦντος.

50. Ἐκ τούτου κατέλυσαν μὲν οἱ Συρακόσιοι τὸ
ναυτικόν· οὐδὲν γὰρ ἦν ἔργον αὐτοῦ, μεγάλαι δὲ δαπά-
ναι τοῖς πλέουσι καὶ στάσεως ἀφορμαὶ τοῖς ἄρχουσι·
τὴν δ᾽ ἄκραν ἐπολιόρκουν, ἐξοικοδομήσαντες τὸ περιτεί-
2 χισμα. Μηδενὸς δὲ τοῖς πολιορκουμένοις βοηθοῦντος,
ἐπιλ<ε>ίποντος δὲ σίτου, τῶν δὲ μισθοφόρων γινομένων
πονηρῶν, ἀπογνοὺς ὁ υἱὸς τοῦ Διονυσίου τὰ πράγματα
καὶ σπεισάμενος πρὸς τὸν Δίωνα, τὴν μὲν ἄκραν ἐκείνῳ
μετὰ τῶν ὅπλων καὶ τῆς ἄλλης κατασκευῆς παρέδωκεν,
αὐτὸς δὲ τὴν μητέρα καὶ τὰς ἀδελφὰς ἀναλαβών, καὶ
3 πέντε πληρωσάμενος τριήρεις, ἐξέπλει πρὸς τὸν πατέρα,
τοῦ Δίωνος ἀσφαλῶς μὲν ἐκπέμποντος, οὐδενὸς δὲ τῶν
ἐν Συρακούσαις ἀπολ<ε>ίποντος ἐκείνην τὴν ὄψιν, ἀλλὰ
καὶ τοὺς μὴ παρόντας ἐπιβοωμένων, ὅτι τὴν ἡμέραν
ταύτην καὶ τὸν ἥλιον ἐλευθέραις ἀνίσχοντα ταῖς Συρα-
4 κούσαις οὐκ ἐφορῶσιν. Ὅπου γὰρ ἔτι νῦν τῶν λεγομένων

κατὰ τῆς τύχης παραδειγμάτων ἐμφανέστατόν ἐστι καὶ
μέγιστον ἡ Διονυσίου φυγή, τίνα χρὴ δοκεῖν αὐτῶν
ἐκείνων τὴν τότε χαρὰν γενέσθαι, καὶ πηλίκον φρονῆσαι
τοὺς τὴν μεγίστην τῶν πώποτε τυραννίδων καθελόντας
ἐλαχίσταις ἀφορμαῖς;

51. Ἐκπλεύσαντος δὲ τοῦ Ἀπολλοκράτους, καὶ τοῦ
Δίωνος εἰς τὴν ἀκρόπολιν βαδίζοντος, οὐκ ἐκαρτέρησαν
αἱ γυναῖκες οὐδ' ἀνέμειναν εἰσελθεῖν αὐτόν, ἀλλ' ἐπὶ τὰς
θύρας ἐξέδραμον, ἡ μὲν Ἀριστομάχη τὸν υἱὸν ἄγουσα
τοῦ Δίωνος, ἡ δ' Ἀρετὴ κατόπιν εἵπετο δακρύουσα καὶ
διαποροῦσα, πῶς ἀσπάσηται καὶ προσείπῃ τὸν ἄνδρα,
κοινωνίας αὐτῇ πρὸς ἕτερον γεγενημένης. Ἀσπασα- 2
μένου δ' αὐτοῦ πρῶτον τὴν ἀδελφήν, εἶτα τὸ παιδίον,
ἡ Ἀριστομάχη προσαγαγοῦσα τὴν Ἀρετὴν "Ἠτυχοῦ-
μεν" ἔφη "ὦ Δίων, σοῦ φεύγοντος· ἥκων δὲ καὶ νικῶν 3
ἀφῄρηκας ἡμῶν ἁπάντων τὰς κατηφείας, πλὴν μόνης
ταύτης, ἣν ἐπεῖδον ἡ δυστυχὴς ἐγὼ σοῦ ζῶντος ἑτέρῳ
συνελθεῖν βιασθεῖσαν. Ὅτ' οὖν σὲ κύριον ἡμῶν ἡ τύχη
πεποίηκε, πῶς αὐτῇ διαιτᾷς ἐκείνην τὴν ἀνάγκην; Πότε- 4
ρον ὡς θεῖον ἢ καὶ ὡς ἄνδρα σ' ἀσπάσεται;". Τοιαῦτα
τῆς Ἀριστομάχης λεγούσης, ὁ Δίων ἐκδακρύσας προ- 5
σηγάγετο φιλοστόργως τὴν γυναῖκα· καὶ παραδοὺς αὐτῇ
τὸν υἱὸν ἐκέλευσεν εἰς τὴν οἰκίαν τὴν αὐτοῦ βαδίζειν,
ὅπου καὶ αὐτὸς διῃτᾶτο, τὴν ἄκραν ἐπὶ τοῖς Συρακοσίοις
ποιησάμενος.

52. Οὕτω δὲ τῶν πραγμάτων αὐτῷ προ[σ]κεχωρηκό-
των, οὐδὲν ἀπολαῦσαι πρότερον ἠξίωσε τῆς παρούσης *
εὐτυχίας, ἢ τὸ καὶ φίλοις χάριτας καὶ συμμάχοις δωρεάς,
μάλιστα δὲ τοῖς ἐν ἄστει συνήθεσι καὶ ξένοις ἀπονείμαί
τινα φιλανθρωπίας καὶ τιμῆς μερίδα, τῇ μεγαλοψυχίᾳ τὴν
δύναμιν ὑπερβαλλόμενος. Ἑαυτὸν δὲ λιτῶς καὶ σωφρόνως 2
ἐκ τῶν τυχόντων διώκει, θαυμαζόμενος ὅτι, μὴ μόνον
Σικελίας τε καὶ Καρχηδόνος, ἀλλὰ καὶ τῆς Ἑλλάδος
ὅλης ἀποβλεπούσης πρὸς αὐτὸν εὐημεροῦντα, καὶ μηδὲν
οὕτω μέγα τῶν τότε νομιζόντων, μηδ' ἐπιφανεστέρας περὶ
ἄλλον ἡγεμόνα τόλμης καὶ τύχης γεγονέναι δοκούσης,

3 οὕτω παρεῖχεν ἑαυτὸν <ἐν> ἐσθῆτι καὶ θεραπείᾳ καὶ
τραπέζῃ μέτριον, ὥσπερ ἐν Ἀκαδημείᾳ συσσιτῶν μετὰ
Πλάτωνος, οὐκ ἐν ξεναγοῖς καὶ μισθοφόροις διαιτώμενος,
οἷς αἱ καθ' ἑκάστην ἡμέραν πλησμοναὶ καὶ ἀπολαύσεις
4 παραμυθία τῶν πόνων καὶ τῶν κινδύνων εἰσίν. Ἀλλ'
ἐκείνῳ μὲν Πλάτων ἔγραφεν, ὡς πρὸς ἕνα νῦν τῆς οἰκου-
* μένης τόπον ἅπαντες ἀποβλέπουσιν, αὐτὸς δ' ἐκεῖνος,
ὡς ἔοικεν, ἀφεώρα πρὸς ἓν χωρίον μιᾶς πόλεως, τὴν
Ἀκαδήμειαν, καὶ τοὺς αὐτόθι καὶ θεατὰς καὶ δικαστὰς
ἐγίνωσκεν οὔτε πρᾶξιν οὔτε τόλμαν οὔτε νίκην τινὰ
θαυμάζοντας, ἀλλὰ μόνον, εἰ κοσμίως καὶ σωφρόνως
τῇ τύχῃ χρῆται, καὶ παρέχει μέτριον ἑαυτὸν ἐν πράγμασι
5 μεγάλοις ἀποσκοποῦντας. Τοῦ μέντοι περὶ τὰς ὁμιλίας
ὄγκου καὶ τοῦ πρὸς τὸν δῆμον ἀτενοῦς ἐφιλονίκει μηδὲν
ὑφελεῖν μηδὲ χαλάσαι, καίτοι τῶν πραγμάτων αὐτῷ
χάριτος ἐνδεῶν ὄντων, καὶ Πλάτωνος ἐπιτιμῶντος, ὡς
εἰρήκαμεν, καὶ γράφοντος, ὅτι ἡ αὐθάδεια ἐρημίᾳ σύνοι-
6 κός ἐστιν. Ἀλλὰ φύσει τε φαίνεται πρὸς τὸ πιθανὸν
δυσκεράστῳ κεχρημένος, ἀντισπᾶν τε τοὺς Συρακοσίους
ἄγαν ἀνειμένους καὶ διατεθρυμμένους προθυμούμενος.

53. Ὁ γὰρ Ἡρακλείδης αὖθις ἐπέκειτο· καὶ πρῶτον
μὲν εἰς συνέδριον παρακαλούμενος, οὐκ ἐβούλετο βαδίζειν.
ἰδιώτης γὰρ ὢν μετὰ τῶν ἄλλων ἐκκλησιάζειν πολιτῶν.
2 Ἔπειτα κατηγόρει τοῦ Δίωνος, ὅτι τὴν ἄκραν οὐ κατέ-
σκαψε, καὶ τῷ δήμῳ τὸν Διονυσίου τάφον ὡρμημένῳ
λῦσαι καὶ τὸν νεκρὸν ἐκβαλεῖν οὐκ ἐπέτρεψε, μεταπέμ-
πεται δ' ἐκ Κορίνθου συμβούλους καὶ συνάρχοντας,
3 ἀπαξιῶν τοὺς πολίτας. Τῷ δ' ὄντι μετεπέμπετο τοὺς
Κορινθίους ὁ Δίων, ἣν ἐπενόει πολιτείαν ῥᾷον ἐλπίζων
4 καταστήσειν ἐκείνων παραγενομένων. Ἐπενόει δὲ τὴν
μὲν ἄκρατον δημοκρατίαν, ὡς οὐ πολιτείαν, ἀλλὰ παντο-
* πώλιον οὖσαν πολιτειῶν, κατὰ τὸν Πλάτωνα, κολούειν,
Λακωνικὸν δέ τι καὶ Κρητικὸν σχῆμα μειξάμενος ἐκ
* δήμου καὶ βασιλείας, ἀριστοκρατίαν ἔχον τὴν ἐπιστα-
τοῦσαν καὶ βραβεύουσαν τὰ μέγιστα, καθιστάναι καὶ
κοσμεῖν, ὁρῶν καὶ τοὺς Κορινθίους ὀλιγαρχικώτερόν τε
πολιτευομένους, καὶ μὴ πολλὰ τῶν κοινῶν ἐν τῷ δήμῳ

πράττοντας. Ὡς οὖν μάλιστα πρὸς ταῦτα τὸν Ἡρακλεί- 5
δην ἐναντιώσεσθαι προσεδόκα, καὶ τἆλλα ταραχώδης καὶ
εὐμετάθετος καὶ στασιαστικὸς ἦν, οὓς πάλαι βουλομένους αὐτὸν ἀνελεῖν ἐκώλυεν, τούτοις ἐπέτρεψε τότε·
καὶ παρελθόντες εἰς τὴν οἰκίαν ἀποκτιννύουσιν αὐτόν.
Ἐλύπησε δὲ σφόδρα τοὺς Συρακοσίους ἀποθανών· ὅμως 6
δὲ τοῦ Δίωνος ταφάς τε λαμπρὰς παρασκευάσαντος, καὶ
μετὰ τοῦ στρατεύματος ἑπομένου προπέμψαντος τὸν
νεκρόν, εἶτα διαλεχθέντος αὐτοῖς, συνέγνωσαν, ὡς οὐ
δυνατὸν ἦν ταρασσομένην παύσασθαι τὴν πόλιν Ἡρακλείδου καὶ Δίωνος ἅμα πολιτευομένων.

54. Ἦν δέ τις ἑταῖρος τοῦ Δίωνος ἐξ Ἀθηνῶν,
Κάλλιππος, ὅν φησιν ὁ Πλάτων οὐκ ἀπὸ παιδείας, ἀλλ᾽ ἐκ
μυσταγωγιῶν καὶ τῆς περιτρεχούσης ἑταιρείας γνώριμον
αὐτῷ γενέσθαι καὶ συνήθη, μετασχὼν δὲ τῆς στρατείας
καὶ τιμώμενος, ὥστε καὶ συνεισελθεῖν εἰς τὰς Συρακούσας
πρῶτος τῶν ἑταίρων ἁπάντων ἐστεφανωμένος. Ἦν <δὲ> 2
καὶ λαμπρὸς ἐν τοῖς ἀγῶσι καὶ διάσημος. Ἐπεὶ δέ, τῶν
πρώτων καὶ βελτίστων φίλων τοῦ Δίωνος ἀνηλωμένων
ὑπὸ τοῦ πολέμου καὶ τεθνηκότος Ἡρακλείδου, τόν τε
δῆμον ἑώρα τῶν Συρακοσίων ἔρημον ἡγεμόνος ὄντα, καὶ
τοὺς στρατιώτας τοὺς μετὰ Δίωνος προσέχοντας αὐτῷ
μάλιστα, μιαρώτατος ἀνθρώπων γενόμενος, καὶ παντά- 3
πασιν ἐλπίσας Σικελίαν ἆθλον ἕξειν τῆς ξενοκτονίας. ὡς
δέ φασιν ἔνιοι, καὶ τάλαντα προσλαβὼν εἴκοσι τοῦ φόνου
μισθὸν παρὰ τῶν πολεμίων, διέφθειρε καὶ παρεσκεύαζέ
τινας τῶν ξένων ἐπὶ τὸν Δίωνα, κακοηθεστάτην ἀρχὴν καὶ 4
πανουργοτάτην ποιησάμενος. Ἀεὶ γάρ τινας φωνὰς τῶν
στρατιωτῶν πρὸς ἐκεῖνον ἢ λελεγμένας ἀληθῶς ἀναφέρων
ἢ πεπλασμένας ὑπ᾽ αὐτοῦ, τοιαύτην ἐξουσίαν ἔλαβε διὰ
τὴν πίστιν, ὥστ᾽ ἐντυγχάνειν κρύφα καὶ διαλέγεσθαι
μετὰ παρρησίας οἷς βούλοιτο κατὰ τοῦ Δίωνος, αὐτοῦ
κελεύοντος, ἵνα μηδεὶς λανθάνῃ τῶν ὑπούλως καὶ
δυσμενῶς ἐχόντων. Ἐκ δὲ τούτων συνέβαινε τοὺς μὲν 5
πονηροὺς καὶ νοσοῦντας εὑρίσκειν ταχὺ καὶ συνιστάναι
τὸν Κάλλιππον, εἰ δέ τις ἀπωσάμενος τοὺς λόγους αὐτοῦ
καὶ τὴν πεῖραν ἐξείποι πρὸς τὸν Δίωνα, μὴ ταράττεσθαι

μηδὲ χαλεπαίνειν ἐκεῖνον, ὡς ἃ προσέταττε τοῦ
Καλλίππου περαίνοντος.

55. Συνισταμένης δὲ τῆς ἐπιβουλῆς, φάσμα γίνεται
τῷ Δίωνι μέγα καὶ τερατῶδες. Ἐτύγχανε μὲν γὰρ ὀψὲ
τῆς ἡμέρας καθεζόμενος ἐν παστάδι τῆς οἰκίας, μόνος ὢν
2 πρὸς ἑαυτῷ τὴν διάνοιαν· ἐξαίφνης δὲ ψόφου γενομένου
πρὸς θατέρῳ πέρατι τῆς στοᾶς, ἀποβλέψας ἔτι φωτὸς
ὄντος εἶδε γυναῖκα μεγάλην, στολῇ μὲν καὶ προσώπῳ
μηδὲν Ἐρινύος τραγικῆς παραλλάττουσαν, σαίρουσαν δὲ
3 καλ<λ>ύντρῳ τινὶ τὴν οἰκίαν. Ἐκπλαγεὶς δὲ δεινῶς, καὶ
περίφοβος γενόμενος, μετεπέμψατο τοὺς φίλους καὶ
διηγεῖτο τὴν ὄψιν αὐτοῖς, καὶ παραμένειν ἐδεῖτο καὶ
συννυκτερεύειν, παντάπασιν ἐκστατικῶς ἔχων, καὶ
δεδοικὼς μὴ πάλιν εἰς ὄψιν αὐτῷ μονωθέντι τὸ τέρας
4 ἀφίκηται. Τοῦτο μὲν οὖν αὖθις οὐ συνέπεσε. Μεθ᾽
ἡμέρας δ᾽ ὀλίγας ὁ υἱὸς αὐτοῦ, σχεδὸν ἀντίπαις ὤν,
* ἔκ τινος λύπης καὶ ὀργῆς μικρὰν καὶ παιδικὴν ἀρχὴν
λαβούσης ἔρριψεν ἑαυτὸν ἀπὸ τοῦ τέγους ἐπὶ τὴν κεφαλὴν
καὶ διεφθάρη.

56. Ἐν τοιούτοις δὲ τοῦ Δίωνος ὄντος, ὁ Κάλλιππος
ἔτι μᾶλλον εἴχετο τῆς ἐπιβουλῆς· καὶ λόγον εἰς τοὺς
Συρακοσίους ἐξέδωκεν, ὡς ὁ Δίων ἄπαις γεγονὼς ἔγνωκε
τὸν <υἱὸν> τοῦ Διονυσίου καλεῖν Ἀπολλοκράτην καὶ
ποιεῖσθαι διάδοχον, ἀδελφιδοῦν μὲν ὄντα τῆς ἑαυτοῦ
2 γυναικός, θυγατριδοῦν δὲ τῆς ἀδελφῆς. Ἤδη δὲ καὶ τὸν
Δίωνα καὶ τὰς γυναῖκας ὑπόνοια τῶν πραττομένων εἶχε,
3 καὶ μηνύσεις ἐγίγνοντο πανταχόθεν. Ἀλλ᾽ ὁ μὲν Δίων,
ὡς ἔοικεν, ἐπὶ τοῖς κατὰ τὸν Ἡρακλείδην ἀχθόμενος, καὶ
τὸν φόνον ἐκεῖνον, ὥς τινα τοῦ βίου καὶ τῶν πράξεων
αὐτῷ κηλῖδα περικειμένην, δυσχεραίνων ἀεὶ καὶ βαρυνό-
μενος, εἶπεν, ὅτι πολλάκις ἤδη θνήσκειν ἕτοιμός ἐστι καὶ
παρέχειν τῷ βουλομένῳ σφάττειν αὐτόν, εἰ ζῆν δεήσει
μὴ μόνον τοὺς ἐχθρούς, ἀλλὰ καὶ τοὺς φίλους φυλαττό-
μενον. Τὰς δὲ γυναῖκας ὁρῶν ὁ Κάλλιππος ἐξεταζούσας
4 ἀκριβῶς τὸ πρᾶγμα καὶ φοβηθείς, ἦλθε πρὸς αὐτὰς
ἀρνούμενος καὶ δακρύων, καὶ πίστιν ἣν βούλονται

διδόναι βουλόμενος. Αἱ δ' ἠξίουν αὐτὸν ὀμόσαι τὸν 5
μέγαν ὅρκον· Ἦν δὲ τοιοῦτος· καταβὰς εἰς τὸ τῶν
Θεσμοφόρων τέμενος ὁ διδοὺς τὴν πίστιν, ἱερῶν τινων
γενομένων, περιβάλλεται τὴν πορφυρίδα τῆς θεοῦ, καὶ
λαβὼν δᾷδα καιομένην ἀπόμνυσι. Ταῦτα ποιήσας ὁ 6
Κάλλιππος πάντα, καὶ τὸν ὅρκον ἀπομόσας, οὕτω
κατεγέλασε τῶν θεῶν, ὥστε περιμείνας τὴν ἑορτὴν ἧς
ὤμοσε θεοῦ, δρᾷ τὸν φόνον ἐν τοῖς Κορείοις, <παρ'>
οὐδὲν ἴσως τὸ περὶ τὴν ἡμέραν τῆς θεοῦ ποιησάμενος, ὡς
ἀσεβουμένης πάντως, εἰ καὶ κατ' ἄλλον χρόνον ἔσφαττε
τὸν μύστην αὐτῆς ὁ μυσταγωγός.

57. Ὄντων δὲ πλειόνων ἐν τῇ κοινωνίᾳ τῆς πράξεως,
καθεζομένου Δίωνος ἐν οἰκήματι κλίνας τινὰς ἔχοντι μετὰ
τῶν φίλων, οἱ μὲν ἔξω τὴν οἰκίαν περιέστησαν, οἱ δὲ
πρὸς ταῖς θύραις τοῦ οἴκου καὶ ταῖς θυρίσιν ἦσαν.
Αὐτοὶ δ' οἱ προσφέρειν τὰς χεῖρας μέλλοντες Ζακύν- 2
θιοι παρῆλθον ἄνευ ξιφῶν ἐν τοῖς χιτῶσιν. Ἅμα
δ' οἱ μὲν ἔξω τὰς θύρας ἐπισπασάμενοι κατεῖχον, οἱ δὲ
τῷ Δίωνι προσπεσόντες κατάγχειν ἐπειρῶντο καὶ συντρί- *
βειν αὐτόν. Ὡς δ' οὐδὲν ἐπέραινον, ᾔτουν ξίφος· οὐδεὶς 3
δ' ἐτόλμα τὰς θύρας ἀνοῖξαι. Συχνοὶ γὰρ ἦσαν ἔνδον
οἱ μετὰ τοῦ Δίωνος, ὧν ἕκαστος οἰόμενος, ἂν ἐκεῖνον
πρόηται, διασώσειν ἑαυτόν, οὐκ ἐτόλμα βοηθεῖν.
Διατριβῆς δὲ γενομένης, Λύκων ὁ Συρακόσιος ὀρέγει τινὶ 4
τῶν Ζακυνθίων διὰ τῆς θυρίδος ἐγχειρίδιον, ᾧ καθάπερ
ἱερεῖον τὸν Δίωνα κρατούμενον πάλαι καὶ ἐλιττόμενον *
ἀπέσφαξαν. Εὐθὺς δὲ καὶ τὴν ἀδελφὴν μετὰ τῆς 5
γυναικὸς ἐγκύμονος οὔσης εἰς τὴν εἱρκτὴν ἐνέβαλον.
Καὶ συνέβη τῇ γυναικὶ τλημονέστατα λοχευθείσῃ τεκεῖν
ἐν τῷ δεσμωτηρίῳ παιδάριον ἄρρεν· ὅπερ θρέψαι καὶ
μᾶλλον παρεβάλοντο πείσασαι τοὺς φύλακας, ἤδη τοῦ
Καλλίππου θορυβουμένου τοῖς πράγμασιν.

58. Ἐν ἀρχῇ μὲν γὰρ ἀποκτείνας τὸν Δίωνα,
λαμπρὸς ἦν καὶ κατεῖχε τὰς Συρακούσας· καὶ πρὸς
τὴν Ἀθηναίων ἔγραφε πόλιν, ἣν μάλιστα μετὰ τοὺς
θεοὺς ὤφειλεν αἰδεῖσθαι καὶ δεδιέναι, τηλικούτου μύσους

2 ἁψάμενος. Ἀλλ' ἔοικεν ἀληθῶς λέγεσθαι τὸ τὴν πόλιν ἐκείνην φέρειν ἄνδρας ἀρετῇ τε τοὺς ἀγαθοὺς ἀρίστους καὶ κακίᾳ τοὺς φαύλους πονηροτάτους, καθάπερ αὐτῶν καὶ ἡ χώρα κάλλιστον μέλι καὶ κώνειον ὠκυμορώτατον 3 ἀναδίδωσιν. Οὐ μὴν πολὺν χρόνον ὁ Κάλλιππος ἔγκλημα τῆς τύχης καὶ τῶν θεῶν περιῆν, ὡς περιορώντων ἐξ ἀσεβήματος ἄνθρωπον τηλικούτου κτώμενον ἡγεμονίας 4 καὶ πράγματα· ταχὺ δ' ἀξίαν δίκην ἔδωκεν. Ὁρμήσας μὲν γὰρ Κατάνην λαβεῖν, εὐθὺς ἀπέβαλε τὰς Συρακούσας· ὅτε καί φασιν αὐτὸν εἰπεῖν, ὅτι πόλιν ἀπολω-5 λεκὼς τυρόκνηστιν εἴληφεν. Ἐπιθέμενος δὲ Μεσσηνίοις, καὶ τοὺς πλείστους στρατιώτας ἀπολέσας, ἐν οἷς ἦσαν οἱ Δίωνα κατακτείναντες, οὐδεμιᾶς δὲ πόλεως αὐτὸν ἐν Σικελίᾳ προσδεχομένης, ἀλλὰ μισούντων ἁπάντων καὶ 6 προβαλλομένων, Ῥήγιον κατέσχεν. Ἐκεῖ δὲ λυπρῶς πράττων, καὶ κακῶς διατρέφων τοὺς μισθοφόρους, ὑπὸ Λεπτίνου καὶ Πολυπέρχοντος ἀνῃρέθη, χρησαμένων ξιφιδίῳ <τῷ αὐτῷ> κατὰ τύχην ᾧ καὶ Δίωνα πληγῆναί 7 φασιν. Ἐγνώσθη δὲ τῷ μεγέθει (βραχὺ γὰρ ἦν, ὥσπερ τὰ Λακωνικά) καὶ τῇ κατασκευῇ τῆς τέχνης, εἰργασμένον γλαφυρῶς καὶ περιττῶς. Τοιαύτην μὲν οὖν τίσιν Κάλ-8 λιππος ἔδωκε. Τὴν δ' Ἀριστομάχην καὶ τὴν Ἀρετήν, ὡς ἀφείθησαν ἐκ τῆς εἱρκτῆς, ἀναλαβὼν Ἱκέτης ὁ Συρακόσιος, εἷς τῶν Δίωνος φίλων γεγονώς, ἐδόκει 9 πιστῶς καὶ καλῶς περιέπειν. Εἶτα συμπεισθεὶς ὑπὸ τῶν Δίωνος ἐχθρῶν, καὶ παρασκευάσας πλοῖον αὐταῖς, ὡς εἰς Πελοπόννησον ἀποσταλησομέναις, ἐκέλευσε κατὰ πλοῦν ἀποσφάξαντας ἐκβαλεῖν εἰς τὴν θάλασσαν· οἱ δὲ ζώσας ἔτι καταποντισθῆναι λέγουσι καὶ τὸ παιδίον 10 μετ' αὐτῶν. Περιῆλθε δὲ καὶ τοῦτον ἀξία ποινὴ τῶν τετολμημένων· αὐτός τε γὰρ ὑπὸ Τιμολέοντος ἁλοὺς ἀπέθανε, καὶ θυγατέρας δύο προσαπέκτειναν αὐτοῦ Δίωνι τιμωροῦντες οἱ Συρακόσιοι, περὶ ὧν ἐν τῷ Τιμολέοντος βίῳ <τὰ> καθ' ἕκαστα γέγραπται.

NOTES.

[L – S⁹ = revised edition of Liddell and Scott's Lexicon, 1940.]

1, 1-2. ἄρα γ': "when ἄρα is found where ἄρ' οὐ might have been expected, the appeal for confirmation is made the more confidently because less obviously stressed " (Denniston, *Greek Particles*, p. 46). The addition of γε makes the question more definite.

" Shall we say, Sosius Senecio, that just as—according to Simonides— Ilium felt no anger against the Corinthians for having served along with the Achaeans against her, because they too (the Ilians) had a zealous ally in Glaucus, a Corinthian by origin, so neither Greeks nor Romans are likely to find fault with the Academy, since they gain equal credit from this treatise, which embraces the Lives of Brutus and Dion, of whom, since the latter had attended Plato's lectures, and the former was reared in Plato's doctrines, both, as if from one and the same wrestling-school, set forth to engage in the greatest contests? "

1, 1. Σιμωνίδης, the lyric poet, 556–468 B.C. ; Κορινθίοισιν (Ἴλιον) οὐ μανίει οὐδὲ Δαναοί (*Frag.* 36 Diehl). According to Aristotle, *Rhetoric* 1, 6, 24, the Corinthians took the phrase as the reverse of a compliment, for it implied that they were not taken seriously as warriors !

Sosius Senecio was a member of the ruling class at Rome under Trajan and Hadrian. Son-in-law of Frontinus (who from 74 to 78 A.D. was *legatus Augusti in Britannia*), he was *consul ordinarius* in the years 99 and 107. In the latter year the war with the Dacians ended, and Dacia became a Roman province. It has been supposed that the public statue of Senecio, mentioned by Dion Cassius (68, 12, 2), was set up to commemorate his services at the time.

Plutarch dedicated his *Progress in Virtue* and his *Table-talk* to Senecio. In the latter he remarks : " Readers must not be surprised if when addressing you I have brought together some observations which you yourself made (*Mor.* 629). In the *Lives* Senecio is addressed by name in *Thes.* 1, *Demosth.* 1 *and* 31 as well as in the present passage. In *Aemil.* 1, Plutarch, without mentioning a name, uses the second person singular, and similarly in *Agis* 2. As in both these passages he seems to be referring to Senecio, it has been suggested by Ziegler that the *whole* series of Parallel Lives was dedicated to him, the actual dedication being assumed to have occurred in the lost Life of Epaminondas, which may be supposed to have been the first of the series since Plutarch was a Boeotian and Epaminondas the great Boeotian hero. (See Ziegler, *Plutarchos von Chaironcia*, col. 52).

οἱ περὶ Γλαῦκον, ' Glaucus ': by a common post-classical usage this periphrasis may stand simply for the person named ; cf. οἱ περὶ Λέντλον ὑπατεύοντες, *Lentulus the consul*, in *Pompey* 59. (The usage recurs below 5, 5 ; 22, 2 ; 22, 3). Sisyphus and Bellerophon were the Corinthian ancestors of Glaucus—*Il.* 6, 144–211.

Ἀκαδημείᾳ (MSS. Ἀκαδημίᾳ corrected by Sintenis). In Arist. *Clouds* 1005, εἰς Ἀκαδήμειαν κατιὼν ὑπὸ ταῖς μορίαις ἀποθρέξει, a long *penult* is required, as in other verse passages. The name is derived from that of the Attic hero, Academus (Eupolis, *Frg.* 32). Such names follow the analogy of abstract nouns in -εια, formed from adjectives with stems in -ες, the suffix -ια, pronounced *yă*, being added : ἀλήθειᾰ = αληθεσια εὐμένειᾰ = ευμενεσια . Thus it appears that the name of the Phrygian town Εὐμένεια is a regular formation (it was so named in honour of King Εὐμενής), but the name Ἀκαδήμεια (like Ἀλεξάνδρεια, Μαρώνεια, etc.) is based on a false analogy.

πλησιάσας, frequently, as here, of the relation of pupil to teacher, e.g., Isocr., 1, 30 : Plut. *Demosth.* 2. Brutus' teacher was a Platonist, Antiochus of Ascalon (*Brut.* 2).

1. 3. φρονήσει καὶ δικαιοσύνῃ, placed first as the emphatic words of the sentence.—Plato, *Rep.* 5, 473 c : " unless philosophers become kings, or those now called kings genuinely engage in philosophy, and political power and philosophy are combined together, there is no respite from evils " : also *Epistle* 7, 326 A : " In praising philosophy I was forced to assert that the various classes of mankind will have no rest from evils till those who study philosophy attain to political offices, or the class which exercises power in the cities really and truly studies philosophy." (Cf. also *Ep.* 7, 325 D ; *Rep.* 5, 499 B ; 6, 501 E). In the Epistle Plato adds : " such was the opinion I held at the time of my first crossing to Italy " (388–387 B.C.). This does not mean that at this date the *Republic* was already written. The evidence from style, which puts the *Republic* in the middle group of dialogues, implies a later date. Moreover in its description of Tyranny there appear to be allusions to the Tyranny of Dionysius I. " Plato may have coined the phrase about Philosophers and Kings long before he used it in the *Republic* (generally dated *c.* 375), or else he merely remembered his state of mind before he visited Sicily." (Field, pp. 72, 129, 130).

1, 4. *Hippomachus* appears in Aelian, *Var. Hist.* 2, 6 as a pedantic martinet. κἄν (for καί) Richards : a potential sense is required. ἕπεσθαι : " it is natural that their principles should *accompany* (i.e., be associated with) their actions " as the *paedagogus* accompanied boys to and from school.

2, 1. [οὖσαι αἱ αὐταί] deleted by Sintenis as introducing *hiatus*.

2, 2. " For both were cut off before the end to which they had proposed to dedicate the gains acquired from many great contests, without their having been able to attain it." < τυχεῖν > Richards : an infinitive with μὴ δυνηθέντες is required to complete the sense ; but being emphatic the inf. should come at the beginning of the clause as in *Arat.* 51, ἀμύνασθαι μὴ δυναμένῳ. The use of μή for οὐ in temporal, causal or attributive clauses is frequent in post-classical Greek. For the sentiment cf. vv. 3–4 of the epigram on Dion attributed to Plato in Diog. Laert. 3, 30 :

> σοὶ δὲ, Δίων, ῥέξαντι καλῶν ἐπινίκιον ἔργων
> δαίμονες εὐρροίας ἐλπίδας ἐξέχεαν.

2, 3. Plutarch thought the purpose of the *daimones* in appearing to Dion and Brutus was " to shake and overthrow their virtue." Hence tr. τὸ δαιμόνιον " the Spirit-World." φάσματα : see *Dion* 55, *Brutus* 37.

2, 4. "Those who try to do away with such notions " were the Epicureans. In *Brut.* 37, Cassius, " using the arguments of Epicurus " offers a *natural* explanation of Brutus' apparition, adding, " it is not credible that *daimones* exist—or if they do, that they have a human form or voice, or the capacity to affect us."

μή after verbs of ' saying ' is common in Plut. and is found occasionally in earlier writers as Xenophon, *Mem.* 2, 39. The transposition of ἄν to follow προσπεσεῖν is suggested by Ziegler in order to avoid *hiatus*.

δαίμονα πονηρὸν . . . ἔχοντας : " because they have in them an evil *daimon*, Superstition." [εἶναι] an evident adscript, due to a copyist who misunderstood the sense. For a similar insertion see *Tit. Flam.* 21. Δεισιδαιμονίαν, *Superstition*, the meaning in post-classical writers. The article is omitted with abstract nouns when personified, as in 8, 4 ; *Timol.* 36.

2, 5. οὐκ οἶδα, as in *Phocion* 32, 7, has the construction of verbs of *apprehension* : " I am not sure that we may not be compelled . . . ."

2, 6. βελτίονας μοίρας : Plut., like Plato, held the rational soul of man to be immortal : *daimones* are destined to extinction. In *Mor.* 419, *Cessation of Oracles*, a speaker representing the author's attitude observes : " You admit *daimones* exist, but by refusing to believe them mortal you no longer retain the notion of *daimones* ; for in what do they differ from deities *if . . . in their essence they possess incorruptibility*? " Later on (ch. 17), sailors voyaging near the Echinades hear a miraculous voice proclaiming, " Great Pan is dead."

2, 7. *Two* parallel lives form a unit, here called λόγος, in 1, 1 γραφή, in *Demosth.* 3 and *Pericles* 2, βιβλίον. Hence Bryan changed βίῳ to βίων.

Supplementary Note I.

Plutarch's reference to Zoroastrianism (2, 5–6).

The story of how one evening Dion was alarmed by the apparition of an Erinys, and how some days later his son committed suicide is told in ch. 55, on the authority (it may safely be assumed) of Timaeus. The historian, no doubt, understood " the sweeping of the hall " as portending the extinction of Dion's family as a retribution for his share in the murder of Heracleides (recorded in *Dion*, 53) ; but Plutarch, while accepting the story of the

Erinys as fact, tacitly rejects the inference that the apparition foreboded divine vengeance. At the same time he explicitly puts aside the ' natural ' explanation which might have been expected to appeal to the author of the tract, ' On Superstition.' He thinks we may be forced to adopt " that very outlandish doctrine of very ancient thinkers, that *evil and spiteful daimones out of envy towards good men and a desire to shake and upset their virtue bring upon them distractions and fears.*"

The passage is explained by a statement found in Plutarch's *Isis and Osiris* (*Mor.* 369 D).

" A very ancient opinion has come down from theologians and law-givers ... that the sublunary Kosmos is derived from a combination of two opposing principles, and is therefore inconsistent and variable.

Some think there are two rival deities ; others that the better is God and the other a *daimon*,—as Zoroaster, who lived 5,000 years before the Trojan War. He called the one Oromazes and the other Arimanios."

Of Zoroaster's actual date and doctrine C. Huart writes (*Ancient Persia and Iranian Civilization* Eng. Trans., 1927, p. 168) :—

" The Parsee tradition places his life between the 7th and 6th centuries B.C., and this date is now almost universally accepted, for the Gathas [Hymns] mention the name of the Prophet, and in view of the archaic character of the language it is hard to place them after the time of the first Achaemenids at latest. The Orientalist West is even more precise and specifies a period from 660 to 583 B.C."

According to Zoroaster " Ahriman commands the Divs or demons. He is the evil creator, and *his inventions are impediments.* Where Ahuramazda created life, Ahriman created death."

The italicised words correspond to Plutarch's reference to evil daimones *impeding* the activities of good men.

Plato in the second book of the *Republic* had maintained against the poets that God is altogether good and the cause of nothing that is harmful to men ; the *daimones* he treated in a spirit of poetic allegory as, for example, Eros in the *Symposium*. But later on he ' felt constrained ' to assert that in addition to the *best soul* there must be assumed " at least one other with contrary powers " (*Laws*, 896 E).

This doctrine was not adopted by Plato's successors in the Academy or by the Stoics, among whom the notion of a being that is wholly the expression of an evil principle—like the Druh of Persism or the Satan of Judaism—is not found.

But Xenocrates, taking over from Plato the view that beings inter-mediate between gods and men actually exist, taught that they are of mixed nature, and that unedifying stories told about the gods, and savage or gloomy religious rites, were inspired by evil *daimones*. Xenocrates' teaching was popularised by Plutarch in his *Isis and Osiris*, his *Face in the Moon*, his *Cessation of Oracles* and *Delphic E*, where it is maintained that these intermediate beings, subject to ultimate extinction, have been granted by the gods the management of the phenomenal world, acting as their ministers in the control of Oracles, *but may be tempted to sin through pride or jealousy.*

When Plutarch speaks of dualistic doctrine as 'most outlandish' he is adopting the standpoint of the ordinary Greek.

3. This chapter appears to be based on Timaeus except Sect. 3 which is taken from Plato *Epistle* 8, 353 B.

3, 1–2. **Hermocrates** had been the leading spirit in Syracuse during the war with Athens. After the victory he sailed with a force to the Aegean to support Sparta. During his absence the extreme democrats became powerful in the Syracusan ecclesia, and when the Spartans had been twice defeated, —at Cynossema in 411 (Thuc. 8, 104–6) and at Cyzicus in 410 (Xen. *Hell.* 1, 18),—the Syracusans dismissed Hermocrates from his command and sent him into exile.

In 409 the Carthaginians invaded Greek Sicily. They destroyed Selinous and besieged Himera, which the Syracusan generals were unable to relieve.

In 408 Hermocrates returned to Sicily, but the Syracusans refused to have him back (Diod. 13, 63). He then with a small force engaged in guerrilla fighting against the Carthaginians at Panormus and Motya, but his friends were unable to get his banishment revoked. He then tried with the help of partisans within Syracuse to force his way into the city, but was killed with most of his followers (407 B.C.). But Dionysius escaped, being taken for dead, and a year or so later, in 406–5, made himself tyrant, and married Hermocrates' daughter—Diod. 13, 96, 3.

3, 2. ἀποστάντες οἱ Σ : Dionysius had seized power when the Carthaginian capture of Acragas had frightened the Syracusans, but when he failed to take Gela and Camarina, a rebellion arose among the 'horsemen,' an aristocratic body. They hurried home, attacked Dionysius' house, and so ill-treated his wife that she killed herself (405 B.C.)—Diod. 13, 112, 4 : 14, 44, 5.

δύο γυναῖκας ἅμα : it is not disputed that the elder Dionysius was a bigamist, but the statement here and in Diod. 14, 45, that he married *both women at the same time* is not to be relied on. Diodorus drew the Sicilian part of his fourteenth book from Timaeus ; but in Book 16, ch. 6 (based on Ephorus,—see Introd., Sect. 3), Doris of Locri is described as the *first* and Aristomache of Syracuse as the *second* wife.

Beloch 3, 2, 102, rightly (in my opinion) rejects both statements. Aristomache's father, Hipparinus (he argues) was the leading noble of Syracuse : it is out of the question that he gave his daughter in marriage on terms so repugnant to Greek sentiment.

Beloch thinks that Dionysius actually married Aristomache shortly after the death of his first wife, the daughter of Hermocrates. As Dion was born in 408 B.C. [see note on παρηκμακώς, 23, 5], his sister was probably very young when she married, which might account for a period of childlessness. It was only (in Beloch's view) when Dionysius feared they were likely to have no offspring that, like Anaxandridas, king of Sparta, in similar circumstances (Hdt. 5. 40), he took as a second wife, Doris of Locri.

Ἱππαρίνου : in Diod. 16, 6, as here by Plutarch, H. is described as εὐδοκιμώτατος τῶν Συρακοσίων: Aristotle however thought poorly of him. In *Pol*. 5, 1306 A he remarks:

" Changes occur in an oligarchy when the oligarchs dissipate their private property by extravagance ; they then want to innovate, and either try to instal themselves as tyrants, or else some other person, as Hipparinus did when he installed Dionysius." Hipparinus died a wealthy man (Nepos *Dion* 1).

πρωτεύσαντος : " who had been the leading man." συνάρξαντος from Plato, *Epist*. 8, 353 A ; but Diod. 13, 94 (source Timaeus), makes no reference to a *colleague*. Novotny suggests that Hipparinus was appointed to a position of inferior status. He cites Thuc. 2, 85, 1, etc., for the title στρατηγοί given to the σύμβουλοι of Spartan admirals ; Plato (loc. cit.) states that Hipparinus' function was to act as *adviser* to Dionysius.

3, 4. When Plutarch in the course of his narrative turns away from his authority *to insert a piece of information derived from a different source*, we commonly find the qualifying word λέγεται, or λέγουσι or φασι, In the *Dion* statements thus qualified occur in reference to remarkable behaviour,—here ; 5, 7 ; 7, 7 ; 9, 2 ; 13, 4 ; 20, 4 : remarkable sayings— 13, 5 ; 17, 9 ; 58, 4 ; remarkable coincidences, or marvels,—24, 5 ; 58, 6.

In chapters 22–54 this use of λέγεται occurs only once, i.e., in 24, 10, which, we are informed below, was taken from Theopompus. Yet the stories of the ox in 26, 7 and the wolf in 38, 1, are the sort of material which we frequently find qualified by λέγεται. The reason for its absence would seem to be simply that Plutarch found *these* stories in Timonides, and merely reproduced them in their original context. It seems likely that the ' λέγεται passages ' were taken by Plut. from collections of material which he had brought together. Such collections, are mentioned in *Mor*. 457 and 464.

For Dionysius' bigamous *ménage* see also Aelian *Var. Hist*., 13, 10 ; but Aelian's remark " one wife followed him on his campaigns, the other received him on his return " shows that the excerpt is not taken from Plutarch. Both authors, it would seem, were drawing on Timaeus.

3, 5. ὑπῆρχεν, it was her good fortune : so Dem. *De Cor*. 257, ὑπῆρξεν ἐμοὶ φοιτᾶν εἰς τὰ προσήκοντα διδασκαλεῖα. (The transposition of ὑπῆρχεν here to avoid hiatus was made by Latte).

πρὸς τὸ γένος : against the prejudice caused by her (foreign) origin.

3. 6. καταφαρμακεύειν here probably means ' bewitch,' not ' drug,' as Doris' mother was presumably living with her husband at the Italian Locri.

[In V. H., 13, 45, Aelian has the strange statement " Διονύσιος τὴν μητέρα διέφθειρε φαρμάκοις." It looks as if the words τῆς Λοκρίδος have fallen out. Aelian's notice would then represent a variation in the tradition].

4. 1–2. Apparently from Timaeus.

4. 1. ἀπὸ τῆς ἀδελφῆς : so in Eur. *Andr.* 203 the heroine asks ironically, " Do the Greeks love me "Εκτορος γ' ἄπο,—on Hector's account?"

4. 2. In Nepos, *Dion* 1, 2, Dionysius' gifts to Dion are mentioned. The *aor.* part, δόντας (as Reiske saw) is required by the sense.

4. 3-5. From Plato *Epist.* 7, 326 D-328 A.

4. 3. θείᾳ τινὶ τύχῃ . . . κατ' οὐδένα λογισμόν : for the absence of the copula cf. *Timol.* 20 αἰσχρῶς κατ' οὐδένα λογισμόν : also Demetr. 38, *Artox.* 8 (Koch).

παραβαλόντας : from the meaning " to lay a boat alongside " the verb developed the sense, *arrive* : cf. *Demetr.* 39, παραβαλόντος εἰς Θήβας, also in *Dem.* 31.

The date of Plato's first visit to Sicily may be inferred from *Epist.* 7, 327 A, σχεδὸν τεσσαράκοντα ἔτη γεγονώς. Hermodorus, Plato's pupil, is cited by Diog. Laert. 3, 6, for the statement that he was 28 when Socrates died (399 B.C.).

4. 4. Plato, *Epist.* 7, 326 E, remarks, " it is likely that one of the Powers above was planning to lay the foundation of the existing state of affairs." The reference to ' liberty ' is due to Plutarch. Liberty came to Syracuse with Timoleon after Plato's death.

Plato's account of his meeting with Dion is to be found in *Epist.* 7, 327 A.

[See Supplementary Note iii below.)

4. 6-7. " For he, having been bred in servile manners under a tyrant, and sated on the one hand with a life of inferiority and insecurity, and on the other with the retinue of servants which the newly enriched affect, and tasteless luxury and a manner of life that finds its ideal in pleasures and material advantages, had no sooner got a taste of Reason and the Philosophy that guides to virtue than his spirit burned within him, and judging with the innocence of youth from his own obedience to the claims of the ideal, that the same arguments would produce a similar effect on Dionysius, he exerted himself and contrived, by securing for him a period of leisure, that he should meet Plato and give him a hearing."

[This story probably is derived from Timaeus : see Supplementary Note ii below].

4. 6. μεστὸς approximates in sense to our slang phrase, ' fed up ' : so in *Arat.* 30 Lydiades μεστὸς ἦν τῆς ἐκ μοναρχίας βαρύτητος : in *Numa* 6, the Romans are described as μεστοὶ θριαυβῶν.

νεοπλούτου : cf. the νεόπλουτα δεῖπνα of *Lucullus* 40 ; and contrast ἀρχαιόπλουτος in Aesch. *Agam.* 1043.

4. 7. τῇ περὶ αὐτὸν εὐπειθείᾳ : *his own obedience.* In *Epist.* 7, 327 B, Plato similarly writes τοῦ θανάτου τοῦ περὶ Διονύσιον.—The use here of the personal **αὐτόν** where ἑαυτόν might be expected is justified by the contrast with Διονύσιον (for this usage see on 33, 2).

The simple infinitive after διεπράξαντο is found also in *Tit. Flam.* 7.

ποιησάμενος : the middle voice indicates that, while acting in the interest of Dionysius, Dion was himself an interested party : so, too, in

51, 5, τὴν ἄκραν ἐπὶ τοῖς Συρακοσίοις ποιησάμενος : cf. *Eur. Bacch.*
440, τοὐμὸν εὐτρεπὲς ποιούμενος, where see Dodds' note.

5. 1-2. The theme here attributed to Plato was evidently suggested
by the *Republic.*

5. 5. σπεύδοντες for σπεύδοντα, Lindskog : The MS. reading represents
Plato as eager, which would be an anticlimax. <οὔπω> Ziegler.

Πόλλιν : in Xen. *Hellen.* 4, 8, 11, Pollis is described as ἐπιστολεύς of
the Lacedaemonian fleet : in 5, 4, 61, his defeat by Chabrias the Athenian
is related : in Aelian, *Hist. Animal.* 11, 9, it is stated that when an earth-
quake followed by a tidal wave occurred at Helice in Achaea (373 B.C.),
Pollis went down with his ship.

5. 6. βλαβήσεσθαι γὰρ οὐδὲν : the remark is ironical.   Plato taught
that virtue is the health—the right order—the true polity of the soul,
which by its aid can transcend misfortune.   This doctrine is expounded
in the Ninth Book of the *Republic.*

5. 7. διὸ καὶ ... " and that is said to be why Pollis ... " Cf. *Pericles*
8, where Plutarch explains why P. was called ' Olympian.' φέρων ἀποδόσθαι :
for this idiomatic use of the *pres.* part. cf. 14, 7 ; 24, 6 ; *Mor.* 27 D.

The Aeginetans had been expelled from their homes by the Athenians
at the start of the Peloponnesian war, but, after Aegospotami, were
restored by Lysander. They remained at peace with Athens till 389, when
they were induced by the Spartans to raid Athenian commerce (*Hellen.*
5, 1, 1). The war continued till the Peace of 387. The Spartan commanders
mentioned by Xenophon as concerned in this war *do not include Pollis.*

ψήφισμα : there was no uniform practice in Greece respecting the treatment of prisoners of war. In 431 B.C. the Plataeans killed their Theban
captives : in 416 the Athenians killed the adult males of Melos ; but the
Spartans taken at Sphacteria in 425 were merely detained till the Peace
in 421.   Later on, the Spartan Callicratidas refused to sell Greeks into
slavery.

Supplementary Note II.

The Story of Plato's Enslavement at Dionysius' Instigation.

The authorities for the enslavement are:

1. Diodorus 15, 6, where it is implied that the sale was carried out
at Syracuse : presumed *source,* Ephorus or Theopompus:

2. Nepos, *Dion* 2 (without details of place or time) : source, Timaeus:

3. The present passage, where the locality is Aegina ; source apparently
Timaeus.   [See below].

4. Diogenes Laertius 3, 18-21, following in the main the same lines
as Plutarch, but with two different accounts of Plato's liberation.

5. A fragment, found at Herculaneum, of Philodemus, *Index Academicorum* (1st cent. B.C.), where the locality of the sale is given as Aegina :
in the extant portion there is no reference to Dionysius or to Pollis.   On
this document see G. C. Field, p. 18.

There are also two passages in Aristotle—cited below—which have been connected with an enslavement of Plato at Aegina.

Among modern writers A. E. Taylor regards the whole story as "barely possible but very improbable " : E. Meyer rejects the part that implicates Dionysius but is prepared to accept the sale of Plato at Aegina : the majority,—Grote, Holm, Gomperz, J. B. Bury, Cornford [C. A. H., VI, pp. 133 and 315], Robin, Harward, Laistner—accept Dionysius' complicity as fact.

I think Meyer is right. The sale of Plato at Aegina is supported by the Philodemus' fragment mentioned above, also by Diogenes' *second* account of what happened at Aegina : " Some say that Plato was brought before the Ecclesia, and they decided to sell him as a prisoner of war. Anniceris of Cyrene chanced to be present. He ransomed Plato for 20 minae and sent him to his companions at Athens, refusing a refund of the money."

The relevant passages of Aristotle are *Physics* 2, 199 B, [cited by Diels *Abh. Berlin Akad.* 23, 1 (1882)], and *Metaph.* 5 [4] 30, 1205 A, brought to my notice by Dr. M. Tierney :—

(1) "The end and the means to it may come by chance ; for instance, we say that a stranger has come by chance, paid the ransom, and gone away, when he acted as if he had come for that reason, though it was not for that reason that he came. And this is due to accident, for chance ranks among accidental causes."

(2) "We say, it happened to some one to go to Aegina when the cause of his going was not that the place was his destination, but that he had been driven out of his course by storm, or captured by pirates."

The one fact that seems to be established about Plato's misadventure is that he was sold in the Aeginetan market. There is no *convincing* evidence that Dionysius had anything to do with it.

That the Diodorus story has nothing to commend it is obvious enough : Dionysius takes Plato to ' the slavemarket '—presumably in Syracuse : his friends buy him out and send him back to Greece with the warning, " a wise man's way with tyrants is either fair speech or rare speech." (This jingle was used, according to Plutarch, *Solon* 28, by Aesop to Solon).

Plutarch's story is remarkable for its abrupt termination, which suggests that it was taken from a Sicilian historian concerned to illustrate by examples the wickedness of Dionysius. The obvious authority to have been reproduced here by Plutarch was Timaeus. As appears from the mention in Nepos, he had dealt with the subject. During his long residence at Athens, Timaeus, it may be presumed, had learnt what was believed at the Academy about Plato's misadventure at Aegina ; as a Sicilian he would have been familiar with the Syracusan tradition known to us through Diodorus. It may be suggested that he made a conflation of his two sources.

If Dionysius was responsible for Plato being sold at Aegina he must have employed an agent. By consulting the Hellenica of Xenophon, Timaeus might have learnt that a Syracusan squadron was supporting

Sparta in the Aegean in autumn 387. The squadron, he might reasonably infer, was sent in answer to an appeal from Sparta. If he had some grounds for thinking Pollis to have been the person through whom the appeal was made, he would have felt free to represent Pollis as Dionysius' intermediary at Aegina.

Obvious objections to the story are (1) Dion must have known that Sparta was supporting Aegina against Athens and hence would not have proposed to send the Athenian Plato home on a Spartan trireme : (2) the discourse attributed to Plato is evidently based on the fifth book of the *Republic*, where the cowardice of tyrants is emphasised : (3) it is not in the least likely that either Dionysius or Pollis divulged what passed at their ' secret interview,'—which appears in fact to have been invented in order to account for the continuance of good relations between Dion and Dionysius.

Of the version in Diogenes 3, 18–20, there is nothing that can be regarded as historical except the already cited alternative account of the Trial Scene at Aegina. Plainly fictitious is the scolding-match between Tyrant and Philosopher ; likewise the first version of what happened at Aegina, in which the Aeginetans take Plato out of Pollis' custody, try him on a charge which obviously could not apply to him, and when someone in jest remarked that he was a philosopher, let him go free.

We may conclude that Plato, shortly after leaving Sicily in 387, was captured by Aeginetan privateers in circumstances which have not transpired. He was offered for sale as a slave, purchased by Anniceris —mentioned as a friend of his in a different connexion by Aelian, V. H. 2, 27,—and set at liberty.

5, 8. By inserting καί before πεμπόμενος and deleting τε after ἐθαυμάσθη Laar brought the text into line with Nepos, *Dion* 1, 4: Legationes omnes quae essent illustriores per Dionem administrabantur. Hunc a Dionysio missum Carthaginienses suspexerunt ut neminem unquam Graeca lingua loquentem magis sint admirati.

πεμπόμενος, *when on mission*: a *perfect* sense is sometimes found in the present tense of πέμπω, as in *Dem.* 18, 156 : δὸς τὴν ἐπιστολὴν ἣν, ὡς οὐχ ὑπήκουον οἱ Θηβαῖοι, πέμπει . . . ὁ Φίλιππος. (Kühner, *Griech. Gram.* (Gerth) ii, 2).

5, 9. αὐτοῦ Kurtz (αὐτόν) : the MS. reading is lacking in point. On Gelon cf. Diod. 14, 66, 1 *and* 5 : " No one would venture to compare D. with Gelon ... D. had no sooner gained the citizens' confidence than he took away their freedom." For praise of Gelon, cf. also Diod. 11, 67 ; Polyaen. 1, 27, 1 ; Aelian V. H. 6, 11 ; 13, 37 ; all of which passages are generally held to come from Timaeus, whom Polyb. 12, 26b accuses of exaggerating the prosperity of Syracuse under Gelon.

6, 1. Dionysius I had two sons, Dionysius and Hermocritus, by his Locrian wife, Doris : by Dion's sister, Aristomache, he ultimately had two sons, Hipparinus and Nysaeus, and two daughters, Sophrosyne and Arete.

Thearidas in 384 B.C. headed the Syracusan legation to the Olympic Games, when Lysias (Diod. 14, 109) incited the spectators to ' demonstrate ' against the Tyrant.

6, 3. Nepos, *Dion* 2 ; 4–5 : " Dionysius patri soporem medicos dare coegit." Plutarch declined, however, it would seem, to represent him as responsible for his father's death. In C.A.H. vi, p. 272, the story is rejected altogether by Hackforth, because Dionysius II on his accession retained Dion in his service.

Diodorus, 15, 74, reproducing an earlier authority, states that Dionysius I died of a fever brought on by hard drinking after his victory in the dramatic contest at the Attic festival of the Lenaea.

This story also has been doubted because he was reputed to be notably temperate (Cic. *Tusc. Disput.* 5, 20). Also the Lenaean festival was held in January ; but *in February* 367 a treaty was concluded between Dionysius and Athens.

If Diodorus is correct in dating Dionysius' death in the Olympian year, August 368—August 367, it follows that he cannot have died shortly after the Lenaea ; or else the news of his death had not reached Athens in the following month.

6, 5. τὸν ἀπὸ **Καρχηδόνος** κίνδυνον : war against Carthage had been declared by Dionysius in 368, but after his naval defeat at Drepanum a truce had been made (Diod. 15, 73). ὑποσχόμενος : Beloch, comparing this passage with 7, 2, infers that Dionysius I had made Dion *nauarchos* in succession to Thearidas.

πλεούσας, ' on the water ' : cf. *Demetr.* 20, ἀποδεῖξαι τὰς ναῦς πλεούσας : also Dem. *Meidias* 568.

The war was not actually concluded till six months later, after Dion's banishment (cf. 16, 6). By the settlement the Carthaginians recovered all that they had lost in 392 B.C.; so we find the town of Minoa at the mouth of the Halycus mentioned as a Carthaginian possession in 357 (25, 12).

The Empire of Dionysius II consisted of (1) Sicily E. of the Halycus, part being directly subject to him, part in dependent alliance :

(2) the ' toe ' of Italy, of which the greater portion had been given by Dionysius I to Locri, the home of his wife, Doris. Young Dionysius at a later date restored Rhegium which his father had destroyed in 387.

(The Tarentines and other members of the Italiot league were in alliance with Syracuse.)

(3) Iapygia (cf. 25, 2) was under his control; and Apulia seems to have been within his sphere of influence :

(4) A number of places bordering on the Adriatic (11, 5–7 n).

7, 1. μεγαλοψυχίαν, ' generosity.'

7, 2. λαμπρότητι, ' munificence ' as in Demosth. 565, 22, τίς ἐστιν ἡ λαμπρότης ἢ τὰ σεμνὰ ἀναλώματα τούτου ;

μειράκιον is used loosely, for Dionysius in 367 was about 29, and had a son old enough in 356 to be left in charge of the garrison on Ortygia (ch. 37).—μειράκιον is defined by Philo Mech. 1, 26 as a youth ἄχρι γενείου λαχνώσιος, ἐς τὰ τρὶς ἔπτα.

ὑπερχόμενον, (cf. 14, 5) "worming his way into . . ." 'Αριστομάχης παῖδες Hipparinus and Nysaeus.

7, 4. ῥεμβώδεις, random occupations : the verb ῥέμβεσθαι, to roam, is used metaphorically in Pomp. 20.

7, 5. φιλάνθρωπος, gracious. The word is first used in Aesch. Prom. in a literal sense of the god Prometheus : also of Hermes in Aristophanes, Peace, and of Eros in Plato's Symposium. It is applied to rulers in Xen. Cyrop. 8, 29. In Plut. φιλανθρωπία (also plur. φιλανθρωπίαι) may mean 'largesse' as in Cleom. 32, Solon 2, Dion 52, 1. [See further de Ruyter, Mnemosyne 49, 3 (1931)].

οὐκ ἐπιεικείᾳ τινὶ μᾶλλον: "not through any reasonableness so much as . . . "—an idiom common in Thucydides. νεμομένη, spreading (like animals that move as they graze) is often used metaphorically of disease (as here of slackness) and of fire (cf. περινέμεσθαι, 46, 4). περὶ τὸ μειράκιον = τοῦ μειρακίου as in 4, 7.

ἀδαμαντίνους, Diod. 16, 5, 3, speaks of "the tyranny said by his father to have been bound with adamant." The phrase comes from Aesch. Prometheus 6. According to Lucian Adv. Indoct. 15, Dionysius obtained a writing-desk which had belonged to Aeschylus in the vain hope of deriving inspiration therefrom.

7, 7. Aristotle's Constitution of Syracuse is cited in Athenaeus 10, 435e, for the statement that Dionysius II "was sometimes drunk for 90 days on end."

8, 1. ἐπαχθής offensive,—from Plato Epist. 7, 327 B. αὐθάδειαν might be rendered 'self-sufficiency': it implies a disregard of other people's opinions. Plato warned Dion in Epist. 4 that αὐθάδεια ξύνοικος ἐρημίᾳ. In Repub. 590 A it is joined with δυσκολία and in Laws 950 B, "states which forbid intercourse with foreigners will be thought τρόποις αὐθάδεσι χρῆσθαι.'

8, 2. ἀμέλει (don't bother) came to be used in the sense of Lat. sane.

8, 3. διατεθρυμμένῳ, here, as in 52, 6, 'pampered' by flattery ; in 41, 4, used in literal sense, 'break in pieces.' κατεμέμφετο της ὁμιλίας, "blamed him for his behaviour in society": with the causal gen. the simple verb is usual. χρειῶν, services. It is governed by τοῖς δεομένοις.

8, 5. ἂν ὀρθοῦν (Ziegler) not ἀνορθοῦν : the maintenance, not the restoration of the Government was in question.

9, 2. λυχνίας: classical writers use the form λυχνίον or λυχνεῖον. A similar hobby is attributed to Aeropus, a fourth century King of Macedon; also to Louis XVI of France.

9, 3. προβεβλημένος, on his guard (like a weapon held 'at the ready').

ἐᾶν (Ziegler) presumably dropped out after ἀφελεῖν. A pres. inf. is needed to denote repeated action.

πλαστῶν : the sense ' hairdresser ' is not found elsewhere, but Professor Stanford refers me to κεροπλάστης used by Archilochus, *Frg.* 57 (quoted in *Mor.* 976) of "one who shapes hair into a queue or pigtail ". The word, abbreviated to πλάστης may have retained in Sicily the meaning ' hairdresser'. Plutarch's authority here is probably Timaeus.

9, 4. It was the practice of the Dionysii to have visitors searched before admission : see Aelian *Var. Hist.* 4, 18 (cf. 19, 2, below).

ὁραθέντα for ὀφθέντα is found in Aristotle.

9, 5. Leptines had a chequered career. For a number of years prior to 389 he was in command of the navy. But by a settlement which he arranged between the Thurians and Lucanians he lost the tyrant's favour and was deprived of the command (Diod. 14, 102). Later when he married his daughter to Philistus he was banished from Sicily, but his influence at Thurii was so great that D. found it advisable to restore him to favour, and married him to one of his daughters (Diod. 15, 7). In 383 Leptines perished in the disaster at Cronium (Diod. 15, 17). It was said Dionysius might have saved him, but would not.—Aelian, *Var. Hist.* 13, 45.

9, 6. Here, as in 9, 2, Dionysius is depicted as regarding ' men of sense ' as inevitable opponents.

9, 8. [ὄντα], Bryan. Its omission is regular after ἀποφαίνω = ' represent.' μὴ is found in post-classical Greek after ὅτι, *because.*

10. The arguments are obviously Plutarch's own reflections, based on Plato's speculations in the *Timaeus.* Plut. had written an essay (*Mor.* 1021), *On the creation of the soul in the Timaeus.*

10, 1. The perfect part. of διαλωβᾶσθαι is used here in passive sense, as in *Caesar* 68.

10, 2. θειότατον παράδειγμα : i.e., the Idea of the Good in the Republic. The future μηχανήσεται after ὅπως is used since the action is continuous as in Plato, *Gorgias* 481, A : παρασκευαστέον ὅπως (ὁ ἐχθρὸς) μὴ δῷ δίκην, ἐάν τε θανάτου ἄξια ἠδικηκὼς ᾖ, ὅπως ἀθάνατος ἔσται, εἰ δὲ μὴ, ὡς πλεῖστον χρόνον βιώσεται. (On this ground Schaefer corrected the text from aor. to fut.).

10, 5. τῷ μὲν σώματι ἀμπεχόμενον: cf. τοῖς σώμασιν ἠσκημένοι, 22, 8. The unusual construction here with ἀμπέχεσθαι may be explained by the antithesis. Otherwise we should expect τὸ σῶμα with the participle as middle, ' having his body clothed.'

κατασκευῆ (cf. 15, 4) *furniture.*

11, 1–3. Based on Plato, *Epist.* 7, 327 D–329 B ; 3, 316 C.

11, 1. ἔστιν οὕστινας: here irregularly for ἔστιν οὕς which is normal except in negative or interrogative sentences (in their nature indefinite): but cf. *Xen. Anab.* 1, 8, 20, ἔστιν ὅστις . . . κατελήφθη.

11, 2. γράμματα here = ἐπιστολαί as in *Pompey* 20, Cato *Min.* 60 : more often used of a single Letter.

Archytas' appeal in fact related to Plato's *third* visit (*Ep.* 7, 339 D).

περιφερομένης. *turning dizzy* : used in *Caes.* 32 of Caesar at the Rubicon.

11, 3. The words of Plato, *Epist.* 7, 328B are : μὴ δόξαιμί ποτε ἐμαυτῷ παντάπασιν λόγος μόνον ἀτεχνῶς εἶναί τις, ἔργου δ' οὐδενὸς ἅν ποτε ἑκὼν ἀνθάψασθαι.   Hence Sintenis read **λόγος** for ἐν λόγοις here.   (ἐν λόγοις εἶναι would mean *to engage in speculation*, as in *Phaedr.* 59 A). Plato's phrase led evidently to misunderstanding, for in the passage cited there is a marginal variant λόγῳ.

δι' ἑνὸς ἀνδρός : Plato has πείσας ἕνα μόνον.   The governing element in the State corresponds to the rational element in the soul.

11, 4. **πολεμοῦντες** quarrelling, as in Xen. *Cyrop.* 1, 3, 11.   Sections 4–7 are evidently based on Timaeus.

11, 4. *Philistus* is stated in *Nicias* 19 to have been a ' spectator ' of the war between Athens and Syracuse, which suggests that he was born after 430 B.C.   Diod. 13, 5, 5, remarks that the Syracusans had their parents and children as θεατὰς τῶν ἀγώνων.

In 406, when Acragas had fallen to the Carthaginians, Dionysius wished to have the Syracusan generals executed for having failed to save the town. His impetuosity led him into a breach of order for which he was fined, but Philistus urged him to proceed, promising himself to pay the fines incurred (Diod. 13, 91).   Henceforth Dionysius and Philistus were close friends.

ἀντίταγαμα, ' a counterbalancing force ': also of persons (as here) in *Nicias*, 2 ; *Lucullus*, 38.

11, 5. **ἄκραν,** the castle built by Dionysius on Ortygia, at the point (it would seem) where the artificial isthmus joined the ' Island ' (Diod. 14, 7).

The story respecting the relations of Philistus with the mother of Dionysius was probably one of the slanders circulated by Timaeus (cf. 36, 1).   Some 1,400 years later Tzetzes repeated it in his *Chiliades.*

11, 5–7. Wilamowitz, *Platon,* 1, 511, has suggested that in fact Philistus' banishment was merely nominal, and that he was employed as Dionysius' vicegerent in the Adriatic region ; for Diod. 15, 7, connects him with Thurii, and Plut. *Mor.* 685 D with Epirus, while Pliny, *Nat. Hist.* 3, 121, mentions ' Fossiones Philistinae ' at Adria near the mouth of the Po.   A further suggestion by Laqueur, P-W, *art.* Philistus, is that Philistus was required by Dionysius to leave Sicily owing to friction with Dion.   It is implied in Diod. 15, 7, that with the Tyrant's brother, Leptines, he was banished in 386–5, and recalled with him some years later ; but Plut. and Nepos (following Timaeus) are certainly right in representing Philistus as recalled by the younger Dionysius, for his absence (it has been observed) is required to explain Dion's pre-eminence at the time of young Dionysius' accession.

11, 6. [τοῦ Λεπτίνου] deleted by Kurtz as an adscript.   In *Timol.* 15 Plut. refers to the lamentations of Philistus (in his History) over the poverty endured by Leptines' daughters, accustomed to the affluence of the *tyrannis.*   **εἰς τὸν 'Αδρίαν,** the *Adriatic* in which Plut. would have included the 'Ιόνιος κόλπος which Strabo calls μέρος 'Αδρίου—cf. also

Acts of Apostles 27, 27. τὰ πλεῖστα τῆς ἱστορίας: this was divided into three parts: (1) ending with the siege of Acragas in 406, (2) with the death of the elder Dionysius in 367, (3) comprising the first five years of Dionysius II (Diod. 15, 89). The third part was in two books. It is nowhere mentioned by Plut., who refers to (1) in *Nic.* 1 ; to (2) in *Dion.* 35, 7.

12, 1–2. διεπεφύκει : *permeated* : in *Cic.* 14 Plut. writes of Sulla's veterans, διαπεφευκότες ὅλης τῆς 'Ιταλίας. ἐτύγχανον οὖσαι διαβολαί . . . " reports prejudicial to Dion and accusations were in fact made by other persons to the Tyrant, to the effect that he . . . " This statement (probably from Timaeus) is valueless, for Dion remained in the tyrant's service for some four months, and Heracleides for some four years. The two were at this time οἰκεῖοι, *Epist.* 3, 318 C. *Theodotes* was uncle of H.

12, 2–3. ὡς ἔοικε, introducing what is merely an inference of Plutarch. καταλύσας ἐκεῖνον : This construction recurs, comp. *Dion and Brut.* 3 ; also in passive, Thuc. 1, 18.

13, 2. On Plato's reception see Aelian, *Var. Hist.* 4, 18, (probably from Timaeus).

13, 3. σχηματισμός, attitude.

ἕκαστα τῶν χρηματιζομένων: cf. in a papyrus of 3rd cent. B.C. ἔντευξις κεχρηματισμένη, ' a petition decided.'

13, 4. τυραννεῖον in sing. or plur. is used in Diod. and Plutarch only of the palace of the Dionysii (Holden). κονίορτος, from the sand on the floor, in which geometrical figures were drawn.

13, 6. ἐκ συνουσίας ὀλίγης, ' after a brief association ': emphatic, and so at beginning of sentence. With μεταβέβληκε τὴν γνώμην cf. μεταβάλλειν ἑαυτὸν in Pl. *Rep.* 381 B. τὸ μειράκιον : the subject placed at the end of the sentence has a secondary emphasis (cf. 56, 6).

14, 3. The term *sophist*, here applied by Dion's detractors to Plato, is used of Socrates in Aeschines 1, 173. It is regularly applied to teachers who take pay. πολλάκις τοσοῦτοι, as in Plato *Rep.* 330 B, for the usual πολλαπλάσιοι.

Dionysius' ships of war are given as 600 also in Diod. (16, 9, 2) and Aelian (V. H. 6, 12), but 500 in Nepos, 5. His cavalry numbered 10,000 (Diod. and Nepos) ; 9,000 according to Aelian : his infantry the authorities all give as 100,000. Parke, however (p. 114, x. 4), thinks these figures " at best represent some hypothetical estimate *for all his mercenaries*, not merely for the mercenaries on the Island of Ortygia." δορυφόρων, *spearmen.*

τὸ σιωπώμενον ἀγαθόν : the *indescribable Good* which Plato in Rep. vi refuses to define. Outside philosophical circles Plato's ' Good ' was a subject of talk. Amphis the comic poet makes a slave say to his master, " what benefit you expect from this woman I can no more understand than *Plato's good* " (Diog. Laert. 3, 27).

In *Epist.* 7, 341 B, Plato thus refers to the ultimate doctrine of Philosophy : " there will never be a treatise of mine on the subject. It does not admit of being put into words like other subjects of study ; but a̠ er much converse on the subject itself and community of life (between teacher and pupil) a light kindled as from a leaping flame suddenly rises in the soul and thereafter sustains itself. Yet *if the subject were to be handled in speech or writing, I know it would be best done by myself.* But I do not think that what is called a thesis would be good for people generally, except for the few who with a little direction can find it out for themselves."

Yet Simplicius recorded that Plato once gave a lecture on *The Good*, of which accounts were written by Aristotle, Xenocrates and others.

[Reference may be made to H. W. B. Joseph, *Knowledge and the Good in Plato's Republic*, 1948.]

διὰ γεωμετρίας: in *Rep.* 578 B education is defined as the diversion of the intellect from shadows to realities, i.e., from sensuous phenomena to the Ideas or Forms. 'Socrates,' therefore, insists on Geometry, Mathematical Physics, Theory of Music and Astronomy, which rouse reflection by the apparent inconsistencies which they exhibit. In A. E. Taylor's words : " to conceive abstractions and to reason systematically about them is a pre-requisite to the apprehension of the Idea of the Good."

14, 4–7. On Dion's deportation, see Supplementary Note iii.

The story of the intercepted letter was evidently taken by Timaeus from Philistus' History.

In *Epist.* 7, 329 C, Plato wrote : " it was perhaps in the fourth month that Dionysius accused Dion of plotting, ... and putting him on board a *small boat* expelled him ": Nepos, however, speaks of " a *trireme* to convey him to Corinth. Timaeus apparently had persuaded himself that Dionysius treated Dion just as later he himself was treated by Timoleon.

Plutarch, as usual, followed Plato.

15, 3. After **κελεύειν** a dat. is often found in post-classical prose, but rarely, if ever, in the Lives. [*Tit. Flam.* 20 is obviously corrupt.]

Nepos, like Plutarch, states that Dionysius sent Dion his movable property.

15, 4. **πομπή**, *retinue* (of slaves). In *Demetr.* 30 a queen leaves Athens μετὰ πρεπούσης πομπῆς.

κατασκευὴ περὶ τὴν δίαιταν, 'service for his table': cf. *Anton.* 6, σκευαὶ τῶν περὶ τὴν δίαιταν.

Supplementary Note III.

The first recorded event of Dion's career is his meeting with Plato, which, as already stated, took place in 388–7, Dion being then a youth of twenty, and Plato about forty. In *Epistle* 7, 327, Plato speaks of the teaching which he imparted to Dion, and its effect on his character :

" When I met Dion ... I indicated the line of conduct I thought best for men, advising him to follow it in practice ... Dion was one who found it easy to learn anything, and at that time he showed his capacity, especially in his grasp of the teaching I gave him. Indeed he responded to my counsels with a keenness and ardour such as I have never found in any young man with whom I came in contact ; and he resolved to live the rest of his life differently from most of the Sicilian and Italian Greeks, with his mind set on virtue rather than on pleasure or any form of luxury. In consequence his mode of life proved somewhat disagreeable to those who conformed to the practices customary at the tryant's court ; and this continued to the death of Dionysius."

Plato represents his teaching as wholly concerned with moral principles. He evidently had no wish to cause a breach between Dion and his brother-in-law, the Tyrant.

There was no breach. Indeed Dion's strictness of conduct may have been a positive recommendation to Dionysius, who, according to Plato (322 A), had reason to complain of the behaviour of his own kinsmen and dependents :

" Dionysius (in the cities which he had recovered from the barbarians) was unable to establish a loyal government, whether composed of strangers or of his own kinsfolk . . . whom he had raised to affluence. Neither by persuasion nor by instruction, neither by benefits conferred nor by ties of kindred, could he make any of them fit to serve in the administration." But in Dion he found a minister who was loyal, honest and efficient. Dion's position in course of time became unassailable, as Philistus may have discovered to his cost (see note on *Dion*, 11, 6).

There came a change, however, when the younger Dionysius succeeded his father ; and Dion was consulting his own interest when he urged the young man to invite Plato to Sicily, and to place himself under his tuition. Plato afterwards (*Epist.* 7, 328 D) described Dion's situation at this time as one of no small danger.

Dionysius' invitation to Plato was followed (as we learn from the Seventh Epistle) by a letter from Dion, who urged Plato to come " before others should turn Dionysius to a course that was not the best." He enlarged on the tyrant's desire for instruction, his own high position in the Government, and the prospect that his nephews would be attracted to Philosophy, and would have a good influence on Dionysius. " Now, if ever (he concluded) our hopes will be fulfilled of the same persons becoming philosophers and rulers of great cities." [1]

Plato and the education of Dionysius.

It has been held by a number of modern scholars that Plato's aim was to train Dionysius to become the philosophic ruler of a ' prerogative ' state, such as that described in the *Republic*. Thus Barker represents him as going to Sicily " with high hopes of training a king to become a philosopher wise enough to regulate affairs by that living play of reason which he held to transcend so greatly the dead letter of the Laws." But in fact it was Dion, not Plato, who cherished ' high hopes.' Plato writes : " My own opinion so far as the young men were concerned, was full of apprehension,

---

[1] What Plato really meant by his dictum about philosophers and kings is considered in Supplementary Note V.

though Dion's judgement I knew to be naturally stable ... I was in two minds about going, but at last I decided that now was the time to put in practice the views I had formed about *laws* and a constitution " [7 328 B].

If Plato in this passage had in mind a ' prerogative ' state it is hard to see why he spoke of ' laws.' In a later passage, 357 D, when dealing with the situation which had arisen after Dion's death, Plato proposed that persons from other states should be invited to draw up a code of laws for Syracuse. " This course," Plato remarks, " is akin to that which Dion and I sought to follow, but second best ; the first is that which was originally attempted in conjunction with Dionysius himself." This passage has been rightly explained by G. R. Morrow : " Plato is here speaking not of three different courses but of *two* ; ' what Dion and I tried to accomplish ' is one and the same with ' what was attempted in conjunction with Dionysius.' "

The constitution which the young Tyrant, aided by Plato and Dion, might have promulgated, would have been bestowed on a united people. Since then, however, Syracuse had been distracted by faction and civil war, the wounds of which were not yet healed.

It is to be inferred that Plato's purpose in 367–6 B.C. was to train Dionysius to become the efficient *ruler of a law-bound state*. To this end he proposed to instruct him in what he had made essential studies in the Academy,—the mathematical sciences and ' dialectic ', which he regarded as the Pathway to Reality.

So Dionysius began with Geometry (*Dion* 13, 4). He did not pursue it for very long. In the Third Epistle, written some ten years later, Plato reminded him of a conversation [3; 319] :

" You asked me if I remembered on my first arrival bidding you restore the Greek cities ... and I asked you was that the only advice I gave, or was there something else as well. To which you replied with a forced laugh, ' you told me to do all these things after I had received instruction,—or not at all.' I said, ' you remember very well.' and you continued, ' you meant when I had received instruction in Geometry,— was it not? ' "

Beloch has remarked : " Plato went to work somewhat pedantically, and refused to recognise the difference between the Academy and the Royal palace ": and Grote long before had said much the same. It is possible that if Plato had left Geometry alone, and started to help Dionysius to draw up the proposed legislation, things might have gone better. Dionysius would have felt he was ' getting somewhere,' and would have acquired knowledge as he went along. " What we have to do when we have learnt it we learn by the process of doing it." said Aristotle. And seeing that Dionysius ' had a wonderful passion for Honour,' Plato might have engaged him in a task which if successfully accomplished would have brought him fame throughout the Greek world. As Aristotle puts it : " A benefactor instinctively develops affection for one whom he has benefited, as well as satisfaction in his own activities." So Dionysius by bestowing a constitution on Syracuse might have discovered a new bond of sympathy between himself and his fellow-citizens, and realised the gratification which arises from the sense of attainment.

But the real cause of the breach between Dionysius and Plato was not the tyrant's dislike of Geometry, but his suspicion, fostered by Philistus, that Dion was intriguing to supplant him.

Beloch, it is plain, thinks that Philistus was justified. He observes (3, 1, 131) : " Dion was pursuing in secret the design of expelling Dionysius from the throne to gain power for himself or for his nephews. To pave the way for this Plato was summoned to Sicily, and came in the honest belief that he could set up his Ideal State, without any suspicion that he had been made a tool in a political intrigue."

Yet Dion, ten years later, when he had an opportunity of attaining absolute power by executing his chief opponents let them go free.

Dion's banishment. To end the war which in 368 B.C. had broken out between Carthage and Dionysius I, commissioners had arrived from Carthage (*Dion* 14). To these Dion wrote urging them to attend no conference at which he should not be present. Why Dion acted in this way Plutarch has not explained ; but it may be inferred that Dionysius, having no plausible pretext for getting rid of him, had been trying to carry on the negotiations behind his back.

The notion of writing a letter in such a situation is evidence that Dion was unused to intrigue ; otherwise he would not have forgotten Dionysius' spies (cf. ch. 25), who intercepted the letter and provided the Tyrant with an excuse for deporting him. Thus Philistus won the first round. Later on Dionysius went further than the occasion demanded. If he had not invaded Dion's private rights it is unlikely that Dion would have invaded his empire.

Holm has suggested that *Laws* 4, 709–10 is based on Plato's experiences at Syracuse : " Come, legislator, what social conditions must we grant to make you competent to model your society by your own efforts? " " Give me a tyrant ... young, of retentive memory, quick to learn, bold and high-souled. But if these advantages are to be of any service they must be accompanied ... by temperance in the popular sense of the word ... and you must add, good fortune in that there is among his contemporaries a legislator with whom chance has brought him into contact. ... The readiest starting-point would be autocracy ... An autocrat desiring to change the tone of public life has no laborious task ; he has only to take in his own person the first steps on the road." [2]

The qualities, however, which Plato demanded in the young Tyrant who was to be associated with the ' legislator of distinction ' are, it should be observed, just those in which Dionysius II was conspicuously lacking.

[2] Condensed from Taylor's translation.

16. Based mainly on Plato, *Ep.* 3 and 7.

16, 1. Cf. *Ep.* 3, 315E ; 7, 329E. **φιλανθρώπου**: see note on 7, 5.

16, 2. **ψαῦσιν**: Reiske for ψαύειν: the transposition of τε is due to Latte.

In *Mor.* 768B we read that a modest woman would prefer the embrace of a bear μᾶλλον ἢ ψαῦσιν ἀνδρὸς ἀλλοτρίου. **μόνος ἀξιῶν . . . ἀντερᾶσθαι**: In *Ep.* 7, 330A Plato says that Dionysius wished him to prefer *his* friendship to Dion's. **ἕτοιμος . . . ἐπιτρέπειν τὰ πράγματα** : for this statement the only basis is Plato's remark in *Ep.* 3, 316A that at first he took part in some of D.'s political acts. With **προτιμῶντι** sc. αὐτῷ as in 16, 5 and *Arat.* 40.

16, 3. **αἰδουμένου τοὺς ἀποτρέποντας ὡς διαφθαρησομένου** : " feeling abashed before those who tried to divert him, because he thought he was likely to be ruined." Plato (7, 330B) wrote φοβούμενος τοὺς τῶν διαβαλλόντων λόγους μή πῃ παραποδισθείη (*be entangled*). It is implied that Plato's opponents warned D. that if he subjected himself to Plato's influence he might bring down the monarchy.

16, 4. **πολέμου τινὸς ἐμπεσόντος** : Plato in referring to the circumstances of his departure wrote (338A): ἦν γὰρ τότε πόλεμος ἐν Σικελίᾳ, which Plutarch assumed to refer to a *new* war (not the war with Carthage, which had begun in 368 before the death of the elder Dionysius). A war against the Lucanians is mentioned in Diod. 16, 5 which the young D. waged " without result for some considerable time." I agree with Souilhé that Plutarch's **ἐν Σικελίᾳ** " ne signifie pas nécessairement que la Sicile était le théatre de la guerre." **εἰς ὥραν ἔτους**, i.e., when the sailing season should come round.

16, 5-6. " And though he immediately broke *this* promise he sent off the revenues from his property, calling on Plato to excuse him for the delay (in Dion's recall) because of the war,—when peace was made (he said) he would recall Dion at once—*and to urge Dion to engage in no agitation* . . . " In Plato *Ep.* 7, 338, there is nothing to justify the words italicised.

17, 1-3. Source unknown.

17, 2. *Callippus*, who entered Syracuse by Dion's side (28, 2), afterwards suborned some Zacynthians to assassinate him (54-7) and finally himself perished by treachery (58). **ἄστει**, here probably (as often) of the upper city of Athens in contradistinction to the Peiraeus. **ἄγρον ἐκτήσατο** : Wilamowitz infers that Dion had been made an honorary citizen since only Athenians could acquire land in Attica. **διαγωγῆς**, *recreation*, as in Arist. *Politics*, 1339b.

Speusippus, Plato's nephew, was President of the Academy in succession to his uncle from 347 to 339 B.C. (when he died).

17, 3. **ἐφηδύνεσθαι** (Bernardakis) is the normal form : ἀφηδύνεσθαι (MSS.) is not found before Lucian.

17, 4. *Silloi*, i.e., squinting verses, a satire by Timon of Phlius (3rd cent. B.C.) directed against philosophers, who in Book I engage in a battle ending in victory for Pyrrhon the sceptic. ' A lampoon with unamiable jesting ' it is called by Aelian, *Var. Hist.* 3, 40.

17, 5. Dion's financial help to Plato is mentioned also in *Aristides*, 1. The information is attributed in Diog. Laert. 3, 3 to Artemidorus, a contemporary of Augustus. **φιλοτιμία**, as in Aeschin, 3, 19, of lavish outlay for public purposes.

17, 6. **σόλοικον**, in bad taste—hence our *solecism*: said to be derived from Σόλοι, name of a Cilician town, where the Attic colonists spoke bad Greek—Strabo 14, 2, 28.

διατεθρυμμένον : MSS. have ἐπιτεθρυμμένον which occurs only in authors later than Plut., whereas forms from διαθρύπτω are found four times in the *Dion*. The constant repetition of the syllable ἐπ—may have led to confusion.

17, 8. In 365 B.C. Dionysius assisted the Spartans in taking the border town of Sellasia from the Arcadians—Xen. *Hellen*. 7, 4, 12.

17, 9–10. *Ptoeodorus* is mentioned in Demosth. *De Cor*. 295 in a list of 'traitors to Hellas.' A plot to seize Megara with Macedonian aid was foiled by Phocion.

Valerius Maximus (*c*. 26 A.D.) had referred to the Dion incident (4, 1, *ext*. 3) but gave Theodorus as the name of the Megarian.

18, 1. From Plato *Epist*. 7, 345C, we learn that it was during Plato's third visit, B.C. 361, that Dion's revenues were confiscated by the Tyrant.

18, 2–3. Plato *Epist*. 7, 338C: " Later Archytas visited Dionysius. There were in Syracuse persons who had received some instruction from Dion, and others had learnt from these, becoming stuffed with misunderstood doctrine (παρακουσμάτων). They had talked to Dionysius, thinking he had mastered my teaching . . . He was ashamed that it should get out that he had had no lessons during my visit."

18, 5. **πᾶσαν μηχανὴν αἴρων** : ' pulling every string.' This figure taken from the machinery of the theatre, occurs in Plato, *Cratylus* 425D.

According to *Epist*. 7, 339D, Archytas wrote to Plato that if he refused to pay a second visit to Dionysius, the political relations between D. and himself and his associates at Tarentum would suffer. (There is nothing in Plato about Archytas and his friends ' becoming sureties ' for Plato's safety.)

18, 6. According to Plato, Archedemus was sent *by Dionysius*: Archytas and other Tarentines sent letters (7, 339). **τριήρη** (MSS. τριήρεις): the correction was made by Laar, since Plato (*loc. cit.*, also 3, 317 B) speaks of ' a trireme '.

18, 8. Not derived from Plato.

18, 9. **Σκύλλαν**, Sintenis for **Σικελίαν**. In 7, 345 D-E Plato wrote : " I thought I ought not to feel anger against Dionysius rather than against myself and those who forced me to go for the third time εἰς τὸν πορθμὸν τὸν περὶ Σκύλλαν." Hence Σικελίαν in the MSS. here would seem to be a gloss. The Homeric line quoted by Plutarch reproducing Plato is Odyssey 12, 428, but Plut. has changed the first person to the third.

19, 1. On Philistus, see on 11, 4 ; 14, 5 ; 16, 1.

19, 2. πίστις, mark of confidence. For the searching of visitors, see 9, 4, note.

19, 3. *Aristippus* was a companion of Socrates and probably the person whom (according to Xenophon *Memor.* 2, 1) he rebuked for the luxury of his life. In *Phaedo* 59 C Plato spoke of him as absent in Aegina when Socrates drank the hemlock.

Diogenes L. 2, 66ff. has a number of stories of Aristippus' sojourn with 'Dionysius,' and he may have visited Syracuse on more than one occasion. Aristippus is not mentioned in the Platonic Epistles, and Plutarch's source for this passage and 19, 7 is unknown.

Aristippus was formerly thought to have been the founder of the Cyrenaic school of philosophy, which taught that Pleasure was the only good, but it would seem that he has been confused with his grandson. The writers who represent him as a philosopher are late; the few early references (e.g., Aristot. *Metaph.* 2, 2) depict him as a sophist or rhetorician. Field (p. 160) remarks that if we read the confused account of the origin of the Cyrenaic School in Diogenes or Aristocles we shall see that there was obviously no record of any positive doctrine that could be traced back to Plato's contemporary. In Aristotle *Rhetoric* 1398 B 39 it is related that once when Plato said something that sounded rather 'professorial' Aristippus retorted, "Our friend (i.e. Socrates) never spoke like that."

19, 6. *Helicon* is mentioned by Plato in Epistle 13 as a pupil of Eudoxus the astronomer. In *Mor.* 579 B Plutarch tells how the Delians were ordered by an oracle to 'double' a certain altar, and on applying to Plato for direction were told that Eudoxus or Helicon would explain how it might be done. The mathematical problem involved is the 'duplication of the cube.'

The Eclipse occurred on May 12th, 361.

19, 7. τι τῶν παραδόξων : for this use of the partitive genitive, see on 43, 1.

προλέγω γενησομένους: instead of the normal usage with acc. and inf. or ὅτι the construction is adapted to balance προεῖπεν ἔκλειψιν above.

19, 8. Based on Epistles 3, 318 ; 7, 347–350.

Plato had been transferred to Archedemus' lodging outside the Acropolis during the feast of Demeter when the Acropolis was occupied by women:— Novotny suggests that the festival in question was the Koreia of June 360. Later Plato was moved to the barracks of the mercenaries, after Dionysius had quarrelled with him about the treatment of Heracleides [see on *Dion* 12], who had been forced to flee from Sicily. Here Plato was warned by Athenians serving in the Syracusan fleet that some of the mercenaries were plotting to kill him.

20. Based on some biography of Plato except for the first section, which is taken from Epistle 7.

The retort in 20, 3 attributed to Plato in conversation with the younger Dionysius is alleged by Diogenes L. 3, 21 to have been made in a letter to the elder tyrant. (It is fictitious, any way.)

20, 2. ἀπολεγομένου (*disclaiming*) through the reading of an inferior group of MSS. (Z) is obviously preferable in sense to ἀπολογουμένου (LPQ) (*excusing himself for* . . .). ἑστιάσεσι: Plato, however, in 7, 349 D asserted that after the quarrel over Heracleides (see Supplementary Note VII below), Dionysius never invited him to his house, but merely gave him money for his journey, (350 A).

Supplementary Note IV : *Archytas of Tarentum.*

Aristoxenus' Life of Archytas has not survived, and the modern student is dependent on a very short account in Diogenes Laertius, and some isolated notices in other writers. The Ninth and Twelfth Platonic Epistles are addressed to Archytas, but they are of doubtful authenticity, and even if genuine, are very brief, and of little importance.

Archytas was probably somewhat younger than Plato, but the dates of his birth and death are unknown. He was seven times *strategos* of Tarentum " whereas the law excluded all others from even a second year of office. The Tarentines, although continually at war with Messapians and Lucanians, were never defeated when Archytas was in command."[1]

Tarentum in the fifth century had become a democracy, but according to Aristotle[2] had developed some unique features: " The example of the Tarentines well deserves imitation; by sharing the use of their property with the poor they gain their goodwill. Public offices they divide into two classes—one half filled by election, the other by lot; the latter that the People may have a share, the former that the State may be better managed."

In the notices which appear in later writers, Archytas invariably is represented as a man of ideal character; cheerful and sociable, considerate to servants, kind to children, pure in morals and conversation, yet not unaware of the worse side of human nature.[3]

In science he is remembered as the founder of mechanics as a branch of mathematical physics; he invented the first automaton—a model of a pigeon, which was made to fly by the escape of compressed air from a valve: in Geometry he ranked with Leodamas and Theaetetus as having " enriched the subject with new theorems and arranged the parts in a better sequence."[4] He is also stated to have solved the problem of the " duplication of the cube "; and it would, therefore, have been his solution that Eudoxus or Helicon imparted to the Delians. Archytas was also distinguished in the theory and practice of music.[5]

---

1 Diog. Laertius, 8 chps. 79–83 : Aristoxenus is cited in 82.

2 *Politics*, 5, 3, 37.

3 Cic. *De Amic.* 88 : *De Senect.* 39 : Aelian, *Var. Hist.* 10, 12 ; 12, 15 ; 14, 9 : Plu. *Mor.* 551.

4 Favorinus ap. Aul. Gell. 10, 12, 9.

5 *Eudemi Fragmenta*, ed. Spengel, p. 45.

Horace (Odes, 1, 28), writing nearly three hundred years after his death, alludes to his fame as a scientist:

> Te maris et terrae numeroque carentis harenae
> Mensorem cohibent, Archyta,
> Pulveris exigui prope litus parva Matinum
> Munera, nec quicquam tibi prodest
> Aerias temptasse domos animoque rotundum
> Percurrisse polum morituro.

In philosophy Archytas was classed as a Pythagorean (e.g., in *Dion* 18, 5). The sixth century Pythagoras, though notorious for his religious innovations, was known also as a mathematician, and Heraclitus (*Frag.* 17) referred to his *research*. Among the later Pythagoreans the religious side of the founder's teachings had been dropped; which, as Burnet has suggested, may explain Aristotle's reference to the School as ' the so-called Pythagoreans,' whom in the *Metaphysics* he represents as speculating on the nature of the physical Universe. The ' four elements ' of Empedocles —water, air, fire, earth—they held not to be ultimates but themselves to be composed of particles having the shape of the *regular solids*.[6] This is in accordance with Plato's conception in his *Timaeus*, the one dialogue in which he treats of nature. Aristotle, however, observes that Plato diverged from the Pythagoreans by regarding the One and the Numbers as separate from things, and by introducing the *Ideas*.

Hence E. Frank [7] has inferred that we have only to ' think away ' the uppermost world of *Ideas* from Plato's successive stages of reality, in order to find the complete system of the Pythagoreans, whose world is the world of Plato's second stage, i.e., *the world as the object of Mathematics, Mathematical Physics and Astronomy*.

To Archytas' contributions to Philosophy Aristotle devoted a treatise (no longer extant), as well as compiling a book of " Extracts from the Timaeus and the writings of Archytas." (The extant ethical works attributed to Archytas, like the writings attributed to the Locrian Timaeus are recognised as forgeries).

That Plato in the *Timaeus* dialogue intended his eulogy of the Locrian Timaeus to be in reality a eulogy of Archytas has been convincingly argued by E. Frank. Long ago Holm (2, 86) maintained that in the same dialogue the character " Hermocrates of Syracuse "—of whom it is said, " we must believe the many witnesses who assert that alike by nature and nurture he is competent for all these inquiries "—was meant for Dion. And more recently G. C. Field, referring to the character in the *Euthydemus* who, as being a blend of philosopher and politician, has been generally supposed to represent Isocrates, states the case for identification in words equally applicable to the identification of ' Timaeus ' with Archytas :

---

6 Further references to Archytas' scientific work in P-W *sub voc.*
7 P. 124.

" If Plato realised, as he most have done, what his portrait would suggest to his readers, and yet took no steps to guard against it, we can hardly deny that the allusion was intentional."

Apart from Plato's dialogue nothing at all is known of the Locrian Timaeus, but such eulogies as the following were not composed at random : " Timaeus is our foremost astronomer, who has made it his particular task to learn about the nature of the Universe " (27A); and " Timaeus belongs to a city excellently governed; is inferior to none of the citizens in property and birth; *has held the highest positions in the state; and at the same time has, in my opinion, attained to pre-eminence in every branch of philosophy.*" (20 A.)

But there were, it would seem, some important issues on which Plato and Archytas disagreed. Archytas was a pioneer in applied science, but Plato thought that to make an experimental test in physics showed the experimenter " to be blind to the difference between divine and human nature " (*Timaeus* 68 D). Again, Plutarch (*Mor.* 718) records that Plato blamed Archytas for using mechanical devices in solving the " duplication of the cube." And there was an obvious difference in outlook between the man who invented a rattle to amuse children and the man who wrote in the *Laws* that to make a change in children's games is to introduce an innovation threatening the stability of the state. Nor can we believe that Archytas, who had enjoyed year after year •the confidence of his fellow-citizens (as indicated by his re-election to the *strategia*), and had himself shown that democracy might be an effective form of government, sympathised with the pessimistic attitude to all existing constitutions which Plato exhibits in the *Laws* and even in the *Politicus*.

If the exiled Dion had betaken himself to Archytas at Tarentum, instead of to Plato at Athens, he might have learnt about the actual working of politics much that would have proved to his advantage in his later career.

21, 1–2. τούτοις, i.e., Dionysius' treatment of Plato.

μετ' ὀλίγον χρόνον : when Dion met Plato at Olympia (Aug. 360) and heard of his ill-success at Syracuse he finally decided on war, and " urged me with my relations and friends to prepare for taking vengeance on Dionysius. Our grievance would be breach of faith with a guest ; his own was his unjust banishment." [7, 350 B].

There is *no reference in Plato to Arete's forced marriage* with Timocrates. Nepos, *Dion* 4, records that Dionysius gave Dion's wife to another, *after* he had heard that Dion was collecting forces in Peloponnesus; this would appear to be the true order of the events.

21, 1. ἠνίξατο, ' had hinted '. This is Plutarch's inference from *Epist.* 13, 362 E: " as to what you told me not to mention to Dion, I did not mention it, but I tried to find out whether he would take the matter bitterly or lightly, and it seemed to me that he would be in no slight degree offended." (The date of the epistle, if genuine, is *c.* 364–3).

It may be that, as Taylor has suggested, Dionysius in 366–5 hoped that Dion could be induced to divorce Arete, in order to show that he had no designs on the monarchy. When Plato gave him to understand that Dion's consent could not be obtained, Dionysius abandoned the scheme, but towards the end of 360, when the news reached him that Dion was preparing for war, compelled Arete to marry Timocrates.

21, 2. δι' ἀπορρήτων, *under a seal of secrecy*, as though Dionysius asked Plato to get information from Dion in confidence and then divulge it to him. But in *Epist.* 13 Plato tells Dionysius that he has ascertained Dion's attitude *indirectly*. It seems that Plutarch misunderstood his authority.

21, 2. πυθέσθαι μὴ ... *to enquire whether* ... This use of μὴ is post-classical. Here as in *Arat.* 29 a negative answer is expected; in *Arat.* 8, *Cleom.* 22, an affirmative.

21, 4. ἐπιστολὴν : our 13th Epistle, *c.* 364 B.C.

21, 7. Polyxenus in 387 had commanded a Syracusan force co-operating with the Spartans in the Aegean (Xenoph. *Hell.* 5, 1, 26). His flight may have been due to alarm at the banishment of Leptines and Philistus. In *Inscr. Gr.*[2] ii, 1, 8 he is mentioned along with Dionysius, Leptines and Thearidas.

21, 8. ὥστε ... οὐκ ἂν συνεκπλεῦσαι : this construction, with the negative οὐ, occurs in a clause itself depending on an inf. in indirect speech, when the introductory ὥστε is itself part of the quotation.

Supplementary Note V.

Dion at the Academy : Plato's political doctrine : Dion's projected reforms at Syracuse.

Plutarch in ch. 47, where he is reproducing Timonides, records that Dion claimed to have learnt in the Academy to conquer anger; in *Mor.* 71 he quotes a letter from Speusippus exhorting Dion to adorn Syracuse with the best laws, and so to bring credit to the Academy. Similarly Plato in *Epistle* 4 urged him to make the famous legislators of tradition appear old-fashioned, and to remember that ' those you wot of ' should surpass the rest of mankind as men surpass children. By this phrase Plato evidently means members of the Academy. The years when Dion was a student there under Plato were between 365 and 361 B.C. When Plato returned from Syracuse, where he had stayed from 361 to 360, he found Dion resolved on war with Dionysius.

In the *Republic*, completed c. 375, Plato had expressed the opinion that either philosophers must become kings or those in power must attain to true philosophy (*Rep.* 5, 473: see on *Dion* 1, 3).

By true philosophers Plato meant persons who have apprehended the Idea of the Good, which he describes as the highest object of Knowledge, the cause of Knowledge, Truth and Being, the supreme Idea.

" Our commonwealth," says " Socrates," " will be perfectly regulated only when it is watched over by a Guardian possessing knowledge of the Good."

" The Good is something which every Soul pursues as the end of all action, dimly divining its existence, but unable to grasp its nature with the same clearness as it attains in dealing with other things, and so missing whatever value those other things might have " [*Rep.* 6, 505, *tr.* Cornford]. " The summit of the intelligible world is reached by one who aspires through the discourse of reason unaided by the senses to reach essential reality, and perseveres until he has grasped by pure intelligence the very nature of reality itself " [*Ib.* 7, 531C].

" The master of Dialectic[1] must be able to distinguish the essential nature of Goodness in isolation from all other Ideas: he must fight his way through all criticisms, determined to examine every step by the standard not of opinions but of reality." " One who cannot do this will neither know Goodness itself nor any good thing. If he does lay hold on some semblance of the Good it will be a matter merely of belief not of knowledge, and he will dream away his life in a sleep that knows no waking " [*Rep.* 7, 534].

"Socrates " naturally asks, " Has our commonwealth and its constitution been a mere day-dream? "

" It may be difficult to attain," he answers, " but it is possible, *provided genuine philosophers come into power* " [7, 540].

The Academy was founded about 385[2], that is, about a decade before the completion of the *Republic*; and since in this dialogue the Apprehension of the Idea of the Good is treated as *una res necessaria* it may fairly be assumed that the Academy had been instituted primarily to aid students in gaining that qualification.

In support of this limited view of Plato's object in founding the Academy, Jaeger, *Aristotle* (*Eng. Tr.*, p. 21) writes:

" Modern academies and universities cannot claim Plato as their model ... The notion of a systematic unity of all sciences was foreign to him; and equally foreign to him was the organisation of all subjects for teaching and research ... Plato was concerned exclusively with Being: ... Starting from the Ideas ... he was not concerned to reduce individuals to a system. They lay below the realm of Ideas, and being completely infinite were unknowable ...

The many classifications of plants that Epicrates (the Comic Poet) speaks of were pursued not from interest in the objects themselves but in order to learn the logical relations of conceptions ... In classifying plants the members (of the Academy) no more aimed at producing a real botanical system than Plato in the *Sophist* aims at historical study of real sophists."

---

[1] The explanation of the meaning of *Dialectic* given by Cornford C. A. H. vi, 323 may be cited : ' It is the study of moral concepts with a technique ... aiming at the definition of moral terms. The deductive reasoning of the Intellect is employed in the criticism of ' hypotheses ' advanced by the respondent. These it tests by the consequences to which they lead. The hypothesis is reached by an effort of Intuition to perceive the content of an Idea. If the consequences prove the suggestion to be one-sided it will be rejected and a new definition will be framed. The process will be continued by Intuition and Intellect alternately till the Idea is fully apprehended.'

[2] Cf. Diog. Laert. 3, 20.

Yet Plato, when he found that the 'ideal' statesman was not going to be the solution for the problems of the time, turned to the study of legal institutions. Communities might at any rate be furnished with laws such as a philosopher could approve.

In 366 Plato started to train young Dionysius in the hope that he would set up such a constitution at Syracuse [see Supplementary Note III]. That hope was blasted ; but in 355, when Dion was at the head of the State, a new opportunity seemed to have presented itself. It may be assumed that Dion at the Academy received the kind of education that Plato had planned to bestow on Dionysius.

Plato's interest in political science is fully revealed in the *Laws*, but was already indicated in the *Politicus* (before 360 B.C.).

In this dialogue the reader is first treated to a vivid description of the prerogatives of the Scientific Statesman—another name for the 'true philosopher' of the *Republic*—but is informed towards the end that those who possess the Statesman's qualifications are likely to remain unrecognised; and the cities must, therefore, resign themselves to the impersonal rule of Law.

To proceed to details,—at an early stage a definition of the Statesman is suggested.

" If we call the art of those rulers who employ coercion the 'tyrannical' art, and the voluntary care of 'voluntary bipeds' by the name *political*, are we to assert that the practitioner of this latter art is a true king and statesman? " [This would involve the maxim, " all government should depend on the consent of the governed."]

This definition is not, however, accepted. It is insisted that *Politics* is an art or science comparable to medicine or navigation, and that its practitioners must be judged by the criterion, are they acting in accordance with *Knowledge*?

" The man who possesses the kingly science must be called kingly . . . we must look for the true government in one or two or at most a few persons, . . . and these . . . whether their subjects be few or many in number, whether they be willing or unwilling, whether the government be conducted *with or without written laws*, must be thought of as ruling by some art or science " [*Polit.*, 293 A].

" Physicians are just as much physicians whether they cure their patients with or without the patients' consent, by surgery or cautery or some other painful method; whether they are acting by written rules or without them; . . . provided they treat them for the good of their health and preserve them by making them better than they were before.

Rulers who really are possessed of Knowledge . . . whether they purge the state by killing or banishing some of the citizens, or make it smaller by sending out colonies, or larger by importing citizens from abroad, so long as they act according to science and justice, and benefit the State by making it better—this we must hold to be the only right government " [293 B *and* D].

"*It is plain—in a sense—that law-making belongs to the kingly art, but the best thing is not that the Laws should have authority, but the man who is wise and kingly*' [294 A].

"Take the case of persons who have been subjected to coercion, and as a result have been improved morally in all respects. That these people should complain of ill-treatment is surely the last word in absurdity . . .

"If a man does what is good for the people by persuasion or by other means, is not this the truest criterion of good government? . . . whatever wise rulers do they can commit no error . . . so long as by always dispensing absolute justice with wisdom and knowledge they are able to preserve the people and make them better than they were before " [296 D–E].

"But when a single ruler acts in accordance with neither laws nor customs, but pretends after the manner of the scientific ruler that what is best must be done even if it contravenes written enactments—while all the time it is some form of desire or ignorance that is responsible for his imitation (of the scientific ruler)—surely every such potentate should be called a tyrant " [301 B–C].

Plato adds that the tyrant, the king, oligarchy, aristocracy, democracy, have all arisen because men do not believe that there could ever be any one worthy of such power as he has assigned to the scientific statesman; "and yet they are willing to admit that if such a man should actually arise he would be welcomed."

(Plato has apparently assumed that the Statesman has entered upon office with the assent of the community, but exercises authority without reference to public opinion, simply according to the dictates of ' science.' He admits, however, that cities had failed to recognise persons qualified to rank as scientific statesmen):

"As things now are, since, as we say, there arises no king, like the rulers bred in the bee-hives, [queen-bees] in body and soul at once outstanding, men must meet together and frame written statutes following the traces of the true and genuine form of government."

In this passage *Plato is not denying the existence of persons qualified* to act as scientific statesmen; he is merely insisting on the inability of states to recognise them as being so qualified.

If we may assume that the doctrines inculcated in the *Politicus* had been expounded to students in the Academy during the years that followed Plato's return from his earlier visit to the younger Dionysius; and if we are prepared, like Meyer and unlike Beloch, to accept the Fourth Epistle as an actual letter of congratulation sent by Plato to Dion and his volunteers from the Academy, we can hardly doubt that these volunteers readily saw in Dion a ' genuine Statesman ' in Plato's sense, and persuaded him—if he needed any persuasion—to take the same view of himself, and ultimately to feel assured that he had Platonic warrant for authorising the ' liquidation ' of Heracleides, his implacable opponent.[4]

---

[4] See Supplementary Note VII, after notes on Chapter 53.

Dion's projected reform of the Syracusan constitution.

In *Dion* 53, 3, Plutarch writes: " Dion had in mind to curtail the unmixed democracy and to set up a form of government, based on those in Crete and Laconia, blending kingship with democracy, in which an aristocracy would preside and administer the most important affairs."

His reason for sending to Corinth was that " the Corinthians were somewhat oligarchical in their government and transacted but little public business in the popular assembly."

Plutarch has no more to say on the subject, but the kind of constitution which Dion is said to have been contemplating may be illustrated from the Eighth Epistle and the Sixth Book of the Laws. In the former Plato recommends to Dion's old associates after the expulsion of Callippus (353 B.C.) that in order to reconcile contending factions there should be appointed three titular kings, who should be bound by the Laws in the same way as the rest of the citizens.

The laws—as was previously proposed in the *Seventh* Epistle, 337 C —were to be drawn up by Greeks from Sicily or overseas. Law-Guardians ' exercising control over war and peace ' should be chosen by this Commission in conjunction with the Assembly and Council.

In proceedings involving death, imprisonment or transportation of citizens the Law-Guardians should form the Court [356].

In Book VI of the *Laws* the constitutional provisions for the ' second best ' State[3] are similar to those proposed in the Epistles for Syracuse. There should be established:—

(1) A *popular assembly* taking cognisance of public law-suits. Its consent is required should any change in the laws become necessary. It is to be constituted on a system of classes, based on property qualifications. *No mention is made of deliberative functions.*

(2) A *Council* appointed by a method combining regard for wealth with regard for universal suffrage, and the use of election with the use of the Lot.

(3) Law-guardians, chosen apparently by all citizens from all.

(4) Law-courts which include an element of special knowledge in the ' select judges,' but are largely based on the principle of a popular judicature.

(In Book IX jurisdiction in capital offences rests with the law-guardians and a court chosen from the magistrates on a basis of merit. This corresponds to the provision recommended in *Epist.* 8 for Syracuse.)

If a Constitution based on such conceptions—which, as Burnet noticed, anticipate in some measure the British Constitution as it was in the middle of the 19th century—had come into operation it might have provided the element of stability in which Syracusan democracy was obviously lacking.

22, 1. αὐτοῦ Πλάτωνος ἐκποδὼν ἱσταμένου :

---

3 See Barker, pp. 336, 339.

In *Epistle* 7, 320 D, we are told that Plato explained to Dion why he was unwilling to co-operate with him: " You may invite our friends, but I was in a sense compelled by you to become an inmate of Dionysius' house and to share in his religious observances. He may have thought I was plotting against him along with you, but instead of killing me he had compunction." I am too old to join in a campaign; I shall remain neutral, and available if ever you want to do each other good, but as long as you both desire to do hurt, invite others."

(Plato adds that if the tyrant had handed over to Dion the property that belonged to him, or had become reconciled to him on *any* terms, he (Plato) could have restrained Dion from taking action against him.)

Yet, if the Fourth Epistle is authentic, Plato, in 355 B.C., warmly congratulated Dion on his victory.

22, 2. τὴν παρρησίαν sc. Σπευσίππου.

22, 3. διάπειραν ὑπὸ : so ἀρχὴν ὑπὸ ... in *Pericl.* 9. This construction after an abstract noun of action is not uncommon.

22, 5. εἰς ὃν ' in honour of whom ': cf. τὰ εἰς 'Απολλώνιον, the title of Philostratus' treatise, and see Phillimore's note on p. xvi of his Translation.

Aristotle's dialogue *On the Soul* is lost, but Cicero *De Divinatione* 25 translated a portion of it, from which we learn that when Eudemus on his way to Macedon had reached Pherae in Thessaly he fell ill. During his illness he dreamt that he was addressed by a young man who told him he would soon recover; in a few days Alexander,—then tyrant of Pherae,— would lose his life; within five years Eudemus would return home. Eudemus, who was a Cypriot, understood this to mean ' to Cyprus.'

The first two predictions were fulfilled, but *quinto exeunte anno* Eudemus was killed in battle near Syracuse.

Alexander of Pherae was murdered in 358-7 (Beloch 3, 2, 84); Dion in June, 354 (see note on 23, 5); Callippus held Syracuse during the next thirteen months—to July, 353. Between him and Dion's friends war broke out; the ' friends ' withdrew to Leontini (Diod. 16, 36, 5) after a defeat, and it was presumably in this battle that Eudemus fell. [On Aristotle's lost *Eudemus*, see Jaeger, *Aristotle*, ch. iii.]

Eudemus, Timonides and Miltas probably joined the expedition at Zacynthus. From this point (see *Introduction*) to chapter 53, inclusive, Timonides' Narrative is held to have been Plutarch's authority.

22, 7. οὐ μεῖον ἢ χιλίων: οὐ μειόνων would be more usual, but for the adverb Koch, cf. Thucydides vi, 2, 25, 67 and Xen. *Cyrop.* 2, 1, 6.

According to Diod. 16, 10, 5, the exiles serving in the expedition numbered thirty. The refusal of the rest to take part may have been due, as Beloch suggests, to their belief that Dion meant simply to take over Dionysius' power. How many exiles were in the force later brought by Heracleides is not stated.

22, 8. Coins of Zacynthus bearing Dion's name have been found, and the inference is that he had been made a magistrate of the city (Evans in Freeman 4, 247).

In contrast to Plutarch's 'less than 800,' Diod. 16, 9, 5, speaks of 1,000. Parke (p. 116) supposes that Timonides was thinking only of the veteran mercenaries, exclusive of volunteer helpers or raw recruits.

ὑπεκκαῦσαι in a metaphorical sense occurs first in Plutarch *Mor.* 616E.

23, 1. Polybius 38, 8, 3, has ἀπεγνωσμέναι ἐλπίδες = forlorn hopes.

23, 2. πολέμ<ι>ον [Reiske] is likely to be what Plutarch wrote. προειπεῖν πόλεμον usually = 'proclaim war.'

23, 3. ἐτησίαι, yearly, i.e., periodic, winds. No singular occurs but cf. ἀπαρκτίας, καικίας, etc., formed on the analogy—it has been suggested —of geographical names like Στρυμονίας.

A wind (the 'Maestro') in summer blows down the Adriatic. If on reaching the Mediterranean it met a cyclone, it might be transformed into a mild N.E. wind. ἡ σελήνη διχομηνίαν ἦγε: the moon was bringing on the mid-month, and so was full. For the phrase cf. Aristoph. *Clouds* 17, ἄγουσαν τὴν σελήνην εἰκάδας.

23, 5. παρηκμακώς, 'past his prime.' Ancient authorities disagree as to the exact date of Dion's death. He was murdered on the feast of Kore, which fell in June during the wheat harvest.

In the *Oxyrynchus Papyrus* his death is assigned to the archonship of Callistratus, July, 355–July, 354, and, therefore, must have occurred in June, 354. This dating is now generally accepted. But Nepos, ch. 10, states that he died 'quartum post annum quum in Siciliam redierat,' which, even if we adopt inclusive reckoning, would put his death in 353. Similarly Diodorus 16, 31 (from a chronographical source), dates the murder to the year Ol. 106, 3 = Aug., 354–353.

It would seem that Dion's death having occurred in June, towards the end of the Attic and Olympian year, led the authorities followed by Nepos and Diodorus to assign it to the following year [Beloch 3, 2, 379]. —Nepos represents Dion as dying at 55 : he was actually 54,—and hence at the date of his expedition, 51.

24, 1. "After the libations … the moon became eclipsed. To Dion this was no marvel as he took into account the regular recurrence of eclipses, the meeting of Earth's shadow with the moon, and the interposition of Earth between moon and sun (lit. *earth's barricading against the sun*." The eclipse occurred, Aug. 9, 357.

In *Nic.* 23, Plutarch contrasts Nicias' panic at a lunar eclipse with the behaviour of Dion who 'had learnt astronomy from Plato.'

24, 5. λέγεται : see on 5, 7, and note that the occurrences reported by Theopompus were of the fairy-tale order, in contrast to the stories of the bees (24, 4) and the wolf (26, 9) which Plut. evidently derived from Timonides.

24, 10. The *Philippica* of Theopompus " was a world-history depicted in a series of extensive digressions. Certain of these acquired separate titles (τὰ θαυμασία, etc.)." *Oxford Class. Dict.* art. Theopompus.

ἱστόρηκε *has reported*; in classical writers the meaning is usually *investigate*.

25, 1. The *triakonters* are not mentioned in Diod. 16, 6, 5, or Nepos *Dion* 5: Demosthenes *Lept.* 162 speaks of *one* merchant ship.

ναῦς: this post-classical form of the *nominative* plur. occurs also in *Pompey* 78, ναῦς τινες ἑωρῶντο (Koch).

25, 2. ἐπὶ πνεύμασι : since they had put their voyage *at the mercy of the winds.*

Philistus was evidently appointed *nauarchos* by the Tyrant when Dion was banished. (On Dion's *nauarchia*, see 7, 5).

The chief harbours of Iapygia are those now called Brindisi and Otranto. παραφυλάττειν, 'to be on guard,' as in *Galba* 20.

25, 3. ἀραιῷ, *light*: cf. [Arist.] *De Mundo* 394a 21, ὀμίχλη νέφους ἀραιοτέρα. *Pachynus*, a promontory on the S.E. coast of Sicily.

25, 4. ἂν ἀποσπάσωσι τῆς γῆς ... "*if they draw off from the land* and purposely (ἑκόντες) abandon the cape." I have substituted the intransitive *active aor.,* for which see *Mor.* 971 D ; Xenoph. *Anab.* 7, 2, 11, for the aor. *passive,* since I find no evidence that this could mean anything except ' be forced from.' MSS. L and P² have ἂν μὴ ἀποσπασθῶσι, which shows that a difficulty was felt in view of ἑκόντες in the latter part of the sentence.

25, 6. *Arcturus* is visible in September.

25, 7. *Cercina*, an island lying N. of the lesser Syrtis (Gulf of Gabes), opposite the modern town of Sfax in Tunis. It is some 270 miles from Pachynus.

25, 8. μικρὸν οὖν δεήσαντος: Attic usage would require μικροῦ. Plut. follows the Attic use except where it would cause hiatus or confuse the sense; as in *Romulus* 18 (cited by Koch).

πρὸς κοντόν, *by aid of the punting pole.*

Κεφαλαῖς: now Mesrata or Ras Bushaifa, a promontory N.W. of the Greater Syrtis, some 300 miles from Cercina [P-W *sub voc.*].

25, 9. διαφερομένοις ' tossing about,' as in *Acts of Apostles*, 27, 27. πελάγιοι ἔφευγον, ' sought to escape over the open sea.'

25, 11. θέοντες, in *Mor.* 76c θέοντες ἱστίοις, running before the wind.

Minoa, also called Heracleia Minoa, lay on the S. coast of Sicily, on the E. bank of R. Halycus.

Tetradrachms belonging to the 4th century are frequent [Head, *Historia Nummorum* 124]. They bear the legend Ras Melcart (Melcart being the Phoenician Heracles).

ἐπικράτεια is the designation given by Plato *Epist.* 7, 349 C, to the Punic *dominion* in Sicily.

25, 12. Σύναλος: the names Synalos and Bomilcar occur in an Attic Inscription [Ditt. *Syll. Inscr.*³ 321] referring to a Punic mission to Athens. The name Synalos is explained in P-W as a popular corruption of the Semitic *Jazan El*, ' God has heard.'

In Diod. 16, 9, 4, the governor of Minoa bears the *Greek* name, *Paralos*.

26, 2. ἀναλαμβάνειν *intrans.* ' recoup their energies ': so of ' reviving power ' in *Pyrrhus* 36.

26, 3. ἀποσκευασαμένους, *depositing*: in Polyb. 2, 26, a leader remarks to his band: ταῦτα (δεῖ) ἀποσκευασαμένους αὖθις ἐγχειρεῖν . . .

The number of panoplies, according to Diod. 16, 9, was 5,000.

26, 7–10. We might suppose that the story was told by the messenger on his return to Syracuse after its occupation by Dion.

27, 1. For the settlement of *Campanians* in the town of Aetna see Diod. 14, 15.

27, 3. *Acrae*, about 20 miles W. of Ortygia, founded by Syracuse in 663 B.C.—Thuc. 6, 5. The river *Anapus* flows into the Great Harbour.

27, 5. <οἱ> Ziegler: the art. is similarly omitted by MSS. in *Arat.* 21 ; but cf. *Timol* 20, οὐ γὰρ ἦσαν οἱ σὺν αὐτῷ πλείους πεντακισχιλίων According to Diod. 16, 9, 6, Dion's recruits numbered 20,000.

παρακαλοῦντας : as the subject is unchanged, the nom. would be regular, but cf. *Tit. Flam.* 52, διώδευον . . . οὕτω κοσμίως ὥστε . . . τὸν σῖτον μὴ μεμετρημένους . . . ἀπέχεσθαι τῆς χώρας : *Philop.* 13, συντόνως οὕτως ἐπολεμή-θησαν ὥστε σπείρειν τοὺς στενωπούς, περικεκομμένους τῆς χώρας: also *T. Gracch.* 2.

28, 1. προσαγωγίδας, informers; for the *feminine* ending cf. γύννις, an effeminate man. There were also in the service of the Dionysii women spies, αἱ ποταγωγίδες καλούμεναι, Aristotle, *Pol.* 1313b.

28, 2. According to Bonner and Smith, *Administration of Justice from Homer to Aristotle*, ἀποτυμπανισμός was *execution by a process of garotting*.

In Aristophanes *Plut.* 476 τύμπανα, *drums*, are associated with κύφωνες, *pillories*. The τύμπανον was then something to which the prisoner was bound, and to be identified with the *board* (σανίς), to which, in the *Thesmophoriazusae*, a criminal is fastened by wrists and, arms with a collar round his neck,—which he begs his guard to loosen, as *it is choking him* (920 ff.).

Here, however, Plutarch evidently used the word ἀποτυμπανίζεσθαι in a generalised sense since the spies perished at the hands of ‘those who came across them.’ The word is found in *Mor.* 1049 D in a metaphorical sense, the reference being to an angry deity punishing men for their sins.

Timocrates in ch. 27 was ‘ guarding Epipolae.’ When deserted by his men he rode into the city, but unable to reach Ortygia turned back, leaving Syracuse by a gate in the wall of Epipolae.

28, 4. Dionysius I became Tyrant in 408 B.C.

Supplementary Note VI.

Syracusan Topography : Epipolae : Achradina : the Temenitid Gate. (See *at end of book* Plan of Syracuse).

According to Cicero, *In Verrem* 4, 52–3, Syracuse might be said to consist of four cities:—The Island (Ortygia); Achradina, containing the forum, prytaneum, curia, and temple of Olympian Jove; Tyche, the most densely populated quarter, named from a temple of Fortune; Neapolis, so called because last built, with a theatre at the top of it, two temples (of Ceres and Libera), and a statue of Apollo (known as Temenites).

There is no mention of Epipolae; evidently Cicero did not know it as a 'built up area.'

The region on the mainland enclosed with a circuit wall by the elder Dionysius is divided by nature into an upland plateau in the North and a smaller lowland area in the South East.

The plans in the text-books, which are based on Cavallari-Holm, *Topografia Archeologica di Siracusa*, represent the quarter Tyche, together with the greater part of Achradina and a small portion of Neapolis, as situated on the Plateau.

Against this arrangement K. Fabricius has made a convincing case. His thesis is, *There never was a Syracuse on the Plateau.*

He points out (1) that modern excavation has provided no evidence that any part of the Plateau was a built up area; (2) that the 'Wall of Gelon'—a long line of rock stretching from North to South, parallel to the East coast and about a mile distant from it, and supposed hitherto to have been the base of a wall erected by Gelon or some earlier builder as a defence of 'Upper Achradina' on the land side,—is actually not a wall but a quarry.

"In reality this scarp of rock extends for only 700 metres ... No single dressed block of stone appears which could belong to any possible wall. ... Wheel ruts are distinctly visible at the highest part of the ledge. At different points may be seen rectangular cuttings from which blocks of stone have been broken off; on the highest parts of the rock may be found cisterns, some round, some four-cornered. ... It is a quarry, established on the side of a declivity, out of which the stones on the summit and on the slope of the hill have been cut."

But if the 'Wall of Gelon' is not a real wall there is no longer any reason to believe in the reality of 'Upper Achradina.' We must confine Achradina to the lowland region. Tyche also—which adjoined Achradina (Plut. *Marcellus* 18) must be located here. The name Epipolae will then become applicable to the *whole* of the triangular plateau, which has its apex at Euryalus (Mongibellisi).

The castle on Euryalus. In *Dion* 27, Timocrates and his troops have been guarding Epipolae: in 29 Dion captures Epipolae and 'frees the citizens confined there': in *Tim.* 21, Timoleon sends a force against it. An obvious place to be attacked, defended, used as a prison, is a castle in a lonely situation. On Euryalus such a castle still stands. It covers nearly four acres, and its walls are elaborately dovetailed into the circuit wall of Dionysius.

It is true that Diodorus (14, 8) when describing the building of Dionysius' wall has nothing to say about the Castle; but modern historians are agreed that the Castle was part of the Dionysian defences; [1] and we may assume

---

[1] The existence of this castle, filled with soldiers and their dependents, on Epipolae may explain why Strabo 6, 2, 4 speaks of Syracuse as 'a *pentapolis* in former times.'

that it was the main objective of Dion and Timoleon in their attacks upon Epipolae.

The Hexapyla. This was a gate in the Northern part of the circuit wall, situated at a point where the road from Leontini entered the enclosed area (Diod. 16, 20: Livy 24, 33; 25, 24). It is generally located at the modern Scala Greca (Freeman 4, 501ff.). The name has been conjecturally restored by Ziegler in *Dion* 45, 5.

Achradina and Tyche.

Fabricius limits Achradina to the area adjoining the Little Harbour; Tyche he places between Achradina and the South-Eastern edge of the Plateau.

Many years ago F. Haverfield, *Classical Review*, 3, p. 110ff., had argued that Achradina lay on the low ground North of Ortygia : " The name does not occur in Thucydides, nor in the accounts of the Athenian siege given by Diodorus and Plutarch. It probably came into use after B.C. 400. The most striking point about the allusions to it in Diodorus is the close connexion implied between it and Ortygia (e.g., xi, 72, 73, 76). In Livy we find the same connexion implied between Achradina and Ortygia. The collocation *Archradina atque Insula* is fairly common (xxv, 24, 10; 29, 10, etc.) and the account of the capture of Syracuse by Marcellus in 212 seems to imply that Achradina was on the lower ground; i.e., as Mommsen calls it, ' the city proper on the shore.' "

But Fabricius goes further. Holding that no part of the ' built up area ' was situated on the Plateau, he locates Tyche also on the ' low ground,' in the Northern part of the area assigned by Haverfield to Achradina.

As evidence that Achradina and Tyche adjoined each other he cites Livy 25, 25: " inter Neapolin et Tycham ... posuit castra. Legati eo ab Tycha et Neapoli venerunt:" also Plut. *Marcellus* 18, where Marcellus " made a great rout of the Syracusans, who fled because it was thought that no part of the city had remained uncaptured, whereas in fact the strongest part, named Achradina, held out because its walls made it defensible against the outer city, of which they name one part *Nea*, the other, *Tyche*."

Cicero in the passage cited above speaks of the Theatre as in Neapolis. Fabricius accordingly refers Livy's *inter Neapolin* et Tycham to a spot now known as Groticelli. There Marcellus would have Tyche—as Fabricius has located it—on the East, and Neapolis on the South.

From the passage cited from the *Marcellus* it may be inferred that Tyche and Neapolis alike were separated from Achradina simply by a wall; and their simultaneous surrender recorded by Livy suggests that the two quarters were closely connected.

The Temenitid Gate.

In Thucydides 6; 75 and 100 the name Temenites is applied to a district fortified by the Syracusans during the war with Athens. Cicero mentions a statue of Apollo *Temenites* which he saw in Neapolis, together with temples of Ceres and Libera. The statue, which must have been either within the precinct of the goddesses or adjoining it, gave its name to the surrounding district, afterwards included in Neapolis.

In 396 the Carthaginians occupied the ' suburb ' of Achradina, when they plundered the temples of Demeter and Kore (Diod. 14, 63). This suburb is then to be identified with the ' Temenites ' of Thucydides. It may be assumed that the ' Temenitid Gate ' was situated in a circuit wall built by Dionysius I; and Fabricius thinks it may be identified with a Dipylon of which he found traces in a wall discovered West of the New Cemetery. The fragment he found to be of the same breadth as the Southern section of the Dionysian circuit wall.

29, 2. ἀνῄει, ' went *up* '; although the Syracusan citadel was situated on Ortygia by the sea. But in most Greek cities the fortress was built on a hill. προχύταις : the suggestion of Stephanus that the word implies ' pelting with flowers ' has been generally accepted. It is true that in Eur. *Electra* 803, *Iph. Aul.* 1112, the word is used of barley groats sprinkled on a sacrificial victim. But to throw sacrificial meal at a triumphal procession would be inauspicious, whereas pelting with flowers was a recognised practice at the Games; see Pindar, *Pyth.* 8, 57; 9, 125.

προστρεπομένων, often used of *offering prayers* to a god or hero, as in *Cleom.* 39.

29, 3. Πεντάπυλα evidently the outer portal of the ' acropolis ', which Holm supposes to have adjoined the S.E. corner of the agora.

ἡλιοτρόπιον, a *sun-dial*. In Athen. 5, 207 E we hear of a shi pbuilt for Hiero II, which carried a concave sun-dial ' copied from the one in Achradina.'

29, 4. αὐτοκράτορας στρατηγούς : this office had provided a legal basis for the rule of the Dionysii.—The association of Megacles with Dion is mentioned in Diod. 16, 10.

There is no reason to think that this irregular assembly had any thought of imposing constitutional limitations, or that any time-limit was laid down, —as has been suggested [Westlake, *Cambr. Hist. Journal* VII, 2, (1942)]. If Plutarch had found any such suggestion in his authority he would not have remarked in 35, 5 that Dion was suspected of prolonging the war in order to enjoy a longer period of office. The democrats, however, when they came to control the Ecclesia, found it convenient to assume that Dion had been elected not ' for the duration ', but merely for the unexpired portion of the legal year.

29, 5. τὴν φιλοτιμίαν καὶ τὸ ἀνάθημα ' the ambitious erection' (hendiadys).

29, 6. Dion's wall 'stretched from sea to sea,' Diod. 16, 12, 1.

Holm takes it to have been a prolongation of the wall which the elder
D. had built along the N. shore of the little Harbour. The extension cut
off the S.E. corner of the agora. It is designated as περιτείχισμα (30, 5);
διατείχισμα (30, 6) ; and προτείχισμα, i.e., defence wall of Achradina
(44, 6).

29, 7. In Diod. 16, 11, 3, as here, Dionysius returns ' seven days afterwards.'

For the *panoplies*, see 26, 3. [The insertion of the article is required
as the reference is to particular things already mentioned.]

30, 1. φιλάνθρωποι: " *generous* terms (see on 7, 5) were offered ...
from the Tyrant, who promised moderation in taxes and relief from military
service, unless voted by themselves." μή, (Coraes) is required by the sense.

30, 2. ἄδειαν, (Emperius : MSS. & δεῖ) *amnesty.*

30, 2–5. Diod. 16, 11, 3–5 remarks that the Syracusans were keeping
negligent watch. He does not refer to the mercenaries. Polyaenus 5, 2, 7
also refers to the tyrants ' stratagem.'

30, 5. σκευωρία, *knavery*, meant originally, according to Pollux, super-
vision of baggage.

30, 7. συνεφρόνουν, *understood*, a sense frequent in Plutarch.

30, 8. From the cross-wall to the gate of the citadel the distance was
a furlong (Diodorus).

30, 9. τὴν χεῖρα : Diod. 16, 12, 4 has τὸν δεξιὸν βραχίονα.

30, 10. Timonides' only recorded appearance in the story.

30, 12. Reiske's correction πολλῷ πλείους is justified by the reference
in 31, 1 to a 'brilliant victory.' Diod. 16, 13, 1 gives Dionysius' losses as 800.

31, 1. ἐστεφάνωσαν has here the generalised sense (found also in the
Attic orator Lycurgus) *rewarded*. See on ἀποτυμπανίζειν 28, 2.

The ' Hipparinus ' letter. Dionysius, in order to produce a breach
between the Syracusans and Dion, wrote Dion a letter urging him to
make himself tyrant. But fearing that it might be ignored if it appeared
to come from himself, he attached to it the superscription, *From Hipparinus
to his Father.*

Hackforth in C. A. H. VI, 280 n, infers that the fact of letters from
the women of the family having been read aloud in the Ecclesia became
known to or was suspected by Dionysius, who assumed that a letter from
Dion's son would be treated in the same way.

31, 2. In *Intro.*, sect. 3 B it is argued that Plutarch was right in
supposing the true name of Dion's son to have been Hipparinus.

31, 4–6. " The other letters, containing many entreaties and suppli-
cations from the women, were read to the Syracusans, while the letter
which seemed to come from the lad, though they objected to its being
opened in public, Dion insisted on opening. It was from Dionysius, in
form written to Dion, but in fact to the Syracusans; it had the appearance
of entreaty and justification, but was composed for the purpose of creating
prejudice against Dion. *For there were reminders ... and threats and stern*

injunctions, combined with lamentations, and, what was most calculated to excite them, demands, (the writer) demanding that Dion should not abolish but take over the Tyranny." The clause as given in the MSS., καὶ τὸ μάλιστα κινῆσαν αὐτόν, ἀξιοῦντος μὴ καθαιρεῖν ... τὴν τυραννίδα, is faulty in two respects :

(1) Plutarch is concerned not with the effect Dionysius actually produced on Dion, but with the effect he *expected* to produce on the Syracusans. Hence I read with Richards τὸ μάλιστ' ἂν κινῆσαν αὐτούς:

(2) a word has fallen out before ἀξιοῦντος as Latte saw. Cf. *Tit. Flam.* 17 ἦσαν δὲ τιμαὶ πρέπουσαι, καί, τὸ τὰς τιμὰς ἀληθινοὺς ποιοῦν, εὔνοια. In the present passage the word most likely to have fallen out before ἀξιοῦντος is ἀξιώσεις. Cf. *Pompey* 58, αἱ Κουρίωνος ἀξιώσεις δημικώτεραι · δυεῖν γὰρ ἠξίου θάτερον : and *Caesar* 30, ἤ γε παρὰ Κ. ἀξίωσις τὸ προσχῆμα τῆς δικαιολογίας εἶχεν · ἠξίου γὰρ ...

Polyaenus 5, 2, 7 (based probably on Ephorus) states that Dionysius released the envoys on the day after the attack on the cross-wall; with them came ' women ' with letters from Arete, Aristomache and others in the citadel. Among these letters was one ' from Hipparion ', in which Dionysius wrote ' like a friend and relation.'

32, 3. Heracleides,—mentioned casually in ch. 11,—had fled for his life to the Carthaginian ' dominion ' during Plato's final visit to Syracuse in 361 B.C. He had been in the service of the tyrant,—*praefectus equitum* according to Nepos—but was held responsible for a mutiny which had broken out among the mercenaries (Plato *Epist.* 7, 348). In 3, 318 C, Plato remarks that both he himself and the Syracusans thought the accusation unjust.

Later H. joined Dion in Peloponnesus. Beloch cites I. G. IV, 1504, where in a list of θεαροδόκοι (persons who looked after the reception of envoys at the temple of Asclepios in Epidaurus) the name Ἡρακλείδης Λυσιμάχου appears along with Dion's.

Diod. 16, 6, 5 records that Dion left Heracleides behind to bring some triremes and merchant ships to Syracuse later, but being hindered by bad weather H. did not arrive till after Dion's entry into the city.

This account is accepted by Beloch (3, 1, 257) who argues that the expedition was financed by Dion.

Beloch regards Timonides' narrative as a late forgery. But if genuine, as I have argued in *Intro.*, Sect. 3. B., it is to be preferred to Diodorus' account. As the troops conveyed to Syracuse by Heracleides served under Dion the quarrel may not have become known to Diodorus' authority, Ephorus.

ἀραρώς, *firm, constant.* It is found in Hom. *Od.* 10, 563, but in prose only in post-classical authors.

32, 4. ἰδιόστολος, ' with an expedition of his own,' as in *Thes.* 26. αὖθις, ' in his turn,' as in Pl. *Charmides* 153 D : αὖθις ἐγὼ αὐτοὺς ἀνηρώτων.

32, 5. μετάγων ῥᾷον αὐτοὺς οἵ <γε> τὸ σεμνὸν τοῦ Δ. ... ἀπεστρέφοντο : " seducing them the more easily since they were turning away from (i.e.,

were repelled by) Dion's solemn air." An indication seems to be required
that the relative clause is causal : (cf. ὅς γε ... ἀπέκτεινε in 3, 6). The
accus. after ἀποτρέπεσθαι is post-classical.

θέλοντες : forms from θέλω, not ἐθέλω, appear in later Greek except
in augmented tenses. τὸ δημαγωγεῖσθαι : " to be flattered by popular arts."
The article seems to have been added to emphasise the antithesis. Its
use with the infinitive after θέλοντες is poetical ; cf. Soph. *Oed. Col.* 443.

33, 1. ἀφ' αὑτῶν, *on their own initiative.* That was how Dion himself
had been appointed.

" It was the natural instinct of Greeks to resort to the place of assembly,
even without special summons, when anything happened that concerned
the whole community."—Bonner and Smith, *Administration of Justice
from Homer to Aristotle*, p. 7.

Nepos *Dion* 6, 3 : " Neque is (Heracleides) minus (Dione) valebat
apud optimates quorum consensu praeerat classi." It looks as if Nepos
misunderstood Timaeus here, for H. was attached to the democratic party.
Timaeus may have remarked that on this occasion the aristocracy favoured
H. no less than the populace.

33, 2. ᾐτιᾶτο, "objected that ... " For the construction, cf. Plato,
Prot. 333d ; *Rep.* 407c. αὐτῷ is substituted for the reflexive pron. to
emphasise the contrast between D. and H. [Kühner-Gerth 1, 564n].

33, 3. ἐν καιρῷ ... " in a crisis needing but a small movement of the
scale to lead to ruin." In Plato *Rep.* 8, 566E a person of unsound physique
μικρᾶς ῥοπῆς δεῖται πρὸς τὸ κάμνειν.

34, 2. εἰ μὴ ... *to think that they do not* ... cf. 13, 6 ; 34, 4.

34, 5. ἀκρίτου, *incapable of judging* : for active sense, cf. *Mor.* 159B.

34, 8. ὡς τετρωμένος (ἂν ἔφευγεν). Sintenis cf. 49, 5 ; also *Caes.* 42 ;
Cic. 17.

35, 2. ὑφ', *subject to* ... Coraes (MSS. ἐφ').

35, 3–7. *Defeat and death of Philistus* : The bias against the Syracusan
democracy evinced by Plutarch's source (Timonides) appears in his reference
to the naval victory a sa *piece of luck.*

Of P.'s end Plutarch refers to three accounts : (1) *He committed suicide,*
according to Ephorus. That this account appears in Diod. 16, 16, 3 is
an argument for assigning the ' Dion chapters ' to Ephorus as source.
(2) Timonides' account, if we are satisfied that his Narrative was authentic,
is obviously to be preferred : *P. was beheaded and his body dragged through
Achradina and cast into the Quarries.* (There are still quarries on the S.E.
of the upland Plateau, N. of Tyche). (3) Timaeus added that he was dragged
by the leg. In Diod. 14, 8, 5 (based on T.), Philistus dissuades Dionysius I
from abandoning the Tyranny by the remark, " you should not fly from
the Tyranny on a horse, but rather fall from it, *dragged by the leg.*" (This,
we are told, was his retort to Polyxenus, who had advised D. to abdicate).

But Diod. in 20, 78 (based on a different authority) states that *Megacles*
used the phrase ' dragged by the leg.' (Megacles may have been a brother
of Hipparinus, Dion's father, as D. later had a brother so named).

It would seem that Timaeus was so much under the influence of super-stitious notions that he insisted that Philistus used the ominous phrase, although P. himself had stated in his History that the speaker was Megacles.

36, 1–2. " Timaeus, however, finding a fair enough pretext (for censure) in the energy and loyalty shown by Philistus in defending the Tyranny, gorges himself on the injurious assertions made to his discredit; but while contemporaries whom Philistus had wronged may perhaps be pardoned for having become so embittered as to vent their rage on his senseless corpse, his reputation (as a writer) makes an appeal to historians of a later date, who have used his narrative and have suffered no harm from what he did in his lifetime, not to reproach him in a tone of insolence and buffoonery with calamities which the best of men is not immune from sharing at the bidding of chance."

τῶν κατ' αὐτοῦ βλασφημιῶν : Timaeus is accused of reproducing the βλασφημίαι current in earlier historians or in oral tradition. The last clause implies that what Plutarch objects to is not the falsity but the *tone* of Timaeus' statements. βλασφημίαι are not necessarily false : cf. Demosth. 9, 1 : δέδοικα μὴ βλάσφημον μὲν εἰπεῖν ἀληθὲς δ' ᾖ.

36, 3. " On the other hand Ephorus is not sound in his judgement when . . ." ὅς, i.e., Philistus. οὐ is regularly inserted after verbs of denying to emphasise the negative character of the statement.

ζηλώσας γένοιτο. This combination is infrequent in prose (but is found, e.g., Plato, *Sophistes* 217C).

πλούτους, *fortunes* : so Plato *Gorgias* 523 C. Philistus envied the luxury, fortunes, power and marriage alliances of tyrants.

ἐμμελέστατος : ἐμμελής lit. ' in tune ', with the derived sense ' appro-priate,' cf. *Demetr.* 2. Translate, " adopts the most fitting attitude ".

37, 1–3. According to Diodorus 16, 16–17, Dionysius asked to be allowed to take his troops and property to Italy.

Plutarch's account gives the impression of being based on a contemporary authority. Such details as those here recorded would not be remembered long by popular tradition.

37, 2. τὸν καλούμενον Γυάροτον (sc. ἄγρον) : " the so-called Plough-land farm." (Contrast γύας ἀνηρότους Aesch. *Prom.* 708.) The reading of the MSS. Γύαρτα (Γύατα) is corrupt : it has no *meaning* and would have to be indeclinable neuter.

Dr. H. W. Parke has observed that the formula ὁ καλούμενος (or ὁ λεγόμενος) is applied only to names which have a meaning : it indicates that they are employed in a particular or metaphorical sense. Thus Xenophon refers to the poisonous henbane as ὁ ὑοσκύαμος καλούμενος : in 25, 8 above we have αἱ κεφαλαὶ καλούμεναι as the name of a place on the African coast. In *Timol.* 9, Ortygia is ἡ Νῆσος καλουμένη and in 18 we find ἡ 'Αχραδινὴ λεγομένη (" the so-called wild pear-tree land," sc. χώρα). So Aristotle referred to Archytas and his associates as the ' so-called Pytha-goreans.'

37, 5. καθίησι, 'employs', a post-classical signification : cf. *Pericles* 7, ῥήτορας ἐτέρους καθιείς.

37, 6. τῶν ξένων τὸν μισθὸν ἀποστερεῖν, to *withhold* the pay : contrast the *aor.* infinitives, ψηφίσασθαι and ἑλέσθαι, denoting momentary action.

According to Diod. 16, 17, 3, the city was short of money. The mercenaries, deprived of their pay, called on Dion "to join them in an insurrection, and take vengeance on their common enemies." He at first refused, but afterwards, compelled by the situation, accepted command of the troops and along with them withdrew to Leontini. (He had evidently persuaded them to abstain from their violent intentions.)

Under Dionysius I the expenses of the army had been defrayed by an εἰσφορά, "which had the character of an extraordinary impost, as it had to be voted on each occasion by the *ecclesia*, although, in fact, it was regularly collected because of the maintenance of a standing army, and hence it counted among the ordinary taxes. As *strategos autocrator* Dionysius had authority to collect it ; even at Athens the *strategoi* collected the direct war-taxes " (Huttl, p. 103).

It would seem that the mercenaries were to have been paid at the end of the campaign ; which might explain why nothing had been done about the matter hitherto.

In 38, 4 we learn that the troops were offered naturalisation, and, as Freeman has suggested, would, as a result of the redistribution of land, have been paid their wages in the form of holdings.

Diodorus speaks of 3,000 mercenaries : this number would include those who had been brought by Heracleides.

Dion's later financial exactions, on which Nepos enlarges in his last chapters, were due apparently to his efforts to wipe off the arrears.

ἐσφάλλοντο μὲν αὐτοί : Heracleides had failed to prevent the departure of Dionysius.

38, 1. ἐξαίσιοι, *portentous*. διοσημίαι : of these 'signs from Zeus' the most significant were lightning, thunder, rain. δεκάπεντε for πεντεκαίδεκα is regular in post-classical writers.

38, 2. In Greek cities, theatres were commonly used for meetings of the Assembly as at Leontini (ch. 43) Corinth (*Arar.* 23) Sicyon (*Ib.* 8), and from the beginning of the fourth century at Athens.

38, 3. ὅσον ὕστερον οἱ πολέμιοι κατέσχον, i.e., the part raided by Nypsius (ch. 41). It was observed afterwards that this corresponded to the area overrun by the ox ! As the ox is said to have alarmed the crowd *in the Theatre*, and the Theatre was in or just west of the Temenites quarter, Nypsius' attack, it may be inferred, was concentrated on Temenites. This throws light on what is meant by the phrase at the beginning of 42, " when the danger *was now approaching* Achradina."

39, 1. ὑπερφαίνομαι is elsewhere followed by the genitive.

39, 2. ὅσον, *only just*. Leontini lies some 20 miles N.E. of Syracuse; it was occupied by the families of the mercenaries whom Dionysius I had planted there (Diod. 14, 78).

NOTES.

87

39, 3. Diod. 16, 7 says that the Syracusan losses were large.

40, 1. πολιτείαις = *grants of citizenship*, as in Aristotle *Ath. Pol.* 54, 3.

ἐπρέσβευον : the use of the active = ' send ambassadors ' is found in Polybius ; e.g., 20, 2 Ἀντιόχου πρεσβεύσαντος οἱ Βοιωτοὶ ἀπεκρίθησαν τοῖς πρεσβευταῖς ...

41–45. *Nypsius' campaign.* In Diod. 16, 18–20 there are few indications of time. From Plutarch it is clear that fighting continued for three days :

First day : N.'s ships while unloading were defeated by the Syracusan fleet (41, 2 ; Diod. 16, 18, 4). The Syracusans started drinking, but during the night Nypsius attacked and broke through Dion's wall (41, 4) ; and burst into the city : the Syracusan strategoi were drunk (Diod. 16, 19, 2). Nypsius' men began to plunder (41, 3 : Diod. 16, 19, 4).

Second day : the raid continued till night-fall, when N. withdrew to thè ' Acropolis ' (44, 1). Dion, recalled (42, 8 ; Diod. 16, 20), resolved to march to Syracuse that night (43, 6).

Third day : before dawn N. launched a formidable attack (44, 5) : Dion arrived and drove the raiders back into the Acropolis (46, 4 ; Diod. 16, 20, 4).

41, 1. ' Nypsius ' = Lat. *Numerius* (Oscan *Numsius* later *Numisius*): I. G. xiv, 894 (Ischia) has Νύμψιος.

41, 4. Diod. 16, 19, 2 refers to N.'s troops " opening the gates ": this is an error, for Dion's cross-wall had no gates !

42, 1. " When such was the position in the city, *and the danger was approaching Achradina*, all thought of the one person left on whom they could rest their hope, . . ." Holm explains that the raiders on crossing Dion's wall had turned left into the Temenites quarter. His inference is supported by 38, 3, where see note.

42, 2. πλήν γε, *however.*

42, 5. ἀπὸ ῥυτῆρος, at full speed (*lit.* away from the rein : see Jebb on Soph. O. C. 899–900). καταφερομένης, 'declining ', a post-classical meaning, as in *Timol.* 12.

43, 1. πολλὰ τῶν δακρύων, *many tears*, a use of the partitive gen. found in Herod. 9, 16 where the same phrase occurs ; also Herod. 9, 61 ; Aristoph. *Wasps* 199, *Peace* 226 ;. So in 22, 5 above τῶν πολιτικῶν πολλοί means ' many statesmen.' ἐκπίπτειν of tears also in *Pelop.* 9, *Mor.* 84D.

43, 4. Syracuse was " a creation of your own ", because the troops were Peloponnesians, and Corinth, the *metropolis* of Syracuse, a Peloponnesian city.

43, 5. εἰ takes fut. indic. in a strong emotional appeal.

44, 1–2. ἀτρεμεῖν : Attic ἠρεμεῖν.

σπουδήν : Sintenis' correction of σχολήν. He cites 45, 1 ἔτυχε οὐκέτι σπουδῇ πορευόμενος. The MSS. reading is mere tautology.

44, 5. κατέσκαπτε : began the demolition of the entire wall (see 41, 4).

44, 7. τοῦ υἱοῦ : inserted by Solanus, cf. 50, 2. (*Apollocrates* despaired of success, and so Nypsius sought " to entomb the Tyranny in the city ").

44, 8. πυροβόλους (Lat. *malleoli*, Holden, *Sulla* 9) : this missile " consisted of a reed shaft, fitted at the top with a frame of wire-work. This was filled with inflammable materials and had an arrow attached to the top ... When directed against an object the arrow stuck into it, and the burning tow set it on fire." Rich, *Companion to Lat. Dictionary*.

44, 9. τὸ καταδυόμενον (sc. μέρος).

45, 5. <'Εξα>πύλων : Ziegler, comparing Diod. 16, 20, 2.

The *Hecatompedos* may be assumed to have been a road 100 feet wide running over Epipolae to Tyche and Neapolis. Pindar *Isth.* 5, 22 speaks (in a metaphor) of ἑκατόμπεδοι κελευθοί.

45, 6. Diod. 16, 20, 4 also mentions Dion as " attacking at many points."

46, 1. For the association of πατήρ with σωτήρ cf. (with Koch) *Camill.* 10, *Sulla* 54, *Aratus* 42, *Pelop.* 33.

47, 2. " The men who had been unfair to him " were Heracleides and Theodotes.

τῆς ἀρετῆς ἡττᾶσθαι : they admitted that they were *overmastered by his virtue* : so Demosth. *De Cor.* 317, τῆς ἀληθείας ἡττώμενος.

47, 3. τοῖς στρατιώταις χαρίσασθαι τὸν 'Η. : *i.e.* to gratify the soldiers by allowing them to execute H. In contrast we find in *C. Gracch.* 4 Κορνηλίᾳ δεηθείσῃ χαρίζεσθαι 'Οκταύιον, " to spare O. at C.'s request."

τοῦ πολιτεύματος, The Government.

δημοκοπίαν (lit. stimulation [κόπτειν] of the people), the reference being to the proposed division of land. Tr. ' mass bribery '. In *Mor.* 802 Plutarch distinguishes δημαγωγία, which implies public speaking, from δημοκοπία, which may consist of public spectacles or banquets or distribution of cash.

47, 4. [' Socrates ' in *Crito* 49B and *Gorgias* 469B–C argued that it is better to suffer injustice than to commit it ; in *Republic* 1, 435 that it is not right to injure anyone ; in 1, 444 that Justice is natural, being produced in the soul as health is in the body by the development among its elements—Reason, Temper, the Desires—of their natural relations of authority and subordination.]

47, 5. " The proof that one has mastered anger, envy and contentiousness is not kindness to friends and good people, but to be merciful and mild towards offenders." For the sentiment, cf. St. Luke 6, 32.

47, 6. κατορθώσεις : " successes in war, even though no human competitor presents himself, are at any rate claimed against us by Fortune."

47, 8. The ' weakness ' is the assertion of irrational elements in the Soul over the Reason.

47, 9. Cf. St. Paul *Rom.* 12, 21 : μὴ νικῶ ὑπὸ τοῦ κακοῦ, ἀλλὰ νίκα ἐν τῷ ἀγαθῷ τὸ κακόν.

48, 1. Diodorus, 16, 20, 6 : " he generously released all his opponents from the charges against them ".

48, 6. ἀκυρώσας : by thus *invalidating* a decree passed by the ecclesia Dion showed that he no longer considered himself bound by the existing constitution. The decree had been passed just before the election of the new strategoi (37, 5).

48, 7. Heracleides begins a fresh 'agitation', pointing to Dion's unconstitutional act as evidence that he is aiming at a tyranny.

48, 8. In *Comparison Timol.and Aemilius*, ch. 2, we are told : "Pharax ... and Callippus ... violated laws and treaties in hope of ruling Sicily ... Pharax acted the courtier to Dionysius (ἐθεράπευε Δ.) after D.'s expulsion from Syracuse ". In *Timol*. 11 Plut. remarks : " Both professed to desire the overthrow of the Sicilian Tyrants but made the calamities which Sicily suffered under them seem like a golden age ". The last clause evidently refers to the years that followed Dion's death.

Pharax is assumed by Beloch to have been an accredited representative of Sparta, while Harward supposes that he was a mere adventurer. Perhaps he began as the former, but developed into the latter.

Heracleides was presumably at Messene to protect corn ships sailing to Syracuse. This would explain why 'faction in the army' resulted in shortage of food at Syracuse. Pharax may have stationed himself at Rhegium to interrupt the passage of the cargo boats.

48, 9. ὑπὸ τῶν φίλων: their second attempt to convince Dion that 'Heracleides must go.'

49. For Heracleides' relations with Pharax and Gaesylus, see Supplementary note VII (following notes on ch. 53).

49, 1. This charge against Dion had been made before (33, 5).

49, 2. ... "And the defeat not having been a serious one, but having occurred rather because (the soldiers) were distracted by one another and by faction, Dion prepared to fight again " : note *gen. abs.* with subj. understood, as often.

49, 4. " The third hour " = 9 a.m. This use of ὥρα = *hour*, has been traced back as far as Pytheas of Marseilles (*fl.* 300 B.C.), the traveller who " sailed round Britain, saw Ireland and *heard* of Norway." He is cited by Geminus (1st cent. A.D.), for a statement in reference to ' high latitudes': "Night becomes quite short ἐν τούτοις τοῖς τόποις, ὡρῶν οἶς μὲν δύο, οἶς δὲ τριῶν, so that after a short interval the sun rises again ".

49, 6. ἀλεξιφάρμακον, *amulet*, cf. *Comp. Dion and Brut.* 4.

49, 7. For Dion as an honorary citizen of Sparta, see 17, 8 n.

πίστεις τὰς μεγίστας <ἐφ'> αἶς : " Gaesylus effected a reconciliation between D. and Heracleides who ... gave the most solemn pledges, *on top of which* Gaesylus himself swore ... "

Between the syllables -ας and -αις, the prep. could have easily dropped out. (αἶς might be taken as dat. of relation with τιμωρός but the construction would be awkward, and the order of the words is against it).

The difficulty was evidently felt by the editor of MS. C who read ἐπώμοσε.

In *Pericles* 30, the only place where ἐπομνύειν = " take an *additional* oath," the vb. is used absolutely ; everywhere else this compound has the same meaning is the simple verb.

50, 1. ἐξοικοδομήσαντες : L-S give ' unbuilding,' which is probably correct ; with the closer investment of the fortress the περιτείχισμα was no longer required.

50, 3. τοὺς μὴ παρόντας, i.e., the dead. ἐπιβοᾶσθαι is the appropriate word for calling upon the deceased at a funeral.

50, 4. ὅπου as a causal conjunction is found occasionally even in classical writers.

πηλίκον (χρὴ) φρονῆσαι ; cf. μέγα φρονεῖν.

51. The story of Dion's meeting with his wife is found also in Aelian *Var. Hist.* 12, 47. Both accounts are probably attributable to Timaeus. (It may be noted that incidents recorded in *Dion* 3, 4 and 13, 2 appear in Aelian with additions, which suggests that Aelian took his extracts not from Plutarch but from Plutarch's source, i.e., Timaeus).

51, 1. οὐκ ἐκαρτέρησαν, ' did not stay ' : this sense is post-classical.

51, 3. In 21, 7 it is stated that Arete had been forced to marry Dionysius' courtier, Timocrates.

51, 4. " Now that Fortune has made you our master, how do you decide in her case about the compulsion? Is it as uncle or also as husband that she shall greet you? " For this use of διαιτᾶν, cf. *Coriol.* 35, οὐ περιμενῶ ταύτην μοι διαιτῆσαι τὴν τύχην τὸν πόλεμον.

ἀσπάσεται, deliberative future, as in Plato, *Rep.* 397D, πότερον πάντας παραδεξόμεθα;

51, 5. διῃτᾶτο, *resided*. The statement that Dion placed the castle at the disposal of the Syracusans is a mistake of Plut. : they would have demolished it. Cf. Heracleides' reproach of Dion in 53, 2.

52, 1. οὐδὲν ἀπολαῦσαι πρότερον ἢ τὸ . . . ἀπονείμαι : " to receive no benefit prior to the distributing . . . "

ἄστει, i.e., Athens.

52, 2. μὴ μόνον Σικελίας . . . ἀποβλεπούσης πρὸς αὐτὸν . . . καὶ μηδὲν οὕτω μέγα τῶν τότε νομιζόντων : " when not only Sicily was fixing a steadfast gaze upon him, . . . and contemporaries thought there was nothing so great as he " . . . For the use of the negative μὴ with a temporal participle see 2, 2 n.—With νομίζειν it is sometimes found even in classical Greek.

ἀποβλέπειν lit. to ' look away ' from *other* objects. μέγα : for the neuter cf. *Aratus* 6 : " nothing (οὐδὲν) is more cowardly than a tyrant."

52, 4. τόπον, (MSS. τοῦτον) Koch, comparing Plato, *Ep.* 4, 320D, ὥστε τοὺς ἐξ ἁπάσης τῆς οἰκουμένης εἰς ἕνα τόπον ἀποβλέπειν.

52, 5. καίτοι is sometimes found with the participle in classical Greek; as in Plato. *Rep.* 511D.

Plutarch's citation from *Epist.* 4, 321b, had already been made in 8, 4.

52, 6. " He obviously was subject to a natural disposition hard to temper to graciousness." Cf. ἀμαθία χρῆσθε, Thuc. 1, 68.

53, 1. The *synedrion* was simply a council of Dion's ' Friends ' : cf. 47, 3 ; 48, 9.

Heracleides was out of office since the navy had been abolished (50, 1).

53, 2. " He did not allow the people to open the tomb when they had set out to do so." (Cf. λύειν ἔδραν, Eur. *Rhes.* 8). In *Tim.* 22 Plutarch writes : " Timoleon did not repeat Dion's experience ... but guarding against the suspicion which had created a prejudice against *him*, made proclamation that any one was free to take part in the demolition of the tyrants' fortification. Accordingly, the Syracusans levelled to the ground the fortress, the palaces and the tombs of the tyrants." On the site T. built a court of justice, " thus pleasing the citizens and showing Democracy triumphant over Tyranny."

53, 4. ἄκρατον δ. the phrase is used, in *Cimon* 15, of Athens after the reforms of Ephialtes and Pericles.

παντοπώλιον, ' a mart.' In *Republic* 8, 557D Plato speaks of democracy as παμπολλαὶ πόλεις ἀλλ' οὐ πόλις, because (as Adam explains), the different varieties of individuals represent as many different constitutions.

For κολούειν (Bryan for κωλύειν), see Arist. *Pol.* 1274a, κολούειν τὴν ἐν Ἀρείῳ πάγῳ ἀρχήν. The Laconian constitution was ranked by Plato among the best of the ' inferior constitutions,' it being a timocracy, ' where Honour is the ruling principle ' (*Rep.* 544c).

In Sparta the element of royalty was represented by the two kings, that of democracy by the Ephors, who were elected by the popular assembly. Ar. *Pol.* 2, 10 : " In the Spartan system under which every citizen is eligible for the Ephorate the people can share in the highest offices."

In Crete, " the Kosmoi (or chief magistrates) are drawn from a limited number of families." " The only power of the Cretan *Assembly* is to ratify the decisions of the Kosmoi. The Council of Elders is drawn from those who have served as Kosmoi. Their power of acting at their own discretion —and not according to written rules—is a positive danger."

τοὺς Κορινθίους. The government of Corinth was in the hands of a Council with eight *probouloi* at its head. Admission to the council was open to the wealthier citizens, apparently without distinction of birth.

Of the Corinthian Ecclesia nothing is known except as an electoral body. Hence Timoleon's appointment to the command in Sicily is more likely to have been made by the ' *synedrion* ', as Diodorus states (16, 65), than by the *demos*, as Plut. has it in *Tim.* 7 ;—which, in fact, is hardly to be reconciled with his statement in the present passage, " the C. do not transact much of the public business in the popular assembly."

53, 5. The persons whom Dion permitted to assassinate Heracleides were evidently to be found among the ' Friends ': see 47, 3 ; 48, 9. They doubtless included some of the " statesmen and philosophers " of 22, 5.

53, 6. συνέγνωσαν, ὡς οὐ δυνατὸν ἦν ... : " *they came to recognise* that it *had not been* possible for the city to find rest from disorder while Dion and Heracleides were in public life together."

It is implied that the removal of Heracleides was justified on the ground of public security.

We may infer (1) that Plutarch's authority here is still Timonides, and (2) that his Narrative was written very soon after Heracleides' funeral.

If the author had been—as Beloch imagined—a forger writing in the time of Timoleon (or later), he would not, unless he happened to be an artist in realistic fiction, have ventured on a remark so coloured by false optimism; [cf. Intro. III B]. Contrast the statement in Nepos, based on Timaeus, who was here probably reproducing the account of the contemporary Athanis : " quod factum omnibus maximum timorem iniecit ; nemo enim illo interfecto se tutum putabat."

Supplementary Note VII : *Dion and Heracleides at Syracuse.*

It is obvious that in chapters 32–53 Plutarch is reproducing the account of a partisan,—just the sort of narrative that might be expected from Dion's henchman, Timonides, writing to Dion's admirer, Speusippus. Heracleides, we are told, was unbalanced in judgement, and irresponsible; disloyal where questions of authority or personal reputation were at stake; turbulent, changeable and factious; ready to flatter the mob for office and power. To test these assertions we have practically nothing but Plutarch's story.

Plutarch is unsatisfactory in his reference to the quarrel between Heracleides and Dion in Peloponnesus, for he does not say what they quarrelled about : he is incoherent and unconvincing in his treatment of Heracleides' seditious proceedings during Dion's second *strategia* : he is silent as to the political situation at Syracuse at the time of Heracleides' murder : he does not explain the significance of the state funeral.

The real cause of the conflict between the ' Dion party ' and Heracleides would seem to have been that Heracleides was a consistent supporter of Democracy, which Dion wished to ' curtail '. There is no suggestion that Heracleides wanted to become a tyrant. Diodorus (16, 21) observes that the Syracusans who favoured him did so because they were convinced that *he* would never aim at Tyranny, and Plutarch's jibe in 48, 5 admits as much.

Dion's sole aim, according to Plutarch, was the good of the people (though he implies (52, 5) that Dion constituted himself the judge of what their good consisted in) ; while Heracleides' main object, we are told, was to keep himself in power by pandering to the wishes of the majority. But there is no more reason for holding, as many modern critics do, that Heracleides' championship of democracy was insincere, than for believing, as Beloch did, that Dion returned to Syracuse with the intention of making himself Tyrant. Heracleides wished to have Dionysius deposed and democracy re-established, but the one man whose co-operation was necessary to accomplish the first was altogether opposed to the second.

Heracleides and Dion, when both were serving under the Dionysii, had been close friends. In his Third Epistle (318C) Plato wrote to Dionysius II in 357 B.C. : " When you banished Heracleides, unjustly as both the Syracusans and I believed, you complained that now, when Theodotes and Heracleides, Dion's intimates, were under a cloud, I was doing all I could to save them from punishment."

But from 366 to 360 Dion and Heracleides never met. By the time Heracleides joined him in Peloponnesus Dion at the Academy had imbibed Plato's anti-democratic ideals.

Eduard Meyer with his usual insight seems to have been the first critic to grasp that the quarrel between the two Syracusans arose primarily from incompatibility in their political aims.

When Heracleides reached Syracuse Dion's popularity was on the wane. Months had passed, but the island fortress was still in the tyrant's hands.

The new Liberator was welcomed : even while in Dionysius' service Heracleides appears to have been a popular character. If Dion had been blest with any ' political sense ' he would have appointed him *nauarchos* immediately on his arrival.

Heracleides soon justified his appointment by his victory over Philistus. Plutarch indeed (35, 3) speaks of it as a ' piece of luck.' Here, we may suppose, he is reproducing Timonides, who in the Academy would have learnt from Plato to dislike navies and despise seamen.

The victory led to the disappearance of Dionysius from the scene. Leaving his son to hold the fortress on Ortygia he sailed away to Locri, where he took over the government.

People at Syracuse thought the war should have ended with the death of Philistus, and Heracleides lost prestige for having failed to catch Dionysius. But there was a general conviction, in which Heracleides shared, that in fact " everything was over except the shouting." On this assumption the democratic leaders, in the face of Dion's opposition, carried a decree for the redistribution of landed property. They argued that " equality is the starting-point of liberty, as poverty is of servitude." The demand for redistribution was the equivalent of the modern demand for a ' welfare state.'

The notion that Heracleides supported the proposal merely because he wanted to win back his popularity, as Plutarch asserts, is no more reasonable than it would be to suggest that Dion opposed it simply because he was a landlord.

To counter Dion's opposition it was decided to hold an election for new *strategoi*. The Ecclesia chose to regard his tenure of office as expiring at midsummer, the end of the legal year.

Heracleides and the rest of the new *strategoi* were democrats. They offered a settlement to the mercenaries, whose pay was in arrears, but it was refused, and the mercenaries withdrew under Dion to Leontini.

What especially shocked Timonides—to judge from Plutarch's narrative—was the contempt shown by the Syracusans at this crisis for repeated supernatural warnings !

For a few weeks the Syracusans might bask in the sunshine of Democracy. Then a cloud arose from the sea. Nypsius, the new commander of Dionysius' fleet, arrived in the Great Harbour. In spite of a naval defeat he managed to land his troops on Ortygia. On the third day his men had sacked the Temenites' quarter and were advancing on Achrad ina

There was nothing to do but recall Dion. Answering the call promptly, "he came, he saw, he conquered," driving the raiders back into the fortress.

Heracleides and his uncle met him and appealed to his clemency ; the other ' demagogues ' had fled.

Dion might have followed the precedent of 406 B.C., and demanded the punishment of the twenty-four *strategoi* on the ground of incompetence and neglect of duty. But he was not likely to obtain a verdict against them from the Ecclesia.

The ' Friends,' i.e. (presumably) Dion's Academic adherents, wanted to have Heracleides and his uncle put to death without trial. Dion rejected the proposal on moral grounds,—for which he is blamed by some modern critics.

When Dion, on the proposal of Heracleides, was re-elected *strategos autokrator*, and had conceded the naval command to him as before, there was general satisfaction.

The problem of the ' land act ' had now to be dealt with ; but instead of pressing for an equitable compromise Dion annulled the Act on his own authority (48, 6).

His use of the veto was plainly illegal. Freeman (3, 554), writing of the powers conferred upon the elder Dionysius, remarks : " The office was a legal one. The commission given to ' Dionysius simply empowered him to take such military steps as he might think good without consulting colleagues, or asking for decrees of the Assembly at every point.' " [1]

Dion's action no doubt pleased the ' Friends ' who had urged him to remove Heracleides and so free the state from the evils of ' mass-bribery,' but it stood for the negation of Democracy. Heracleides tried to meet the challenge by new methods. [See *Dion* 48, 7 to 49, 7].

The account given by Plutarch of his relations with the Spartans, Pharax and Gaesylus, is based—to say the least of it—on inadequate information.

Harward's description of Pharax as a soldier of fortune supporting Dionysius is certainly right, but the charge that Heracleides sought through Pharax to make an agreement *secretly* with Dionysius, can no more be trusted than the story (in ch. 5) of what passed at the ' secret interview ' between the elder Dionysius and Pollis. When we read of a *secret* interview we require to be told how the facts came to be divulged. All we *are* told is that " when the Syracusan notables suspected this there was faction in the camp." The suspicions of political opponents subsequently reported to one of their own party do not rank as evidence.

In the absence of information it might be conjectured that Heracleides hoped to bring Pharax over to the Syracusan side and to use him as a check on Dion's autocratic behaviour.

We next are told that Pharax appeared with an army in the South

---

[1] Professor T. A. Sinclair refers me to Aristotle, *Pol.* 3, 1285 b, who defines the Spartan kingship as a permanent military command, and adds, " A permanent general is possible in any form of government."

of Sicily. Dion went out to meet him " with the Syracusan militia " and sustained a slight reverse because the men from the fleet insisted on his fighting before his preparations were complete ; whereupon Heracleides sailed back to Syracuse. Dion, however, on hearing that his intention was to shut the gates of the city on him and his army, set out in haste and reached Syracuse before him. It is hardly credible, since Dion's army is said to have consisted of Syracusans, that Heracleides had such an intention.

Then Heracleides sailed away and by chance (it is implied) came across a Spartan named Gaesylus, who said he had come to take command of the ' Siceliots,' as Gylippus had done in the war against Athens. It has been suggested by Meyer that actually Gaesylus had been sent by Sparta in answer to a request from Heracleides for a Spartan commander-in-chief. (Plato in *Epistle* 4 reports that a letter from Heracleides had been received at Sparta).

Accepting this hypothesis we may infer that Heracleides' object in his sudden return to Syracuse was to meet Gaesylus and put his case before him.

The result was, however, that Gaesylus declined to interfere with Dion's authority, and instead effected a reconciliation between the two Syracusans.

It is important to observe that *Plutarch records no further activities of Heracleides.*

Then came, in quick succession, the demobilisation of the fleet—by which Heracleides ceased to hold office ; and the surrender of Ortygia to Dion. The war was over and Syracuse was free.

On hearing the news Plato sent Dion the Fourth Epistle : " . . . Try to surpass the famous Lycurgus, and Cyrus, and everybody else that has been noted for character and statesmanship. At Athens they say your cause is likely to be ruined by the ambition of yourself, Heracleides, Theodotes and other notables . . . If any one shows such a tendency then do *you* play the part of a physician. You may think it absurd that I should say these things which you know well enough yourself. Put forward, all of you, your best powers, and *if you need anything write to me.*"

The confidence here expressed by the author of the *Politicus* in Dion's capacity to overshadow the glory of the famous legislators of ancient times inevitably suggests that Dion, in the writer's opinion, possessed the qualification of a ' scientific statesman,' (just as the reader of the Seventh Epistle (341D ; 345C) feels that Plato claimed this qualification for himself).

But it is the prerogative of the Statesman in that dialogue, under the guidance of Wisdom and Justice, to ' purge ' the State by killing or banishing citizens without regard to custom or written law ; and this is precisely how Dion dealt with the recalcitrant Heracleides.

The public funeral of Heracleides is inexplicable except on the supposition that Dion held himself to be a Statesman in Plato's sense.

It does not appear that Dion consulted Plato (as he was invited to do in the Fourth Epistle) on any of his political problems. If he had asked his advice about Heracleides, and followed it, his fortunes might have had a happier issue.

Less than a year after Dion's death Plato wrote in the Seventh Epistle (331D) :

" A man of sense should not use violence against his country by changing the constitution when the best one cannot be brought into operation without banishment or slaughter of citizens: rather should he keep quiet and have recourse to prayer ... "

But this is not the teaching of the *Politicus* [see Supplementary Note IV] nor is it, we may be sure, the teaching that had been imparted to Dion in the Academy.

It is the worst of great thinkers, as John Bright once said, that they so often think wrong.

54–58. Source, Timaeus [*Intro*. 3A].

54. *Callippus'* conspiracy : C. though mentioned in 17, 2 and 28, 3 is here formally introduced,—as Heracleides was in 32, 3 though mentioned in 12, 1. In each case the earlier and later notices are taken from different sources.

Dion's last days. According to Nepos, *Dion* 7, " Dion, after having got rid of his adversary, behaved with greater lawlessness in dividing among the soldiers the property of known opponents. When this had been distributed he began to be short of money, as his day-to-day expenses were considerable . . . and he had nothing left to take except the possessions of his friends " : (based on Timaeus, who himself probably drew upon Athanis, the democratic contemporary historian). On this subject Plutarch has nothing to say.

The charge against Dion of financial oppression appears to relate to his collection of the *eisphora* (war-tax) in order to pay his mercenaries, whose wages the *ecclesia* had withheld in 355 [37, 6].

54, 1. Plato, *Epist*. 7, 333E : " Dion . . . brought with him two brothers from Athens, who had become his friends not through philosophy but from the ordinary companionship from which most friendships develop, —based on entertaining and initiation into the Mysteries. When these noticed that Dion was being misrepresented to the Greeks of Sicily as planning to make himself Tyrant, they became (I might say) authors of the murder, since they stood in arms behind the murderers."

Nepos, *Dion* 8, names the brothers Callicrates (an obvious error for ' Callippus ') and Philostratus. Callippus' association with the Academy was insisted upon by later writers : Diog. L. mentions him as a disciple of Plato along with Speusippus, Dion, Xenocrates, and Aristotle, while Athenaeus 11, 508E writes (from a source unsympathetic to Plato) :

" Callippus, a pupil of Plato and fellow-pupil of Dion, seeing that Dion was trying to appropriate to himself the ' monarchy ', killed him and when he had himself attempted to rule as tyrant, was slaughtered ". In the *Index Academicorum* of Philodemus, however, his name does not occur.

(Plato merely asserts that it was not through Philosophy that Dion and Callippus became friends). περιτρεχούσης : ' current,' i.e., *ordinary* companionship (from Plato, *Ep.* 7, 333E).

54, 2. μιαρώτατος: *sine ulla religione* (Nepos).

In *Rhetoric* 1, 12, 1373 a Aristotle refers to Callippus' conspiracy. Among the classes of persons to whom men do wrong Aristotle includes " those against whom the wrong-doers have a grievance, and with whom they are at variance, like Callippus, when he acted as he did to Dion." Aristotle adds : καὶ γὰρ τοιαῦτα ἔγγυς τοῦ μὴ ἀδικεῖν φαίνεται.

But what was the nature of Callippus' grievance Aristotle does not say.

54, 4. ὑπ' αὐτοῦ : for the use of the *personal* pron. see on 35, 7. In Nepos 8 we learn that Dion had agreed to a plan by which C. was to pretend to be his enemy in order to win the confidence of disaffected persons.

54, 5. In Nepos, 8, this answer is given by Dion to his wife and sister when they warn him of C.'s proceedings.

55, 1-2. The story of the Apparition, though not found in Nepos may be attributed to Timaeus (see Supplementary Note I, p. 47). μόνος πρὸς ἑαυτῷ τὴν διάνοιαν : the same phrase is found in *Phocion* 5. διάνοιαν, acc. of closer definition. καλλύντρῳ τινί : so in Plato, *Protag.* 304D, a sophist is described as κάπηλός τις, " a sort of retail-trader."

55, 3. *The death of Dion's son.* In *Ep.* 8, 355E and 357C Plato speaks of ' the son ' as alive after his father's death, at the time when his cousin Hipparinus " was engaged in the liberation of Syracuse ", i.e., during the earlier months of 353. (See 58, 4 *note*) : but in *Mor.* 119 (*Consolatio ad Apollonium*) the lad is said *to have fallen* from the roof and so perished ; and this version is repeated in Aelian *Var. Hist.* 3, 4. The *Dion* story agrees with Nepos, *Dion* 4, and is, therefore, attributable to Timaeus, but Plutarch has omitted the statement that the young man had been encouraged in vicious habits by Dionysius.

I think those modern critics are right who hold that Plato when he wrote *Epist.* 8 had not heard of ' the son's ' death, and, therefore, assumed that he was assisting his cousin in his efforts to liberate Syracuse. Plato's remarks are somewhat oracular and do not suggest that he was in touch with Syracusan affairs. In 355E–356A he suggests that in the interest of peace three titular kings should be appointed, Dion's son; Hipparinus, son of the elder Dionysius ; and the former tyrant, Dionysius II. In 357 A–C he represents the deceased Dion as referring to the plans for the betterment of Sicily which he had intended to carry out before he died : " these plans (he adds) are not impossible, ἃ γὰρ ἐν δυοῖν τε ὄντα ψυχαῖν τυγχάνει καὶ λογισαμένοις εὑρεῖν βέλτιστα ἑτοίμως ἔχει, ταῦτα δὲ σχεδὸν ὁ κρίνων ἀδύνατα οὐκ εὖ φρονεῖ. By the ' two minds ' I mean the mind of Hipparinus, son of Dionysius, and the mind of my own son, τούτοιν γὰρ συνομολογησάντοιν, τοῖς γε ἄλλοις Συρακοσίοις, οἶμαι, ὅσοιπερ τῆς πόλεως κήδονται, συνδοκεῖν."

In the first of the two passages which I have left in the Greek λογισαμένοις should be translated (as by Bluck, p. 165), " when they have weighed the matter up " (*not* " now that they have . . ."). If they had already done so the plans would have been 'ready waiting,' not to be approved, but to be put into execution. The second passage is to be rendered accordingly, "if these two come to an agreement the rest at least of the Syracusans —of those at any rate who care for their country—are of one accord, I am sure." Bluck further draws attention to the use of the particle γε, which shows that the main clause does not give the *result* of an agreement between the two. I may refer also to *Ep.* 7, 337C, where Plato is speaking of proposed laws (which in fact never were adopted) : τεθέντων δὲ τῶν νόμων ἐν τούτῳ δὴ τὰ πάντα ἐστίν. Here also we find the present indicative, although the future might be expected.

55, 4. ἀντίπαις : in *Aem. Paul.* 22, Plutarch uses this word to describe Scipio Aemilianus in reference to the year 168 B.C. He was then 17, having been born in 185. (See on 13, 6.)

56, 1. Ἀπολλοκράτην ... ποιεῖσθαι διάδοχον : Nepos, *Dion*, 5, 5, states that, before the citadel was surrendered to Dion, Dionysius offered peace on these terms : Siciliam Dion obtineret, Italiam Dionysius, Syracusas Apollocrates, *cui maximam fidem uni habebat Dion.*

56, 3. εἰ δεήσει : fut. implying a present necessity that something shall be done,—Goodwin *M.T.* 407.

56, 4. πίστιν ἣν βούλονται cf. St. Matt. 27, 15, ἕνα δέσμιον ὃν ἤθελον,— although the indef. rel. pron. would have been appropriate in both passages.

56, 6. ἐν τοῖς Κορείοις : the festival of Persephone occurred in June (harvest)—Diod. 5, 4. ὡς ἀσεβουμένης ... "since she was being sacrilegiously treated in any case, even though the mystagogue [Callippus, it is implied, had initiated Dion into the Eleusinian mysteries] proposed to slay her mystic at some other date."

57, 2. κατάγχειν Coraes, [κατέχειν MSS.].

57, 1-3. "As Dion was sitting in company with his friends in an apartment (οἰκήματι) furnished with a number of dining-couches, some of the conspirators surrounded the house (οἰκίαν) outside, while others were at the folding-doors and windows of the room (οἴκου). And the Zacynthians who were about to lay hands upon Dion entered without swords, wearing only their tunics. At the same time those outside (the room) closed the doors and held them, while the others (i.e. the Zacynthians) fell on Dion and tried to throttle him. When they could not finish the work they kept calling for a sword ; but none of those outside (the room) ventured to open the door, for there were many persons inside with Dion."

For οἶκος, room, cf. ἑπτάκλινος οἶκος (Phrynichus Com. frg. 66).

57, 4. κρατούμενον καὶ ἐλιττόμενον (Schaefer for δειδιττόμενον).— According to Nepos, *Dion* 10, Callippus gave Dion a public funeral. If this is true, C. was following the precedent set by Dion himself in regard to Heracleides.

57, 5. MSS. give καὶ θρέψαι μᾶλλον : the transposition is due to Ziegler. παρέβαλοντο, with inf. as in *Pelop.* 8, 'ventured.'

58, 2. In Plato, Laws 642 C, Megillus the Spartan observes : "the assertion that all good Athenians are pre-eminently good appears to be true ; they alone by divine providence are through a natural instinct good in reality not in pretence."

58, 4. Callippus' rule had been confined to Syracuse. He now attempted to extend it to Catana, some 30 miles N. of the city. Polyaenus 5, 4, agrees with Plut. that Syracuse was captured in his absence. Diod. 16, 36, 5, states, however, that Hipparinus *expelled* Callippus from the city.

ὅτε, *whereupon* : Attic usage would require τότε δέ.

58, 4. πάλιν ἀπολωλεκὼς τυροκνῆστιν εἴληφεν: "I have lost a city and gained a cheese-scraper." Why C. should have thus designated Catana Plut. has not explained, but apparently a play on words was intended. A gloss κατακνῆστις· τυροκνῆστις is found in Hesychius. Perhaps C. made play with the words Κατάνη 'στιν and κατακνῆστιν: e.g. πόλιν ὀλωλεκώς, ἥν, εἴληφα κατακνῆστιν ! (ἣν εἴληφα Κατάνη 'στιν).

58, 5. *Rhegium* (Reggio), devastated by Dionysius I in 387 was after-wards partly restored by his son, who renamed it Phoebia. It was besieged now (353) by Callippus and Leptines, who expelled the Tyrant's garrison,— Diod. 16, 45. <τῷ αὐτῷ> Lindskog : some addition is needed to bring out that the weapon used was the particular one mentioned in 57, 4.

Plutarch had already alluded to Callippus' fate in *De sera Num. vindicta*, (*Mor.* 553D).

58, 8. Dion's wife and sister must have been released when his nephew Hipparinus 'liberated' Syracuse in 353. In 351 H. died and was succeeded by his brother Nysaeus. He in turn was expelled by Dionysius, but in 345 Hicetas was holding the mainland area and besieging Dionysius in Ortygia. Hence Arete and Sophrosyne left Syracuse in 345.

58, 9. The charge made here against Hicetas (as the historian Mitford [1744–1827] long ago pointed out) is unsupported by evidence. He had no motive for the crime. The death of Dion's wife and sister may have been due to accident, or to an attack by pirates. In such a case "party calumny would take the opportunity to asperse Hicetas."

58, 10. ἐν τῷ Τιμολέοντος βίῳ : chapter 31.

Hicetas renewed the struggle with Timoleon who besieged Leontini. But the mercenaries turned against Hicetas, and handed him over to Timoleon, by whom he was executed. Hicetas' wife and daughter were also con-demned to death, and Plutarch remarks that the Syracusans were avenging Dion, "for it was Hicetas who had Dion's wife, sister and child drowned at sea, *as mentioned in the Life of Dion.*" [*Tim.* 33.]

This implies that the *Dion* was written before the *Timoleon*, whereas the last sentence of the *Dion* implied that the *Timoleon* was prior. The problem is further complicated by a false statement in *Timol.* 13 that the fate of the daughters of *Dionysius* is recorded in the *Dion*.

The simplest hypothesis is that this last passage and the final sentence of the *Dion* are both adscripts.

[Ziegler, *Ploutarchos*, p. 262f, *Die relative Chronologie der Biographien* has discussed in detail the problem created by the comparatively numerous *anticipatory* citations found in Plutarch's Lives.]

Something may be said of Timoleon's reorganisation of the Syracusan constitution, whereby democracy was restored with some modifications in the direction of that ' mixed constitution ' of which Plato and Dion had dreamed.

The chief magistrate of the city was the priest of Olympian Zeus, annually elected by lot from three candidates selected by the demos out of three particular ' clans ': but what powers were attached to the office we do not know.

The most influential body was the ' Council of 600 ' for which only the wealthier citizens were eligible.

In all important issues, however, the deciding voice was that of the popular assembly.

The competence of the college of *strategoi* was confined to military affairs. In the event of war with non-Greeks [Carthaginians] a commander-in-chief was to be sought from Corinth.

Syracuse and the other cities of Greek Sicily were restored and strengthened by Peloponnesian colonists and united in a loose federation [Beloch 3, 1, 589–591 with authorities there cited].

But Timoleon's constitution lasted only some 20 years after Timoleon's death, when Agathocles became Tyrant of Syracuse.

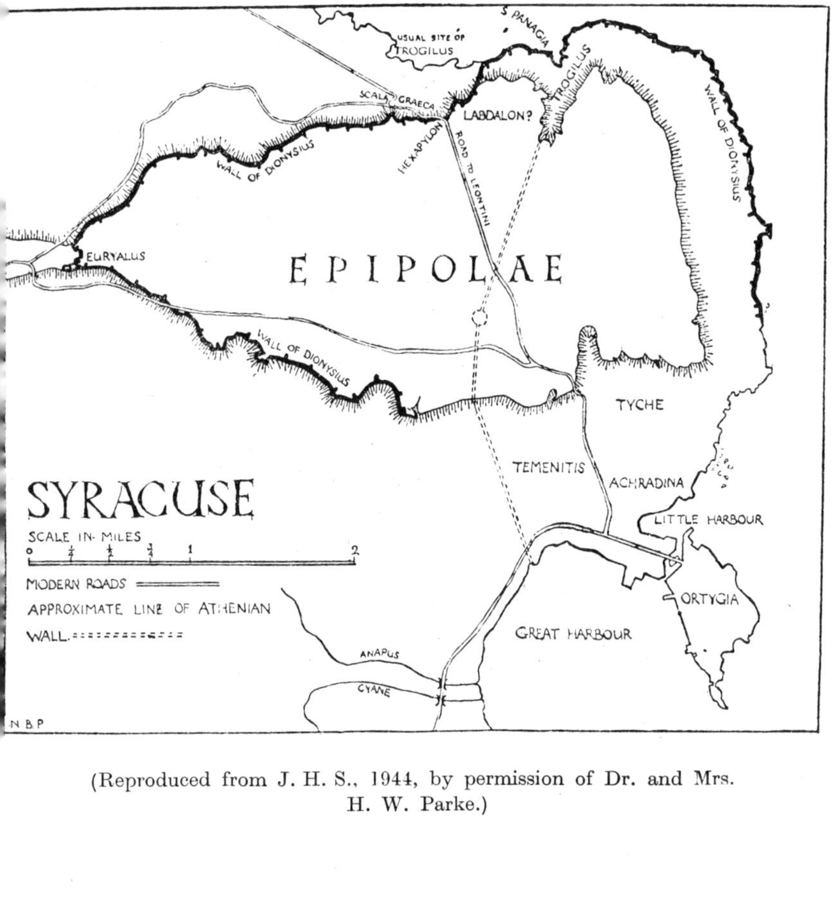
S PANAGIA
USUAL SITE OF TROGILUS
SCALA GRAECA
LABDALON?
TROGILUS
HEXAPYLON
ROAD TO LEONTINI
WALL OF DIONYSIUS
WALL OF DIONYSIUS
WALL OF DIONYSIUS
EURYALUS
EPIPOLAE
TYCHE
TEMENITIS
ACHRADINA
LITTLE HARBOUR
ORTYGIA
GREAT HARBOUR
ANAPUS
CYANE
SYRACUSE
SCALE IN MILES
0 ¼ ½ ¾ 1 2
MODERN ROADS
APPROXIMATE LINE OF ATHENIAN WALL
N.B.P.

(Reproduced from J. H. S., 1944, by permission of Dr. and Mrs. H. W. Parke.)

INDEX I.

A.—NAMES OF PERSONS.

B.—LOCAL NAMES.

II

GREEK

ἀδαμάντινοι δεσμοί, 7, 6; 10, 4.
ἄδεια, 30, 2.
αἴρων μηχανήν, 18, 5.
αἰτιᾶσθαι, object, 33, 2.
'Ακαδήμεια (formation of word), 1, 2.
ἄκριτος (active), 34, 5.
ἀμέλει, 8, 2.
ἀναλαμβάνειν (intr.), 26, 2.
ἀντίπαις, 55, 4.
ἀπὸ, on account of, 4, 1.
ἀπὸ ῥυτῆρος, 42, 5.
ἀποβλέπειν, 52, 2; 55, 2.
ἀπολέγεσθαι, 20, 2.
ἀποσκευάζεσθαι, 26, 3.
ἀποσπάσ[θ]ωσι, 25, 4.
ἀποστρέφεσθαι, w. acc., 32, 5.
ἀποτυμπανίζειν, 28, 2.
ἆρα, 1, 1.
ἀραρώς (ἀραρίσκω), 32, 3.
ἀτρεμεῖν, 44, 2.
αὐθάδεια, 8, 1; 53, 5.
αὖθις, in his turn, 32, 4.

βλασφημίαι, 3, 1.

γράμματα = ἐπιστολαί, 11, 2.

δαιμόνιον, τὸ, 2, 3.
Δεισιδαιμονία, 2, 4.
δεκάπεντε, 38, 1.
δημοκοπία, 47, 3.
δίαιτα, 15, 4.
διαιτᾶν, 51, 4.
διαιτᾶσθαι, 51, 5.
διοσημίαι 38, 1.

εἰς ὅν, in honour of whom, 22, 5.
ἐξοικοδομεῖν, 50, 1.
ἐπιβοᾶσθαι, 50, 3.
ἐπικράτεια, 25, 11.
ἐστιν οὕστινας, 11, 1.
ἐτησίαι, 23, 3.

θέλειν, 32, 5.

ἰδιόστολος 32, 4.
ἱστορεῖν, 24, 10.

καθιέναι, employ, 37, 5.
καίτοι, w. participle, 52, 5.
καταλύειν, depose, 12, 2.
κατασκευή, 15, 4.
καταφαρμακεύειν, 3, 6.
καταφέρεσθαι, 42, 5.
κελεύειν, w. dat., 15, 3.

λέγεται, use of as formula, 3, 4.
λόγος (in reference to a person), 11, 3.
λυχνίαι, 9, 2.

μειράκιον, 7, 2.
μεστός, 4, 6.
μὴ, postclassical use of (1) with participles, 2, 2. (2) after vbs. of saying, 2, 4. (3) after ὅτι, because, 9, 8. (4) = whether, 2, 5; 21, 2.

ναῦς, nom. plur., 25, 1.

οἱ περί, postclassical use of, 1, 2.
ὅπου, as causal conj., 50, 4.
ὁραθείς, 9, 4.
οὐ with inf. after ὥστε in reported speech, 21, 8.

παντοπώλιον, 53, 4.
παραβαλεῖν = arrive, 4, 3.
παραφυλάσσειν, 25, 2.
παρηκμακώς, 23, 5.
πεμπόμενος (on mission), 4, 8.
περιτρέχουσα (ἑταιρεία), 54, 1.
πλάστης, 9, 3.
πλησιάζειν, 1, 2; 11, 5.
πλοῦτοι, 36, 3.
ποιησάμενος (extended use of middle voice), 4, 7.
πολιτεῖαι, 40, 1.
πομπή, 15, 4.
πρεσβεύειν, send envoys, 40, 7.

GREEK TEXTS AND COMMENTARIES
An Arno Press Collection